The Protection
of Children

The Protection of Children

State Intervention and Family Life

SECOND EDITION

Robert Dingwall
John Eekelaar
Topsy Murray

QUID PRO BOOKS

New Orleans, Louisiana

THE PROTECTION OF CHILDREN

Previously published in 1983 by Basil Blackwell Publisher Ltd., Oxford, UK; and in 1995 (in the Second Edition) by Avebury, a division of Ashgate Publishing Ltd., Aldershot, UK and Brookfield, Vermont, USA.

Published in 2014 by Quid Pro Books. Part of the *Classics of the Social Sciences* Series.

ISBN 978-1-61027-236-0 (pbk)
ISBN 978-1-61027-220-9 (ebk)

QUID PRO BOOKS
5860 Citrus Blvd.
Suite D-101
New Orleans, Louisiana 70123
www.quidprobooks.com

Contents

[Page numbers in brackets above reference the original pagination of the 1995 and 1983 editions; they are retained in this republication for continuity in citation and syllabus, consistency with the new ebook edition, and the convenience of the reader. This original pagination is found embedded into the text by the use of brackets. Numbers to the far right above refer to the pagination found at the bottom of pages in this new republication.]

To James, Alice, Edward, Louise, Joshua,
Hannah and the one who was born too late
for the copy deadline

Preface • 2014

The Protection of Children has enjoyed a remarkably long sales life for an empirical study. It is now more than thirty years since the first edition appeared and, of course, many of the institutional details have changed in that time. Its continuing relevance, however, comes from its analysis of the impossible dilemma that confronts child protection services in democratic societies. On the one hand, they are enjoined to respect the autonomy of families and the liberty of parents to decide how best to bring up their own children. On the other, they face societal demands that no child should ever die or experience serious injury, neglect or sexual abuse as a result of parental maltreatment. These goals simply cannot be achieved simultaneously. Our analysis of the institutional solution to this conflict in the form of the 'rule of optimism' is still regularly quoted by journalists and the reports of inquiries into child deaths.

Not many social scientists introduce a phrase into the English language and its subsequent history is instructive about the ways in which the impact of successful sociology becomes invisible. It is also a nice example of how ideas become assimilated into a societal environment that finds it hard to accept the sociologist's focus on systems and organizations.

The project on agency decision-making in child abuse and neglect was conceived by John Eekelaar in the late 1970s, through the SSRC Centre for Socio-Legal Studies. John was already established as a leading academic family lawyer. I joined him as a sociologist with a newly-minted PhD on health visiting, which had introduced me to the institutional context of children's services (Dingwall 1977). Later we received additional funding from the UK Department of Health and Social Security and recruited – she might say 'turned' – one of our key informants, Topsy Murray, from her administrative role in a local authority we were studying.

We came to focus on the process by which health and social service agencies filtered the large population of children with poor lives – under-fed, unloved, occasionally knocked about or indecently handled – to produce the very small number defined as 'serious' and, ultimately, candidates for legal intervention. The agencies had neither the resources, nor the societal backing, to intervene in every troubled family. The UK has a strong commitment to family autonomy and family privacy: children's health and well-being is primarily a matter for parents, not the state. Agencies are resourced on this basis, to deal with exceptional cases. There are no perfect predictive tools so some decisions are always wrong: some interventions will be unnecessary and some children will not receive the protection they need (Dingwall 1989). The death rate from child abuse reflects high-level judgements about the balance to be struck.

Front-line workers, however, have to take this context as given and get on with the practical tasks of picking out those few children that the agency can deal with. This is what we came to describe as the 'rule of optimism'. My colleagues assure me that it was my phrase, although I cannot remember when it first emerged in drafting our report. The term owed something to Scheff's work on decision rules in medical diagnosis but it also echoed the idea of a monastic rule. These were the statements drafted by founders of religious orders that set out the basic principles by which members would live and work.

Our analysis, then, stressed the *organizational* basis of the rule of optimism. It is not written down anywhere but it embeds the unavoidable legal and institutional constraints on professional practice into the culture of their agencies. As the term has taken on a life of its own, however, it has often been turned into a *psychological* label and used to accuse child protection workers of credulity or naïveté. How could they miss things that are obvious with 20/20 hindsight to any journalist, lawyer or case reviewer? It is absorbed into a narrative of 'wet' and woolly-minded liberal professionals who ought to be suspicious of every family they encounter. When they are, as in the Cleveland sexual abuse cases of 1987, the result is, of course, an equal and opposite denunciation of trigger-happy intervention stealing children from loving parents.

The psychological version first appeared in the inquiry into the death of Jasmine Beckford in 1985 and, despite our periodic efforts to correct the record, has regularly resurfaced. The 2013 report on the death of Daniel Pelka in Coventry takes its definition from an Ofsted overview of serious case reviews, for example:

> A frequent lesson from the reviews was that practitioners had been affected by what is known as the 'rule of optimism'. This is a tendency by social workers and healthcare workers towards rationalisation and under-responsiveness in certain situations. In these conditions, workers focus on adults' strengths, rationalise evidence to the contrary and interpret data in the light of this optimistic view. They confuse participation by parents with cooperation (para. 96).

Our analysis of organizational culture has become a 'tendency' of individuals as it has slipped into common currency to the extent that its source no longer needs to be credited.

Psychologizing the rule of optimism makes it into a tool for blaming child protection workers for child abuse deaths. It diverts attention from the contexts in which they have to make difficult decisions with imperfect, limited and fragmented information. An inter-agency system creaking under resource pressures and lacking public support for a more interventionist approach necessarily has to find ways of bounding its work. Sometimes the result is that children die. There are no quick fixes to a complex – and, in a technical sense, wicked – problem. The first step, however, is to see the problem for what it is – and that is not one of weak-minded professionals but of the social licence to operate that governs the agency system.

The impact of this book does not lie in its immediate value in preventing or identifying child maltreatment but in understanding why this is such a difficult task. It contributes to the self-awareness of the professionals involved and to their reflection on the decisions they make every day. As an organizational ethnography, it is also something of a model of what could be achieved in the days when ethical review was satisfied by a few conversations with the directors of the relevant agencies and the professional integrity of researchers.

In preparing this version, we have taken the opportunity to review the text of the Second Edition and to correct a small number of typographical and formatting errors that crept in during the scanning of the original. We are grateful to Pamela Watson for her careful reading of the proofs to detect these. The book is otherwise as it appeared in that edition in 1995 with a postscript reviewing its contribution and subsequent publications by the team.

Robert Dingwall
April, 2014

References

Dingwall, R. (1977) *The Social Organisation of Health Visitor Training*, London, Croom Helm. Reprinted by Quid Pro Books in eformats, 2013. http://quidprolaw.com/?p=4625

Dingwall, R. (1989) 'Some problems about predicting child abuse and neglect'. Pp. 28-53 in Stevenson, O., ed., *Child Abuse: Public Policy and Professional Practice*, Brighton, Wheatsheaf Publishing. Available at https://www.academia.edu/334882/Some_problems_about_predicting_child_abuse_and_neglect

Foreword • 1983

Twenty years ago, when the first scholarly articles on child abuse were being published, and when the very topic of child abuse was being discovered by physicians, lawyers, and the lay public, the abuse of children was thought to be both rare and caused by mental defects in the perpetrators. Two decades of research have demonstrated that both views were misconceptions. Child abuse is not rare, and mental illness and character disorders explain no more than 10 per cent of the instances of abuse.

In the course of scientifically establishing the extent of abuse, an important problem arose, which, to the best of my knowledge, was not identified or addressed by anyone until this volume was prepared by Robert Dingwall, John Eekelaar, and Topsy Murray. The problem is the discrepancy between the number of officially validated instances of child maltreatment and incidence estimates obtained through social surveys. In the United States, the largest number of cases of child maltreatment officially tabulated is not much more than 600,000 cases annually. Yet, survey research (e.g. Straus, Gelles and Steinmetz, 1980) yields an incidence estimate of more than 1.4 million instances of child abuse annually – and this estimate is confined only to instances of physical abuse.

Official reports of child maltreatment significantly and consistently underestimate the actual extent of abuse and neglect of children. As Dingwall, Eekelaar, and Murray correctly point out in chapter 4 of this book, a major fact to be explained is the *rarity of allegations of maltreatment*. This rarity is examined and explained by the authors through a careful ethnographic examination of how front-line agency staff confront, identify, investigate and report instances of suspected maltreatment of children.

It would be a mistake to assume that because this is a study of how clinical personnel label and identify child maltreatment in the United Kingdom, the results are only generalizable to the management of maltreatment in that country. There are important differences between child abuse management in the United Kingdom and the United States, not the least of which is that mandatory reporting of abuse, a fixture in the United States for the last decade, does not exist in the United Kingdom. These differences, however, should not obscure the fact that in both countries, indeed, in virtually every society in which abuse occurs, there is no objective condition which results in total agreement that the condition is abuse. The private and intimate nature of the family as a modern institution means that most abuse and neglect takes place behind closed doors, in the privacy of the home. The official detection of maltreatment nearly always requires a report, an assessment of the condition of the child, an inquest into how that condition arose, and, often, an assessment of family history. This entire process, whether in the United Kingdom, United States, or many other countries, is conducted under what Dingwall, Eekelaar, and Murray call 'the rule of optimism', where clinical staff are required to think the best of parents.

The assumption that maltreatment allegations are rare, in the light of the probable extent of abuse and neglect, the postulate of the 'rule of optimism', and the careful ethnographic examination of how agents of the state identify, investigate and intervene in cases of abuse constitute three major leaps forward in our understanding of the problem of child maltreatment in society. This book does not offer the conventional formulation of child abuse – incidence, causal model, treatment and prevention programmes. It offers much more. In fact, it is only by understanding how child maltreatment cases come to public and official attention, and what aspects of maltreatment or suspected maltreatment cases motivate certain actions by agents of social control, that we can assuredly improve our understanding of, and our ability to manage the tragic and sorrowful problem of, the abuse and neglect of children.

Richard J. Gelles
University of Rhode Island
1983

Acknowledgements

Few projects of this scale – using comparable methodologies – have been carried out in Britain. It may, therefore, be difficult for readers to appreciate the depth of our indebtedness to informants, sponsors and associates. Indeed, it was only in attempting to draft these paragraphs that we, ourselves, fully realized just how many people had contributed in so many ways to the study. We can hardly mention them all but we hope that those we have been unable to name will, none the less, accept that this is no reflection on the significance of their help.

Our first debt must necessarily go to the participating authorities and their staff for accepting and welcoming us into their everyday practice. This was not always convenient and was sometimes intrusive, but our presence was received not merely with tolerance and good humour but with the confidence that a published scrutiny of the complexities of child protection would eventually benefit staff, clients and citizens. Without wishing to diminish the significance of others' contribution we would especially like to thank the then Divisional Nursing Officer and Deputy Director of Social Services in our main study area for their continuing encouragement and personal commitment to facilitating our work.

The study was funded primarily by the Social Science Research Council with a contribution from the Department of Health and Social Security. At a time when the value of social science research is under critical scrutiny, we are particularly pleased to acknowledge the benefits of the SSRC's support by means of the block grant to the Centre for Socio-Legal Studies. This produces the inestimable advantages of continuity and stability of employment with the consequent development of a unique cadre of experienced staff, able to transcend basic disciplines in a common endeavour. While it is hard to disentangle the contributions of specific individuals, we would particularly like to thank Chris Whelan, who assisted with some of the fieldwork, Keith Hawkins, Doreen McBarnet and Mavis Maclean. We are also grateful to Pembroke College, Oxford for releasing John Eekelaar from a significant part of his tutorial duties and for administering the DHSS grant.

We would particularly like to pay tribute to our secretarial staff. In a project like this, secretaries are far more than people who type letters and make coffee. Their role is better understood by analogy with laboratory technicians whose skill, initiative and flexibility are the essential foundation for scientific advance. We have been peculiarly fortunate in the talents of three of our project secretaries, Angela Palmer, Ginny Rosamond and Rosemary Stallan, and one of our interview transcribers, Jean Mason, all of whom have contributed far more than we had any right to expect. We are also grateful to Noël Harris, Jennifer Dix, Caroline Mason and Carolyn Hartley at the Centre for Socio-Legal Studies and to Maureen Hudson, Jill Souch and Katie Span for their home audio-transcription of field-notes and interviews.

Our computerized retrieval system was devised and implemented by Clive Payne, Nick Pomianowksi and their colleagues at the Faculty of Social Studies Computing Centre in Oxford and the extraction of data from social services referral logs was carried out by Ginny Rosamond and Judith Rayner.

We have also had the benefit of conversations with numerous academic colleagues around the country and in North America. We would especially like to acknowledge the contributions of Maureen Cain, Jean Packman, Christine Hallett, Nigel Parton, Celia Davies, Roger Bacon, Richard White, Phil Strong, Peter Manning, David Armstrong, Robert Mnookin and David May.

Finally, we must thank our respective spouses, Pam, Pia and Simon, for their forbearance over the six years of this project.

None of this is, of course, to imply that the limitations of this study should be attributed to anyone but its authors, although we trust that the reader will find in it the virtues of others.

R.D.
J.E.
T.M.
1983

The Protection of Children

Introduction

TORTURE BOY 'TRAGEDY'

The aunt of a three-year-old boy, who was tortured and beaten to death by his mother's lover while police and social workers made fumbling attempts for 22 days to find him, said last night: 'I can never forgive the system for what happened.' . . . vital information was garbled and lost as it was passed between police, the city's social services department and the local National Society for the Prevention of Cruelty to Children. A senior police officer told the inquiry that D___ could have been found within three days if the search had been properly conducted.

Guardian 9.11.1979

BOY SNATCHED AT HOME – FATHER

Police and social workers barged into a living room and snatched seven-year-old L___ W___ from his family, it was claimed last night . . . . The police and social workers had a warrant to put L___ into care. They suspected that he had been 'battered' because of bruises on his face . . . . A spokesman for B___ social services department defended the action: 'It is our duty when there has been an allegation of injury or neglect to inquire and ensure that we act in the best interests of the child . . . .' A police spokesman said: 'When a warrant is issued we have to ensure it is enforced . . . the correct procedure was observed.'

Guardian 3.9.1980

{1} It seems that child protection agencies cannot win. In the first case, an allegation is dealt with in a routine fashion and a child dies. On the second occasion, a suspicion leads to prompt and decisive action. {2} Either way, the social services department finds itself pilloried – for bureaucratic delay or for over-zealous intrusion into family life. In each case, however, that judgement is possible only by reference to a particular model of the relationship between children, families and the state. The first extract implies a view that state agencies have a duty to protect children from the excesses of their adult caretakers; the second, that families have a right to privacy

1

which is sustainable even where the proper legal formalities of obtaining a warrant have been observed.

Such conflicts can be demonstrated not only in newspaper articles but equally in academic and political debates, most conspicuously in the United States but increasingly wherever a nation's health and welfare services are influenced by American experience.[1] They exemplify a relatively long-established sociological observation: that the existence and nature of social problems cannot be separated from the values of those who would identify them.

> The term *social problem* indicates not merely an observed phenomenon but the state of mind of the observer as well. Value judgements define certain conditions of human life and certain kinds of behavior as social problems: there can be no social problem without a value judgement. (Waller 1936: 922 original emphasis)

In the same paper, Waller goes on to suggest that the perception of events as problematic arises from the interaction of two conflicting sets of *mores*. The first of these, the organizational or basic *mores,* 'are those upon which the social order is founded, the *mores* of private property and individualism, the *mores* of the monogamous family, Christianity and nationalism' (1936: 924). Alongside these exist the humanitarian *mores* held by those who feel an urge to make the world better or to remedy the misfortunes of others.

> Poverty is a social problem, when it exists in the midst of plenty or in a world in which universal plenty is a technological possibility. The value judgement passed on poverty defines it as at least in part socially caused and as something which ought to be remedied. A simpleton would suggest that the remedy for poverty in the midst of plenty is to redistribute income. We reject this solution at once because it would interfere with the institution of private property, would destroy the incentive for thrift and hard work and disjoint the entire economic system. What is done to alleviate poverty must be done within the limits set by the organizational mores. (1936: 926) {3}

The simple-minded remedy for child mistreatment might be to license child-bearing and collectivize child-rearing. In a liberal democracy we almost instinctively reject both as authoritarian and dictatorial acts, infringements on the rights of adults to reproduce themselves on such occasions and in such fashions as they think fit. Debates about the proper response to child abuse and neglect are, in substance, debates about the nature of the good society. They are possible only because of the clash of Utopias between humanitarian and organizational moralists.

There is an important implication. In so far as most participants in the debates would, nevertheless, concede the existence of such phenomena as

2

child abuse and neglect, the core dispute is over the point at which intervention may be justified. What this means is that the very definition of mistreatment becomes a relative matter. Where do we draw the line between firm discipline and physical abuse? How is neglect to be distinguished from low standards of parental competence? What marks off sexual abuse from intimate displays of affection between family members? It is on the answers to these questions that advocates of state intervention and family rights ultimately establish their positions. The more we argue for family autonomy, the more latitude we must allow parents in their conduct, and vice versa.

Furthermore, it should be apparent that, if mistreatment is to be defined in this relative fashion, as part of a wider analysis of the nature of our society, then questions about its true incidence or true prevalence become meaningless. Attempts to describe the epidemiology of abuse and neglect and, from that, to make inferences about aetiology are refractions either of the moral judgements of the investigator or of the practical decision-making of child protection agents. We do not wish to argue that nobody has the right to make such judgements, nor are we somehow trying to discount the suffering of many children by treating our response as something which has its origins in the culture of our society. What we do insist upon is that abuse and neglect come to exist as socially recognizable phenomena, and hence as a cause of action, only as a result of processes of identification, confirmation and disposition within health, welfare and legal agencies. They cannot be discussed intelligibly without an understanding of the way in which such processes operate, an understanding which must necessarily be moral rather than technical.

This is not an entirely novel observation. In a somewhat neglected paper, Gelles advocated a similar view of child abuse as social deviance. He spelt out the consequences: {4}

> ... all the cases that make up the data on incidence, all the explanatory analyses and all the prevention and treatment models are influenced by the *social process* by which individuals and groups are labelled and designated as deviants. In other words there is no objective behavior we can automatically recognize as child abuse ... when I speak of the social construction of abuse, I mean the process by which: (a) a definition of abuse is constructed; (b) certain judges or 'gatekeepers' are selected for applying the definition; and (c) the definition is applied by designating the labels 'abuse' and 'abuser' to particular individuals and families. This social process of defining abuse and labelling abusers should be an important facet in the study of child abuse. (Gelles 1975: original emphasis)

Unfortunately, such arguments have had little practical effect. In a recent review of research on child mistreatment during the 1970s, Gelles

(1980) remarked on a continuing methodological weakness in the readiness to define child mistreatment in terms of 'those instances in which the victim became publicly known and labelled by an official or professional' and argued that this should be corrected in future work. Gelles, himself, has carried out a number of studies of violent acts within families which could be the basis for identifications of child abuse, based on survey data, latterly from a nationally representative US sample of households (e.g. Gelles 1974, 1978). One might also mention the ingenious attempts of Giovannoni and Becerra (1979) to map the diversity of commonsense definitions of mistreatment by the rating of vignettes presented to samples of social workers, paediatricians, lawyers, police officers and the general public in Los Angeles.

Nevertheless, the processes involved in selecting incidents from a candidate population or applying definitions elicited in response to hypothetical cases remain obscure. The study reported here attempts to fill that gap in demonstrating how such processes generate the perception of child mistreatment current in our society. England[2] is taken as an example of advanced liberal democracies as we seek to answer questions like: What sort of social problem is child mistreatment? Whose job is it to respond to this problem? How does that work shape and define the problem? We shall describe how children are actually identified as having been mistreated and chronicle their passage through a variety of health, welfare and legal agencies. At each stage, we shall point to the range of available decisions and consider why some cases take one route rather than another. In particular, we shall ask why some cases attract coercive intervention while others do not. {5}

This discussion, we shall argue, encapsulates the interaction between a number of different ideas about the proper nature of our society and about the relations between families and the state. In this respect, the book can also be seen to have a sub-text which explores the compromises which make social regulation possible in a liberal society. We draw this out towards the end of our account in attempting to explain why the present English system takes the form that it does and why *all* systems of child protection in comparable societies are likely to operate in a similar fashion. Finally, we use this theoretical analysis as the basis for specifying a definition of children's rights against which particular institutional arrangements may be evaluated.

1

The Institutional Framework and Research Design

There are two possible ways of starting a book which is mostly about organizations and their members, each of which carries its own presuppositions. We might begin with a formal description of official rules, roles and statuses. Alternatively we could open with an account of everyday practice, what the staff actually seem to be doing. The former might be taken to imply that the most important definitions of organizations and their work are those of the people who create the official structure, in this case the legislators, who draft statutes defining child mistreatment and setting up or licensing agencies to deal with it. The latter might be understood as asserting the primacy of street-level or comparable work, here by social workers, doctors and health visitors making operational decisions about particular children. In either case, we risk being drawn into an irony, of concentrating on the lack of fit between formal and informal aspects of the organizations to criticize either the ignorance of legislators or the deviance of agency staff.

The reality is, of course, that both aspects are important. The statutes relating to child mistreatment constitute the relevant organizations' charters, defining their objectives, legitimizing their intervention into citizens' family life to regulate the quality of child-rearing and empowering them either to trade resources for compliance or to coerce reluctant parents.[1] At the same time, statutes are not self-enforcing. Their application and, hence, their social significance depend upon case-by-case decisions taken by authorized interpreters, not just in the courts but in all agencies having dealings with children. Nevertheless, those interpretations must ultimately be reconcilable with the terms of the organization's charter, if an agency is to fulfil its notional contract with the remainder of its host society.

In choosing to begin with a description of the principal legal provisions and related institutions in England, then, we should not {7} be taken

5

as prejudging their relationship to the way in which members of these organizations work. These formal structures are a final constraint on staff activities but, simultaneously, statutes take on significance only as they are used and organizations exist only through their members' actions. Our motive for starting with an institutional account is entirely pragmatic: that readers who are not familiar with the English system of health, welfare and legal agencies will find our analysis of their practice more intelligible if we first perform a 'naming of parts'.

THE LEGAL PROVISIONS

Most Anglo-American jurisdictions seem to have a broadly comparable set of statutory provisions relating to child mistreatment. Katz et al. (1976), for instance, show that American state laws typically have some sort of preamble which enjoins the promotion of child welfare and establishes the state as a caretaker of last resort where this goal is unattainable. The circumstances which amount to mistreatment are loosely defined but compulsory intervention can only follow a court hearing, under the state's civil procedure. Dispositions available normally include some sort of protective supervision in the child's own home or the transfer of legal custody to a recognized agency.

English legislation follows a similar pattern. At the time of our study, social intervention in family life for the purpose of child protection was founded on three Acts of Parliament: the Children Act (CA) 1948 and the Children and Young Persons Acts (CYPA) 1963 and 1969.[2] The 1963 Act laid an overriding obligation on local authorities – county councils and metropolitan boroughs – to prevent children from coming into their care and empowered them to provide various sorts of family support for that purpose.

> It shall be the duty of every local authority to make available such advice, guidance and assistance as may promote the welfare of children by diminishing the need to receive children into or keep them in care . . . or to bring children before a juvenile court; and any provisions made by a local authority under this subsection may, if the local authority thinks fit, include provision for giving assistance in kind, or in exceptional circumstances, in cash. (CYPA 1963, s. 1(1))

Where this objective is not attainable, however, the authorities have two sets of statutory resources available. {8}

The first set are established by the Children Act 1948, which provides for what is, somewhat inaccurately, known as 'voluntary care'.[3] In fact the care is voluntary only in the sense that children may not be removed from their homes against parental objections. The origins of this Act lie in the

6

duties of Poor Law authorities to receive into their care children who had been orphaned or deserted or whose parents were incapable, whether for physical, mental or moral reasons, of looking after them. While such children are no longer placed in the workhouse, the state still assumes the responsibilities of a residual caretaker. Once a child has come into care, the authority is under a duty to facilitate his or her discharge to the care of parents or near kin. Where this is not consistent with the child's welfare, the authority has the power, under section 2 of the Act, to pass a resolution assuming parental rights over the child. If the parents object, and the authority wishes to persist in the case, the resolution must be referred to a juvenile court for determination. The 1948 Act is most relevant to those mistreatment cases where it is possible to negotiate with parents for the placement of a child with alternative caretakers. It empowers the authority to provide financial assistance and to regulate the placement. If necessary, of course, the authority can take advantage of section 2 powers to detain the child for his or her own protection, should the parents breach the agreed disposition.

Where negotiation is neither possible nor desirable, the authority's actions lie under the Children and Young Persons Act 1969. This provides for juvenile courts to make orders relating to a child's care on application from a local authority, the police or an authorized person. (Only the staff of the National Society for the Prevention of Cruelty to Children enjoy this latter status.) Those orders may be granted where the conditions specified in subsection 1(2) are satisfied in respect of a particular child:

a) his proper development is being avoidably prevented or neglected or his health is being avoidably impaired or neglected or he is being ill-treated; or

b) it is probable that the condition set out in the preceding paragraph will be satisfied in his case, having regard to the fact that the court or another court has found that that condition is or was satisfied in the case of another child or young person who is or was a member of the household to which he belongs; or

bb) it is probable that the conditions set out in paragraph (a) of this subsection will be satisfied in his case, having regard to the fact that a person who has been convicted of an offence mentioned {9} in Schedule 1 to the Act of 1933[4] is, or may become, a member of the same household as the child; or

c) he is exposed to moral danger; or

d) he is beyond the control of his parent or guardian; or

e) he is of compulsory school age within the meaning of the Education Act 1944, and is not receiving efficient full time education suitable to his age, ability and aptitude; or

f) he is guilty of an offence, excluding homicide,

and also that he is in need of care or control which he is unlikely to receive unless the court makes an order under this section . . . . (CYPA 1969, s. 1(2))

We shall adopt the shorthand of agency argot and refer to these respectively as the 'proper development', 'same household', 'moral danger', 'beyond control', 'truancy' and 'offence' conditions.

This collection of mistreated, disobedient and delinquent children reflects the 'unified theory of deviance' (Handler 1973: 42-51) which became established in England during the post-War period. The presenting problems of troubled and troublesome children were all defined as epiphenomenal manifestations of the same underlying family pathology. As Handler (1973: 42-51) and Packman (1975) show, the result was a steady expansion and integration of services for families and children, from the Children's Departments set up under the 1948 Act to the present day generic social services departments described later in this chapter. While few other jurisdictions seem to collapse the statutory categories together to quite the same degree, the practical overlap is often considerable. These will, of course, almost invariably all be defined as juvenile court matters and dealt with under similar procedures even if there is a greater separation of social work services for probation, school welfare and child protection.

If a local authority receives information suggesting that there are grounds for bringing proceedings on a child in their area, the 1969 Act requires that the report be investigated unless the authority is satisfied that inquiries are unnecessary. If it is substantiated, proceedings must follow, unless the authority determines that such action would not be in the child's interest or in the public interest. Where emergency action is needed, the authority's staff, like any citizen, may apply to a justice for a *place of safety order*, empowering them to remove a child and detain him or her in a place of safety. The applicant must establish a *prima facie* case under section 1 (2a-f) and the order cannot extend for more than twenty-eight days. A police officer of the rank of inspector or above has a similar power {10} to detain a child for up to eight days. Either type of order may be converted at a hearing before a full juvenile court to an *interim care order*. Although these are civil proceedings, such orders can be thought of as analogous to remands. The child's detention continues, but the interim order must be reviewed by the court every twenty-eight days until a full hearing can be arranged. At each renewal objections may be lodged.

The court hearings themselves will be discussed in more detail later. For the present, we need only note that they are adversarial in character and that the parties are the local authority (or whoever else has applied) and the child. This opposition reflects the original assumption of the drafters of the 1969 Act that most cases would involve delinquent children. Although these cases were to be transferred to a civil jurisdiction, the

8

model procedure retains many criminal features. In fact, the 1969 Act remains the high-water-mark of the attempt to decriminalize juvenile offences. Most of its criminal jurisdiction was effectively removed by the incoming Conservative government and has never been restored. The basic design contrasts with the common pattern in the United States, where parents typically form the respondent party, and generates numerous procedural anomalies which we shall examine in due course. As the courts resolve these, however, the practical differences in procedure appear to diminish considerably.

Only two of the dispositions possible under the 1969 Act are of any real significance for abuse and neglect cases: supervision and care orders. *Supervision orders* last for three years and require the authority to appoint a person to 'advise, assist and befriend' the child (CYPA, 1969, s. 14). They do not confer a right of entry to the child's home, nor do they allow the supervisor to remove the child, other than through a place of safety procedure. However, the authority can return to the court and ask for the supervision order to be converted into a care order without reestablishing the original grounds. *Care orders* transfer all the powers and duties of a child's parents to the local authority for an indefinite period, terminating on the child's eighteenth birthday. The authority has almost entirely unfettered discretion over its management and placement of the child.

Both the 1948 and 1969 Acts define fairly closely the circumstances in which local authorities can intervene and the criteria which the justices should look to in evaluating the propriety of any particular action. Where, however, a child is thought to be in need of protection but his or her case is not covered by the relevant Acts, the {11} authority can resort to wardship. This is a common law, as opposed to a statutory, jurisdiction of the Family Division of the High Court. The only test is whether a judge can be convinced that it would be in the best interests of the child to make an order transferring parental rights to the court, to be discharged under such arrangements as he thinks fit. This is a uniquely flexible procedure but it offers considerable scope for uncontrolled judicial discretion.

Probably the most conspicuous difference between England and the United States is over mandatory reporting laws, requiring professionals to notify suspected mistreatment to a designated agency. All American states have such statutes but they do not exist anywhere in the United Kingdom. Once again, though, this may not be a matter of great practical significance. The basic principles in England were stated by the report of the public inquiry into the murder of Susan Auckland by her father.

> We consider that doctors working in hospitals . . . should be able to recognise evidence of a situation where a child not at present injured may be at risk, and when they see such evidence should at once notify the social services . . . [A] general practitioner should be able to recognise

9

evidence of a situation where a child might be at risk, and should not hesitate to notify either a health visitor, or the social services, or both, if he finds evidence of that kind . . . . It is the health visitor's duty to seek the assistance of the social services or the general practitioner or both if she sees a situation in which this is necessary. (Auckland 1975: paras 254, 259, 270)

Anyone failing to report relevant information to the local authority's social services department is likely to face public censure and professional or organizational disciplinary action, sanctions which seem as likely to be effective as the rarely-invoked civil or criminal penalties prescribed in the USA, although the latter can be useful for inter-agency bargaining.

The principles embedded in the formal charters under which Anglo-American health, welfare and legal agencies operate can be summarized as emphasizing the residual nature of state intervention. Substitute care is a last resort and, where possible, a purely short-term measure while parents are assisted into a condition where their children may be returned. The occasions on which compulsory measures can be taken are defined in statute and subjected to the check either of elected representatives, as in the English section 2 procedure, or more commonly the courts. It is only within these limits that agencies enjoy such legitimation as the legislature can confer on their interventions into family life. {12}

THE AGENCY SYSTEM

Statutes, as we have observed, are not self-enforcing. They depend upon people identifying cases of non-compliance and initiating appropriate action to mobilize the remedies available. The particular difficulty with mistreatment, though, is that children lack the civil status, and often the physical capacity, to seek redress on their own behalf. Others must do this for them. While this was originally a matter for voluntary associations of concerned citizens in both the UK and the USA, the responsibility has increasingly been assumed by various state agencies.

In England, powers and duties under child protection legislation are concentrated in the hands of local authority social services departments and discharged largely by certified social workers. Child protection is a high-cost, high-risk area for local authorities and it is important for the defence of their actions, whether to auditors or press critics, that duly qualified staff are seen to be taking the key decisions. Although social workers make extensive professionalist claims, social services departments are organized on classically bureaucratic principles. Nowhere is this more important than in child protection, where most departments have elaborate procedural rules and detailed provisions for accountability upwards. At the same time, these departments are dealing with a multitude of other client groups, including the elderly, the physically and mentally handicapped, the chronically sick and disabled and the mentally ill. Child protection must press its claim for departmental time and resources in competition with these other demands. Conversely, the departments face the problem of arriving at a defensible allocation of their services.

While social services departments command most of the relevant powers and resources, social workers make relatively few initial identifications of possible cases of mistreatment. The reason for this is quite simple: social services are essentially reactive rather than proactive.[5] That is to say, most of their cases result from referrals, either from other agencies or from would-be clients themselves. The latter is an unusual route for a child protection case. On the whole, people do not refer themselves for abusing or neglecting their children but for financial difficulties, housing problems and the like. As we shall show, once a referral is established on the latter grounds, it can be difficult for a social worker to perceive child protection issues within it. {13}

Although cross-national comparisons are always somewhat hazardous, it does seem arguable that England enjoys a rather more coherent and better-resourced system, with a greater stress on public-sector agencies, than many comparable countries. De Francis's (1972) survey of American provisions in 1967 noted a similar decline in voluntary associations' involvement but found that there had been no corresponding growth in the child protection activities of public welfare agencies. By his criteria, fewer than 10 per cent of the states offered near-complete geographic coverage. Between two-thirds and four-fifths of the staff involved lacked graduate training in social work. While the states had enacted mandatory reporting laws with great enthusiasm, this had not been matched by a corresponding willingness to vote funds for responsive services. Although subject to stringent financial economies in recent years, English social services still appear to be operating from a higher resource base.

The most important single source of referrals in our study was the health care system. In the county where most of our fieldwork was conducted, health service workers identified 53 per cent of the children under five referred during the first six months of 1979 to the three social services offices under study. All but a handful of these referrals, in fact, came from health visitors.

In the United Kingdom, the National Health Service provides comprehensive health care for the whole population, free at the point of contact and financed mostly from general taxation. At the time of the study, English hospital and preventive services were organized under three administrative tiers – Regions, Areas and Districts. Regions and Areas both had lay governing authorities, nominated by the Secretary of State for Social Services. Districts were local management units. A number of Areas, however, were too small to justify more than one district. These were recognized as notably more successful than multi-district Areas, and plans were in hand for a reorganization which would, in effect, suppress the Area tier and create District authorities. In selecting localities for our study, then, we focused on single-district Areas which might expect to be least affected by these changes. Within each tier, acute, chronic and community services are separately managed through distinct medical, nursing and administrative lines of authority.[6] Primary care services are organized through Family Practitioner Committees representing medical, dental, pharmaceutical and optical practitioners in territories roughly equivalent to the former Areas.

The community health services embrace both medical and nursing {14} staff. As we have seen, the most important sources of identifications of children in need of protection, at least as measured by social services referrals, are health visitors.[7] They are registered nurses with a specialist post-basic qualification in social science and public health. Most of their work involves the routine screening of the population of children under five, either at clinics or by home visiting. It should be stressed that eligibility for visiting is determined purely by demographic criteria, rather than by any test of need. In 1979, 82.5 per cent of all children in England under five received a visit in their home.[8] The majority of health visitors are now attached to general practitioners, although they remain health authority employees. Health visitors command no particular legal or financial resources and their access to people's homes is entirely voluntary. Partly because of this, we suggest, they have successfully maintained a good deal of autonomy for basic-grade staff, despite the overlay of a bureaucratic management structure in the late 1960s. Other community nurses include school nurses, who assist with the medical screening of schoolchildren, district nurses, who provide clinical nursing care to patients in their own homes, and community midwives, who routinely follow up all women with new babies until about ten days after confinement and who may, themselves, perform some deliveries. Any of these nurses may have assistance from nursing auxiliaries, depending upon local staffing policies.

Medical practitioners may become involved in identifying abuse and neglect at four points: in general practice, at child health clinics, in the accident service and in the maternity services. All of these are dealing with very large numbers of children. Every year about three-quarters of all children under fifteen will see their general practitioner, averaging between four and five consultations each. Child health clinics, for under fives, reach about 80 per cent of all children under one year, although this rate drops sharply after the age of two to less than one-third of those eligible. Between a quarter and a third of all patients in accident departments are children under fifteen. Virtually every birth in Britain involves a doctor at some point.[9]

As we shall show, three factors are important in analysing medical responses: the degree to which the doctors involved have any paediatric training – or other experience of children, their conceptualization of the doctor/patient relationship and their orientation to technical or holistic versions of medicine. The first should be self-evident. The second is partly linked to the employment relationship between the doctor and the NHS. Community physicians and hospital staff are employees, while general practitioners are self-employed {15} and contract with the NHS to provide services. These differences are reflected in the degree to which doctors are willing to think of themselves as agents of the NHS and, indirectly, the state, or as free individuals whose first obligation is to their patient. It can be argued, for instance, that English doctors have maintained their professional autonomy more successfully than have their American counterparts in the absence of mandatory reporting. Katz et al. (1976) found thirty-six states specifically denying doctors any discretion in deciding when the normal confidentiality of the doctor/patient relationship should be breached. On both sides of the Atlantic, doctors seem to have similar difficulties in defining 'the patient' when a parent presents with a mistreated child. The power of adults seems more important than the presence or absence of a specific financial relationship. Finally, the third dimension relates to the degree to which the doctor adopts a view of medicine as essentially biological engineering or as having a broader expertise in the repair of general problems of living.

Beyond this role in identification, we have the hospital paediatric services, who will almost invariably be consulted for specialist opinion on any suspected case of abuse or neglect. It is an important feature of the British medical system that specialist practitioners are available only by means of referrals from general practitioners, except in cases coming through accident services. Areas vary greatly in the rigour with which this is enforced. In some places community medical staff make referrals with a token consultative note to the child's general practitioner. Some paediatricians will accept 'under the counter' referrals from health visitors or social workers. Neither of these practices is, however, universal and the effect is to place the child's general practitioner in a powerful position, especially in relation to non-emergency cases.

Paediatrics is a specialty which has expanded dramatically in recent years, medical staff numbers tripling between 1963 and 1977. Its base has, however, changed significantly with the virtual elimination of infectious childhood diseases by public health measures. There is a discernible tension between technical and holistic responses to this loss of work. Some argue for a greater division of labour concentrating on increasingly specialized attempts to repair particular systems or organs, while others advocate a more community-oriented approach, looking to the prevention of disorder by environmental or individual intervention. Although organizationally distinct, it is convenient to mention child psychiatric services here. These, too, have expanded somewhat in recent years, but provision {16} remains very uneven and any involvement in the assessment of, for instance, emotional or mental development is highly dependent on the availability and interest of the local specialist.

Perhaps the most important thing to remember about medical involvement is that, with the partial exception of general practice, a child's first contact is likely to be with a relatively junior doctor. This has implications in terms of his or her values, aspirations, interests and knowledge, whether through specific training or as a parent. These junior staff are the gatekeepers, making a crucial decision about whether to accept and treat a child's signs and symptoms as presented or to initiate a further investigation.

The health and social services lie at the core of the system of identifying and managing cases of mistreatment. There are, however, a variety of other agencies which are involved with the child population and may feed cases into either organization, usually social services. Among the most important of these are education, police and probation, as statutory services, the NSPCC, a quasi-statutory service, local voluntary bodies like playgroups or mother and toddler clubs and, finally, kin and neighbours.

The same local authorities as provide social services also provide education services for their population. In Britain all children between the ages of five and sixteen should be in school and, thus, available for surveillance by teachers with the support of school health and child guidance workers. Compulsory school attendance is supported by the activities of education welfare officers. These latter were largely recruited to act as truancy officers but, in recent years, their work has taken on a less overtly coercive character and adopted a social work type of approach. Such changes have been reflected, to a degree, in current recruitment and retraining policies. School health and child guidance services can provide a back door for specialist medical assessment, since referral is freely available to school teachers, social workers and health visitors. Education departments have the power to initiate care proceedings for truancy, which may occasionally be significant as an evidentially straightforward means of responding to some cases of mistreatment.

Police forces are managed by separate authorities, whose membership is drawn from councillors elected to local government authorities and from local magistrates. Although some police theorists (e.g. Punch and Naylor 1973) present the force as the twenty-four-hour agency of first resort for social problems, it is not clear how widely this view is shared. The basic orientation of the police is in terms of responding to alleged crimes and in filtering the prosecutable from {17} the unprosecutable. Before sex discrimination legislation took effect, work with children was the prerogative of the women's section of the police, whose training and experience was biased towards welfare matters. This reservoir of skill has now been dispersed so that much seems to depend on the *ad hoc* response of the officers involved with any specific reported case. There may be some contrast with the United States here. Twenty-six of the states designate law-enforcement agencies as the recipients of mandatory reports.[10] Some of these have developed specialized response units like the one in Los Angeles described by Giovannoni and Becerra (1979). With isolated exceptions, police and social services have maintained a rather distant relationship in England, although there has recently been increasingly central government pressure for greater police involvement in mistreatment cases.

Probation officers are employed by yet another authority, the Probation Committee drawn from the magistrates in each local authority area. Nowadays, most probation staff have received what is essentially a generic social work training. The core of their duties with families is the administration of probation orders and the supervision of offenders, but they also have a significant involvement with the welfare of children through their role in furnishing social history reports for divorce proceedings. Any of these tasks may put them in a position to identify possible cases of mistreatment, although, as we shall see, much depends on the degree to which they are actually aware of this opportunity.

We referred to the National Society for the Prevention of Cruelty to Children (NSPCC) as a quasi-statutory body. This reflects its ambiguous position between the state and the voluntary sectors. In some respects it is an independent charity, with its own income through subscriptions, donations and legacies and its own governing body. On the other hand, it has received state grants on a substantial scale from time to time, its practice has a degree of state supervision and it enjoys some of the same legal powers as local authority social services, notably the power to initiate care proceedings for abuse or neglect. The society's operations have two main components. Firstly, there is a nationwide network of inspectors, investigating public complaints about children's treatment. This is, historically, the Society's key role and the one with which it is associated in the public mind. Nowadays, though, its work might be much better characterized in terms of initiating and developing demonstration projects which may provide models for subsequent state sector activities or which may continue under contract with local authorities. {18}

The NSPCC is a large national body, but the voluntary sector also contains a patchwork of local groups, although, again, many of these turn out to rely heavily on discreet financial or organizational help from local authority social services. Playgroups, for instance, have a surprisingly large involvement in the containment of mistreatment. Where a child's development is causing concern, a common move by the social services department is to pay for a playgroup place. The child's condition is then monitored by voluntary workers and his or her attendance record checked. Agency staff, particularly health visitors, can also come in to assess the child more frequently and more thoroughly than might be possible through home visiting. The possibility of such actions is a reflection of the financial support to the playgroup by social services, through payment of fees, subsidized rental of premises and the like, and the department's legal duties to inspect and regulate the quality of the playgroup's provision. Such bargaining power can be used to enlist voluntary helpers in support of social work objectives. Similar considerations apply to some of the self-help groups such as Parents Anonymous. In this area it is hard to discern the sort of autonomous activity which comes to mind when one polarizes service provision into the two conventional categories – state and voluntary.

Finally, we must mention the role of neighbours and kin. They are often unrivalled in their opportunity to identify mistreatment. However, that opportunity may, as we show later, constitute an important constraint on their ability to articulate their observations into an identification. Moreover, their lack of a theoretical basis for reaching such a conclusion may create difficulties in winning sufficient acceptance of their proposed identification by officially-recognized agencies. Again, this point will be elaborated further.

If a child's parents withhold compliance from voluntary intervention the health and social welfare agencies must resort to the courts for authority to act in a more coercive fashion. The juvenile courts in England are simply a special kind of magistrates' court. English magistrates' courts are typical of the lowest level of courts in Anglo-American legal systems. Their jurisdiction is limited to minor offences with fairly low maximum penalties. Characteristically the courts process large numbers of defendants, a high proportion of whom plead guilty and who are dealt with speedily. With the exception of a few metropolitan areas, the magistrates who sit in judgement are all amateurs, in the sense that they are not qualified as lawyers and have other full-time occupations. Legal advice is provided to them by a court official, the clerk. He, or occasionally she, is {19} increasingly likely to be a graduate with a professional qualification in law, but many of the older clerks are still largely self-taught, with the assistance of night classes or correspondence courses. Defendants tend to be represented by solicitors rather than barristers, historically the more prestigious segment of the legal profession. Nevertheless, such courts handle the overwhelming majority of legal work and constitute the commonest point of contact between citizens and the judicial system.

Juvenile courts cover most criminal matters involving children, with the important exception of homicide, and a number of civil matters, including the orders relating to the exercise of parental rights or duties, with which this study is concerned. Cases are heard before a panel of three magistrates who are selected from the more experienced of those hearing adult cases. At least one member of the panel must be a woman. In busy areas, a clerk may specialize in juvenile work, but few parts of the country generate enough cases to allow either solicitors or barristers to concentrate their practice in a similar fashion. Juvenile courts exclude the general public and defendants may not be identified in any press reports. Where possible, courtrooms are reserved for juvenile work and hearings scheduled separately from those of adult cases.

Care proceedings are almost invariably initiated by the relevant local authority social services department, which will normally be represented by a solicitor employed in the same authority's legal department. As the respondent party, the child is entitled to legal aid from public funds and will usually be represented by a solicitor in private practice. Since parents are not parties, they may be represented only at their own expense. While the local authority's solicitor and the court clerk are likely to be involved in such proceedings fairly regularly, they are less common experiences for individual magistrates or private practice solicitors, a fact which has important implications for the conduct of cases. The intricacies of representation under such conditions will be explored later.

Again contrasting England with the United States, one is struck by the social distance between the courts and the rest of the agency system. There seems to be much greater concentration on adjudication and comparatively little on case preparation or management. English courts do not have affiliated social workers, the probation service being deliberately kept at some distance and having little involvement with care proceedings for mistreatment. Representation is left to private practice lawyers, reimbursed from public funds, rather than being assigned to a public defender's office. Finally, once a {20} court order has been made, the local authority's discretion is virtually unfettered. Even the higher courts have consistently refused to intervene in this area.

We should, perhaps, reiterate that these legal and institutional descriptions are not intended to serve as more than a general orientation for our subsequent analysis. As we have indicated, detailed discussions of many points will be required as our argument unfolds. In the process, we intend to show how the official rubrics are translated into practical actions. Before doing so, however, we need briefly to outline the methodology of this study and describe the data on which it is based.

THE RESEARCH STRATEGY

Having recognized the way in which social problems are constructed by a process of definition, we decided from the outset that we should try to avoid either implicitly taking over the view of mistreatment which was current in any particular agency or stipulating our own ideal definition, which we could then use to draw ironic contrasts with the decisions that were actually being made. This study has no interest in telling the reader what mistreatment *really* is. As we have already stated, we think this would be a meaningless enterprise. What we are aiming to do is to show *what the relevant agency staff consider to be mistreatment* and how this constructs a particular population of identified cases.

Our first questions then were: how did front-line workers recognize mistreatment when they saw it and what subsequent actions did that identification provide for? We could not, of course, expect such decision-making to be a simple matter. We knew of the historical tensions and rivalries between agencies, founded on their respective analyses and remedies. Moreover, we recognized that fieldworkers in the public service operate within a legal and organizational context which constructs the data available to them and limits the conceptual or practical options for action through resource-allocation and supervisory decisions. So we decided that any study must be deeply rooted in the everyday practice of the relevant institutions. By contrast with the public inquiry model, we wanted to ensure that our analysis did not displace routine activities from the circumstances which generated them as preferred responses to per-ceived organizational problems.

These interests in the practical basis of agency work directed us to-wards an ethnographic style of research.[11] Such an approach is {21} partic-ularly suited to the study of social processes, since it relies on a continuing involvement of the researchers alongside those people actually involved in the processes. It is possible to chronicle events as they unfold, where others must rely on *post hoc* rationalizations or responses to hypothetical problems. In this sense, the difficulty, which survey research always faces, of how people's statements about what they do may be related to behav-iour in particular instances, is considerably reduced.

We chose to collect our data, then, primarily by direct observation, supplemented by the questioning of informants and by the scrutiny of the documents produced by various agencies. Both of these latter activities depend upon the observational data. This furnishes the base for inductive generalizations to be explored in interviews. For an ethnographer, it should be noted, 'interview' has a rather different meaning than for a survey researcher. An interview is a conversation directed towards a specific goal, which may form part of a period of field observation, a 'natural interview', or may be separated in time or space, an 'informal interview'. In either case, the researcher is exploring a list of topics rather than posing a particular set of questions. It is argued that such an ap-proach goes a long way to resolving many of the problems of meaning which confront the questionnaire designer. Since people respond differ-ently to the same form of words in a question, it may be useful to vary the phrasing in order to ensure that the meaning of the topic being addressed remains consistent. Without a good deal of knowledge about the topic, one cannot formulate relevant questions or interpret the answers.

This same consideration applies to the analysis of documents. If one does not have some understanding of the contexts in which they are written and read and the relevant purposes of writers and readers, then one cannot evaluate their significance. Records, reports or whatever are not literal descriptions of some reality: they are, rather, accounts which organize and, in some sense, create the reality which they describe, within the constraints of some particular occasion on which they are read.

The researcher's observations, questions and inductions are, then, closely united. These data are organized in a dialogue with a general theoretical apparatus developed from previous ethnographies. It is important to stress, however, that this literature is regarded as a source of sensitizing concepts rather than directions. We know, for instance, that records play an important part in many previously-studied organizations. From this, we conclude that it is likely that such documents will repay particular attention in our data collection and {22} analysis. The first injunction, however, is to characterize the meaning of these documents for the people in this study before considering possible similarities and differences with other studies. Our disciplinary literature tells us where to look, but not necessarily what to look for.

This point is worth some emphasis because a frequent challenge to ethnography relates to the possibilities for bias either in the collection of data or in the effects of observation upon the observed. We have already noted the discipline of fidelity to data. However, the possibilities for systematic bias are limited in this study. Where many ethnographies have depended upon a single investigator and his ability to convince an audience of his integrity, we have had the benefit of collaborative data collection. This works in two ways. Firstly, we have different national, academic, intellectual and social backgrounds. There are very few areas of data in this study which are based on the observations of a single team member. Obviously, over five years, we have come to influence each other a good deal. Nevertheless, what is presented here represents data which had been jointly collected and jointly analysed. In that sense, some of the more obvious possibilities for biased reporting are limited. Secondly, we have been obliged to be a great deal more meticulous in our data handling than has conventionally been the case. All our data have had to be collected with an eye to communal use. In practice, this has meant an attempt to achieve near-verbatim accounts in our notes from field observations. For many of the formalized settings like court hearings and case conferences, we have used two investigators taking simultaneous notes which were subsequently combined into an agreed version. The remaining material was dictated from the raw notes on to tape, generally on the evening of the day on which it was collected. The tapes were then transcribed into a standard A4 format. It is, perhaps, worth adding that we adopted a policy of overt note-taking wherever possible. This means that our initial notes were, for the most part, taken as events occurred, rather than being brief scribblings in lavatories or similar secluded corners. Where we conducted interviews, we almost invariably taped them and had similar transcripts prepared. In total, we have something over seven thousand A4 sheets of data containing around two million words.

Analysing such a volume of material presents its own problems. We adopted a computerized retrieval system. The basic principle is similar to that of indexing a book. A preliminary list of topics is drawn up and each sheet of data given a unique reference number. {23} Every page is then read and coded for the topics appearing on it. In this process further topics may be added, although it is generally advisable to wait until a substantial body of data has been collected and an extended provisional list created so that the number of topics introduced during coding is restricted. In this study, the initial coding was divided between Topsy Murray and John Eekelaar, while Robert Dingwall checked every sheet. The code sheets are punched and the computer program used to invert them, producing a list of all the locations at which each topic appears. The topics may be connected by various logical operators for sub-searches. We then took the index and used it to make the thematic searches by hand which form the basis of our subsequent discussions.

Obviously, we can present only a limited selection of this material here. In that sense, the reader must necessarily take our presentation on trust to some degree. However, it should be apparent that in making these particular choices, we have conducted an exhaustive search of our data. This book is not just some collection of anecdotes which support our views, but is the result of a collective, considered attempt to assess, weigh, and interpret a large body of detailed material.

The reader may, however, still be worried about the degree of reactivity. How far can our presence be said to have influenced the phenomena under consideration? We have already alluded to our decision to take field notes openly. In our view, this is desirable both ethically, in that it reminds our subjects that they are being researched, and intellectually. Nevertheless, it plainly aggravates the risk of observer effects. These can, however, be much exaggerated. In a case conference or court hearing, it is easy to merge into a crowd of people, many of whom will be writing themselves. During our agency observations, we spent extended periods with most of the work groups and individuals involved, which allowed them to become accustomed to our presence. More importantly, however, in both of these cases, the people involved had to meet other and more important pressures. Whether over a period of routine work or in managing a crisis, the requirements of task performance take precedence. The threat to a worker from an inadequate response in such a context is more immediate and tangible than the indeterminate threat from a distant piece of research by someone not employed by the agency and with no individual sanction available. In an area like child protection, of course, this is further compounded by the uncertainty and ambivalence in most agencies about their role. Given this, it can be argued that any consistent attempts at impression management {24} by workers would be self-cancelling, since the arguments between intervention and non-intervention are so finely-balanced. Even if researchers were important enough to worry about, acceptable occupational practices are so ill-defined as to defeat most subjects.

In analysing the material we do, in any case, attempt to weigh the significance of each piece of information. We consider, for instance, the context in which someone has spoken, the nature of the occasion, the other members of the audience, the speaker's relation to the people present and his or her stake in the encounter. It should also be remembered that most of our data have been generated by at least two of the team in different locations. We have therefore, also tried to assess whether there are conspicuous discrepancies between, for example, Robert Dingwall and Topsy Murray's observations of health visitors. There is a considerable emphasis in the ethnographic tradition on the importance of analysing deviant cases for what they reveal about proposed generalizations. For the charge of observer effect to succeed, a critic would need to demonstrate a consistent difference between behaviour presented to us and behaviour in our absence, which we have failed to identify.

It is this sifting process which partly accounts for our conservative approach to the quantification of our data. Such an operation necessarily entails assumptions about the homogeneity of the category being summarized by a number, which may be seriously misleading. There is also a risk that quantification will misrepresent the nature of the sampling universe. Our data are produced by theoretical rather than random sampling, which naturally makes us reluctant to venture beyond an ordinal level of measurement in respect of the frequency of events. A detailed examination of one case which agency staff themselves recognized as atypical may actually be more useful for our purposes than ninety-nine cases which present no extraordinary features.

Finally, we should also comment on our resource support. One of the great limitations of much British ethnography has been its small scale, so that studies have often been restricted to what one individual could accomplish within very limited resources. The evidence for its generalizations has, consequently, sometimes been rather thin. With more adequate staffing and secretarial resources, we have been able to introduce an explicitly comparative approach. Although a sample of three local authority areas may still seem small, it was drawn on specific theoretical grounds, selecting localities which were, on the face of it, wholly unlike each other. The basic parameters of {25} the agencies we were interested in are defined by statute. There is, however, considerable scope for variations reflecting the material circumstances of an area – its demography, social geography, industrial and economic organization, etc. – and local cultural and political philosophies. By maximizing these latter contrasts, we could test our inductive generalizations from the data collected in our first authority. In this respect, the comparative fieldwork approached a more conventional model of hypothesis-testing.

THE RESEARCH DESIGN

We have been peculiarly fortunate, under the funding arrangements of our research unit, in being able to follow an evolutionary approach to this study. Rather than specifying a neat design in advance, then, we have, throughout, been able to rethink, modify and adapt our fieldwork in response to our emerging analysis. This flexibility has been a great facilitator but it does, inevitably, mean that our account of the project design may lack some of the (often spurious) elegance of more structured approaches. The most sensible way of proceeding would seem to be through a brief natural history of the study.

The original idea came from John Eekelaar's work on custody after divorce (Eekelaar and Clive 1977), where he became interested in the ways in which lawyers and courts handled issues concerning the welfare of children. Care proceedings under the Children and Young Persons Act 1969 offered another arena where such matters could be studied. In these hearings, evidence relating to the social circumstances of children was, it seemed, reviewed to consider whether the children's interests might be better served by the suspension of parental rights, duties, obligations or whatever in favour of the local authority.[12] John Eekelaar developed contacts with the social services department in Shire, the county where most of the fieldwork was carried out. Shortly afterwards he was joined by Robert Dingwall, who had previously been involved with research on community health services for children (Dingwall 1977a). Together, they also reached agreement with the legal department of Shire County Council and the community nursing division of the Shire Area Health Authority for what turned out to be the first phase of the study.

'Shire' is fairly typical of the English Shire Counties. It has a population of about half a million, a high level of economic prosperity {26} and a traditionally Conservative council. The councillors represent a landed interest with a strong paternalist streak rather than the more abrasive suburban elements which currently mark the party leadership. There has, then, been a greater sympathy with public expenditure than one might otherwise have expected. At one edge, Shire forms part of the London commuter belt and there is, indeed, some long-distance commuting from most parts of the county. About a third of the population live in the county town of Midchester. Like most of the South East, this expanded rapidly in the 1930s and its economy is dependent on employment in light engineering, science and technology. There are some sizeable higher education establishments and a tourist trade but no heavy or depressed industries. Although there are pockets of unemployment in some of the surrounding market towns, the rural areas share this economic buoyancy. The rate of care proceedings for abuse or neglect seems to be somewhat lower than the national average, about 2.5 per ten thousand population under eighteen compared with 4.5 per ten thousand for the whole of England and Wales.

Initially, the main interest of the study was in court hearings, the organization and presentation of evidence and the consequent disposal decisions. Accordingly, it was decided to begin on a case study basis. John Eekelaar and Robert Dingwall observed case conferences, to record what evidence was presented for consideration in discussing whether to bring a case, and court hearings, comparing the evidence presented with that previously discussed. Health visiting and social work records were read as data on the history of the case and key workers, generally health visitors and social workers, interviewed about their perceptions of the case, the factors precipitating intervention at this time and the extent of information which was not used in the formal decision-making of case conferences or court hearings.

Including a number of cases which were picked up during later phases of the study, 27 case files were compiled, covering 34 children, 12 boys and 22 girls, with ages ranging from one child who became the subject of proceedings at birth to another aged fourteen-and-a-half whose welfare was suffering as a consequence of the effects on her mother of a progressive degenerative hereditary condition of the brain. We attended 11 full hearings of care proceedings in the magistrates' court and 25 case conferences. Twelve interviews were conducted with social workers and five with health visitors (sometimes more than one worker was present).

As the research progressed, however, it became clear that it would {27} throw insufficient light on the screening process by which cases came up as care proceedings. It was plain that we would need to look more closely at the passage of cases between agencies, particularly given social services departments' discretion to refuse referrals. We would also need to consider the internal arrangements for supervision and management, since, for many of the fieldworkers involved, case conferences could, effectively, be convened only with the support of a bureaucratic superior. There was then, evidently, filtering going on which resulted in the apparent irrelevance of case conferences as arenas for decision-making as opposed to establishing a commitment to some action effectively decided upon in advance. We therefore decided to undertake a programme of observation within the health and personal social services. In this we proposed to analyse the successive sifting of candidate cases by fieldworkers, by their supervisors, by those making and by those receiving referrals, which led to the identification of children as having been abused or neglected and their allocation between the various disposal options available.

At this stage, DHSS funding became available and the project team was joined by Topsy Murray, a local government administrator with experience in liaising between social services and legal departments and in servicing an Area Review Committee. The second phase of the study was based on a division of labour between Robert Dingwall and Topsy Murray, on the one hand, and John Eekelaar, on the other.

John Eekelaar undertook an analysis of a sample of case records held by Shire Legal and Social Services Departments with a view to determining whether there had been any significant changes in intervention policy over the years since the 1974 reorganization of local government, when the county was created in its present form. This, of course, also allowed some check on possible observer effects on qualitative features of decision-making since the beginning of field-work. Summaries of 25 cases were dictated for further analysis. After completing this, John Eekelaar collected comparative data on local authority solicitors to set with those generated in Shire. Given the small number of solicitors involved in this work in any one authority, it would otherwise have been difficult to distinguish structural features of lawyers' work in local government from personal idiosyncrasies. In total, interviews were conducted with solicitors in 15 local authorities. It may be convenient at this point to add that we also interviewed, at various times, clerks to five magistrates' courts and solicitors from 13 private practices. {28}

Meanwhile, Robert Dingwall and Topsy Murray began a programme of observation with staff in the social work and health visiting services. Three area teams were selected in Shire, together with the most nearly coterminous health visiting sectors. The fieldwork lasted a total of 24 weeks, in the course of which the investigators 'shadowed' three Area Directors, 10 Senior Social Workers, 14 Social Workers, three Senior Nursing Officers, five Nursing Officers and 12 Health Visitors. For the first two areas, Robert Dingwall observed firstline and middle management in both services while Topsy Murray observed fieldworkers. This was designed to provide inter-observer checks and to monitor observer effects. These controls were extended by a partial crossover in the last area, where Robert Dingwall worked on both levels in the health visiting sector while Topsy Murray covered both levels in the area team. Three hundred and twelve households were visited with health visitors and 132 households with social workers. A further 190 health visiting clients were seen at clinic sessions and eight social work clients in group work. Observations were also carried out in the Accident Department at the Victoria Hospital in Midchester and with the Area Review Committee. Members of the team attended seven meetings of the full committee and four meetings of a sub-group charged with revising the inter-agency procedure manual. Finally, we also interviewed two of the consultant paediatricians at the Victoria Hospital and the Principal Medical Social Worker together with one of her staff who had a particular involvement with abuse and neglect cases.

In order to establish the limits of generalization possible from these Shire data, Robert Dingwall and Topsy Murray also spent six weeks in two other local authority areas. Within the constraint already discussed, of coming under single-district health authorities, these were selected to present environments which sharply contrasted with that of Shire.

'County' lies in one of the more remote parts of England. It formerly enjoyed a certain prosperity from extractive industry but the main employment now is seasonal, in the holiday trade, or dependent upon the vicissitudes of the farming and fishing industries. There are a few small military installations. Although its population approaches that of Shire, it is relatively scattered and the largest centres are little more than overgrown market towns. Politically, the council is not strongly partisan in character. Although its general tenor is Conservative, the party whip sits lightly and there is a tradition of independence.[13]

'Borough' is typical of many traditional Labour authorities in the {29} North of England. Its population is again similar to that of County but packed into a small Metropolitan Borough. The main employment is heavy industry, although it has fared better than some in recent years. One of our informants advised us to read *Coal is Our Life* (Dennis et al. 1956) to understand the sort of community we were dealing with. That advice would be highly appropriate. We concentrated on the industrial parts in our fieldwork, although, like many of these boroughs, there were some surprisingly rural areas.

Our methodology changed here somewhat to give greater weight to interviewing, although some observation was carried out in both areas. This was partly practical, to increase the spread of our data, and partly reflected our developing familiarity with the contingencies of everyday practice, which enabled us to move rapidly to relevant lines of questioning. Since we intended to use these data mainly to test our Shire findings, rather than to make substantive comments on either County or Borough, we felt the sacrifice of depth for breadth was justifiable.[14]

In editing the data for publication, we have followed a number of conventions. Obviously, all names have been changed and other non-material personal details modified in order to preserve the anonymity of informants, authorities and clients. Beyond this, we have referred to all doctors and lawyers as male and all nurses as female, since to retain the original sex of informants may have rendered them identifiable. Social workers have been randomly allocated, reflecting the more equal original proportions of male and female informants. We use the terms 'parents' and 'families' fairly loosely. This partly reflects agency usage, but also avoids clumsy circumlocutions. Unless otherwise indicated, then, 'parent' includes cohabitees of an adult biologically related to a particular child and adult caretakers of children not related to them. 'Family' includes all household arrangements within which children are living. 'Children' is used in a similarly commonsensical fashion.

All quotations are as they appear in our notes or transcripts, except in a few cases of grammatical obscurity during descriptive passages in our field notes. In all these data extracts, . . . indicates a pause or hesitation in the original speech and (. . .) indicates that a portion of the original has been omitted. Explanatory interpolations are identified by the letters CSLS appearing at the end of the brackets. Unintelligible passages in interview transcripts are indicated by (-u-).

Our time and resources did not, unfortunately, permit us to include an inner-city area with a substantial West Indian or {30} Asian population. We regret this to some degree. The data from John Eekelaar's legal interviews suggest that there are peculiar features about practice in central London, for instance. However, we feel that the experience of such areas is already well-represented, particularly in the more polemical literature, and that our choices do permit a fair depiction of the circumstances in which the majority of those involved in child protection actually work.[15] This is a point we shall return to in the conclusion, where we argue against many of the more simplistic policies which have been advocated on the basis of exceptional experiences. For the present, however, let us concentrate on documenting practice representative of the greater part of England.

2

The Child as a Clinical Object

{31}
Our basic hypothesis is that abuse and neglect are the products of complex processes of identification, confirmation and disposal rather than inherent in a child's presenting condition and, at least in some sense, self-evident. If this is correct, then we would expect to find areas of uncertainty where the appropriateness of defining a particular child as abused or neglected was a matter for debate. It may be possible to limit these areas by formalizing decision rules. Some authorities, for instance, issue front-line workers with checklists of signs thought to be indicative of mistreatment. Nevertheless, at some point, someone must actually decide whether a child is or is not a member of the class of mistreated children. In designing the study, therefore, we sought to observe occasions on which such choices were made and to question the participants about their decision-making procedures.

To anticipate the argument of the next three chapters, we found that most agency staff distinguished two types of evidence. The first kind is what we have chosen to call *clinical* evidence, that is to say the data which are yielded by examining the child's body, signs, and by the child's reports of his or her physical sensations, symptoms. The second, we have called *social* evidence. Here, the data are thrown up by an investigation of the child's environment, covering matters like the observable quality of relations with parents, the material conditions of the household and the circumstances of the alleged injury or other physical disorder. In either case, contemporary inquiries may be supplemented by searches of records for details of the child's clinical or social history. The former type of evidence is largely, but not exclusively, associated with doctors; the latter, again largely rather than exclusively, with social workers. Health visitors have access to both. Identifications, however, cannot be concluded without inquiry into a third matter, namely, responsibility for the {32} child's condition. Social evidence is of particular importance in this respect, for the inferences which may be made about the moral character of family members.

We did, however, find that some, although a minority, of our informants rejected this model by claiming that there was no uncertainty and that abuse or neglect could be sufficiently inferred from clinical evidence alone. Could we justify our hypothesis in the face of this challenge? Were we over-complicating a simple matter? Further, although this charge was not explicitly made, did the majority view merely represent confused and inadequate professional practice?

'THE BONES TELL A STORY . . .'

The view that clinical evidence is invariably self-sufficient was expressed most clearly in an interview with a consultant paediatrician. He had stated, in discussing referrals, that his main source was the local accident department.

RD: So obviously that must have depended to a considerable degree on the ability of the casualty officers to identify . . .

CONS: They were taught quite intensively after a time and of course the consultants there and the registrars would recognize doubtful cases and ask me if they were worried.

RD: Yes. Did you find this a fairly straightforward thing to get across to them, that, in a sense, certain injuries could be taken as unequivocal signs of abuse?

CONS: Yes. I had one great advantage in that sphere, that's my age. You know, an aged old grandad, people are less likely to dispute with him. I found it very good being grandad.

In the light of the data presented later in this chapter on accident departments, this ready agreement with our proposition, that 'certain injuries could be taken as unequivocal signs of abuse', seemed odd. We therefore brought the interview back to the topic a few minutes later:

RD: No, I was thinking that, you know, it's a very difficult task surely for a house officer in a busy accident set-up like the Victoria, you know, he has very limited social background information on a child. {33}

CONS: I don't. I haven't found this nor did Henry Kempe. The so-called grey areas as far as we're concerned don't exist. And what we would say to the in . . ., you've probably read the instructions that the Area Review Committee issued, the form, haven't you, you know, that if a child under two years of age is injured, seriously injured, then it shouldn't have happened. You know, if it gets seriously injured in a road traffic accident, it shouldn't bloody well have happened because it should be in the back of the car sitting in its little old seat with its whatnots on, you know, I mean I regard that as gross neglect, don't you?

TM: Yes. So any under-two-year-old shouldn't present the injuries or any injuries should be considered suspicious.

CONS: No, no, no injuries at all. And, you know, the explanation is irrelevant because it shouldn't have happened.

We continued probing, but this doctor's position remained essentially unchanged. What he was arguing, in effect, was a principle of strict liability, that any injuries to a child were sufficient to support an allegation of parental neglectfulness, acts of omission or want of care, if not, indeed, actual abuse.

This analysis has some support in the medical literature. Kempe and his colleagues (1962), in their original paper on 'The Battered-Child Syndrome', observe that, 'To the informed physician, the bones tell a story the child is too young or too frightened to tell.' Like most doctors, however, they are cautious about the possibility of identifying abuse or neglect on clinical evidence alone. They stress, for instance, that, 'A marked discrepancy between clinical findings and historical data as supplied by the parents is a major diagnostic feature of the battered-child syndrome.' Similarly, Bamford (1976: 58) remarks, 'The only injuries in abused children that are rarely, if ever, simulated by disease processes are those in which the epiphyses are displaced and small fragments of bone pulled away from their growing ends.' Even this, he notes, can be produced after difficult breech deliveries or over-zealous physiotherapy. Hull (1974) concludes that clinical evidence can do no more than suggest the desirability of a detailed inquiry into the child's social environment. Bittner and Newberger (1981: 205) put forward a similar view, noting that 'the diagnosis is often impossible to make with certainty' and stressing the need for multidisciplinary inquiry into the family history to assess the plausibility of alternative explanations. Finally, Friedman (1972: 90) admonishes, 'there are no pathognomic findings {34} in cases of abuse, and the diagnoses, even to some degree in cases of admitted guilt, are clinical judgements on the part of the physician.'

The majority of our informants, it must be stressed, professed views which were closer to this latter position. The first example is taken from an interview with an area director of social services.

AD: (. . .) the health visitor found a bruise on his cheek and was suspicious for ages, I really couldn't get anybody with me on this. But then eventually when it was felt that this child needed to be seen by a doctor, worried about movement in his left leg, the GP did agree to see it and we were, I called an NAI conference, went all the way down to New Thorpe (. . .) He graciously came in, very prickly. I tried to help him see that the little bruise on his face and the horrific nappy rash, you know, from hip to knees, perhaps seen on his own child mightn't have aroused, he could have said, 'Its feed's all wrong. It's an allergy rash, and the bruise he could have done this by banging his face on a rattle.' I said, 'But seen in context of this family, it's worrying' and eventually he was beginning to soften, but he wasn't convinced you see. Well he refused to go through the normal path of casualty and he sent him to Holborough Hospital to be X-rayed, he was determined that he was going to deal with it himself and not follow it through. I think he was quite shocked to find that the child had a fractured femur, fractured ribs and a pneumothorax, you see.

In a further interview, another consultant recounted a similar story about his attempt to sensitize a local forensic pathologist to the possible contribution of abuse or neglect in cases of sudden infant death. Our informant explained that he had gone to observe a number of autopsies and noticed that, although the weight of the body was recorded, the pathologist appeared to attach no significance to it but immediately made an incision in the chest, opened the lungs to find fluid and recorded the death as the result of a respiratory tract infection. By mapping the weight on a chart showing its statistical distribution at particular ages and adding his own observations on the infant's skin condition, our informant said that he had been able to persuade his colleagues that many of these deaths were due to neglect which left the child vulnerable to infection.

The point which we would draw from these stories is not an ironic contrast between the sharp wit of the tellers and the naiveté of the subjects but rather the importance of the theoretical context within which observations are made. The first consultant reaches his conclusions by drawing on one set of ideas about the nature of childhood and the responsibility of parents. For him, children should {35} exist in a state of biological perfection. The least injury or blemish is a consequence and demonstration of parental failure. The two subsequent accounts offer a more pragmatic approach, where cases are examined in the light of specific hypotheses, with an initial preference for finding a 'natural' explanation, that is to say one which did not involve an imputation of responsibility. The general practitioner and the pathologist looked for sufficient evidence (an extended rash, fluid in the lungs) to confirm particular natural causes (allergy, sudden infant death). Our informants had different hypotheses and brought in other sorts of evidence (the family circumstances, the child's general condition) to open up the possibility of identifying these cases as the result of human agency, specifically neglectful parenting. These data were equally available to all four people but their different starting points led them to different conclusions.

The first consultant bases his argument on the view that an explicit moral code is an essential basis for a good society.

CONS: (. . .) I tried to bring my children up in the fear and nurture of the Lord and some people think that was wrong. You know, you've got to choose your standards and your ethics and your beliefs and you have to teach them to your children. Some people say you shouldn't. You should leave them free to choose. This is a load of rubbish because the children want to know and you've got to tell them. You've got to give them clear standards.

This moral code represents an absolute standard and, as such, may be used to justify the policing of private conduct under the criminal sanction.

CONS: (. . .) There's probably some increase (in sexual abuse CSLS) because of the blatancy of perverts (-u-) to flaunt perversion. They always did flaunt it a bit but the newspapers are letting them flaunt it a bit more (. . .) I don't think that the so-called liberalizing of the laws against sexual perversion have done anything but harm.

Similar moral themes run through a good deal of the published literature. Parton (1981) has discussed this material in detail for the UK: these examples are from the USA.

There is no strata of our society currently giving the problem of abuse and neglect the attention it demands. Violence is glorified rather than abhored on television: schools teach basket weaving rather than child and family development: over $120 billion are spent to defend against {36} a threat from without while our families, the core of our society, are being eroded with the cancer of abnormal rearing practices. Parenting practices in our society are likened to the great tree, standing erect, shielding us from the sun, only to fall one day from internal decay. (Heifer and Kempe 1976: xviii)

. . . the effect of childhood maltreatment very seldom wears off as the abused child grows into adulthood. We must be concerned with the effect of today's battering and neglect upon tomorrow's adults. What we, in our present inaction are doing is permitting our neighbours and our peers to not only mistreat their children but produce a new generation of criminal misfits who are going to turn around and attack us and our children (. . .) it is inextricably linked with unbearable stress, with impossible living conditions, with material or spiritual poverty, with distorted values, with disrespect for human life and with drug addiction, alcoholism, assaults, armed robberies, murders and other ills in the midst of which we live – and for which we must find massive healing. (Fontana 1976: 226)

Where right and wrong are so clearly defined, strict liability may be applied. If all childhood injuries or disorders are evidence of deficiency on the part of parents, it is simply unnecessary to embark on a detailed inquiry into the attribution of responsibility. Moreover, where this moral code is absolute, departures from the ideal cannot be the result of responsible and rational choices but indicate individual psychopathology (cf. Gelles 1973). The extent of such pathology may be used as the basis for a comprehensive moral critique of contemporary society.[1] The majority stance of our informants is altogether more pragmatic in its preference for a case-by-case approach which starts from an expectation that there is a natural explanation for the observed clinical findings and that this can be displaced only by demonstrating a chain of social causality. All parents are respectable and all injuries or disorders in children have a natural cause, unless and until the contrary can be proven.

These two models give us two decision rules set out in figure 1. {37} Rule (a) represents the minority view, that that identification is self-evident while rule (b) represents the majority view that clinical evidence

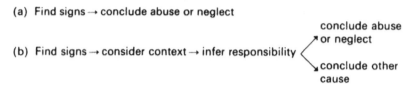

(a) Find signs → conclude abuse or neglect

(b) Find signs → consider context → infer responsibility → conclude abuse or neglect / conclude other cause

Figure 1 Possible decision rules for identifying abuse or neglect

must be supplemented by a broader scrutiny of the child's general state and his or her social environment as a preliminary to attributing responsibility for the presenting signs and symptoms. Which of these characterizes the process of identification?

We have already presented indirect evidence in our informants' anecdotes. To substantiate our case, however, we intend to present direct evidence from our own observations in two settings where social evidence is limited but there is ample clinical evidence available for inspection by doctors, the socially licensed experts in interpreting such material. What picture emerges from environments which are particularly favourable to the operation of the 'self-evident' model of decision-making?

ACCIDENT DEPARTMENTS

In the course of our fieldwork, we collected data on four accident departments in the three areas. One of these departments was a peripheral unit attached to a small general hospital but the other three were all major accident units, each dealing with about 80,000 patients per year. We completed twenty-eight hours' participant observation over a period of six days at the Victoria Hospital in Shire and carried out interviews with both medical and nursing staff elsewhere. This may be a smaller data base than we would ideally have liked: on the other hand, where we can check details with other ethnographic accounts of British accident services, they are remarkably consistent.

For medico-legal reasons virtually every patient who presents at an accident department will, ultimately, be seen by a doctor. Patients follow one of two routes. Most come through the 'front door', that is to say, they arrive at the department other than by ambulance and go to the reception desk. A receptionist records the time of arrival and takes down from the patients basic information like their name, age, sex, address, occupation and name of GP. These records go into a box which is used by the nurses for scheduling. Patients go to a waiting area, are called through into a holding area and then go through to the treatment area as space becomes available. There may be some contact with a nurse at this point but otherwise the patient will be seen by the duty Senior House Officer (SHO) and give a preliminary history. The SHO may send the patient to X-ray or {38} pass him to a nurse to be prepared for examination and treatment. Patients coming through the 'back door' are generally arriving by ambulance and assumed to represent more serious cases. They are admitted directly to the treatment area. If they are not accompanied the receptionist comes round to collect the record information. Such patients will normally be prepared for examination by the nurses before being seen by a doctor. At least initially, they receive priority over 'front door' cases.

What sort of consultations result? This example, from our Shire data, was described by the doctor involved as 'an average consultation for children . . . nothing very exciting'. The patient is an eight-year-old boy, accompanied by a young man whose identity is never, in fact, established by the doctor.

SHO: How did it happen?

BOY: I fell off a swing.

MAN: No. He was pushed over.

SHO: Where does it hurt?

> The boy points to his wrists and the SHO feels them. His next remark is addressed to the boy.

SHO: Did you manage to sleep?

> The boy remains silent.

MAN: No, he hasn't slept very well.

> The SHO writes on the record that the boy fell off the swing and sends them both off to X-ray. The whole consultation has taken about three minutes.

Such interaction closely resembles Strong's (1979a) description of the 'bureaucratic frame', a type of encounter which, he suggests, may predominate in the National Health Service.[2] The idea of a frame is taken from Goffman (1975: 10):

> I assume that definitions of a situation are built up in accordance with principles of organization which govern events – at least social ones – and our subjective involvement in them: frame is the word I use to refer to such of these basic elements as I am able to identify. {39}

Among those elements are the qualities which each party ascribes to the other. In his study of paediatric out-patient clinics, Strong shows how parents are assumed to be honest, competent and caring and the disorders of their children to be natural events. Where the evidence for such assumptions was weak or absent, doctors engaged in various kinds of interactional work which attempted to reconstitute the parents' character within the principles of the frame.[3]

It should be apparent that this encounter centres on the SHO and the boy. The doctor does not seem to respond to the young man's interventions and records the boy's version of the history. When we asked several of the SHOs why they preferred the child's version, they pointed out that the parent or adult companion had often not directly witnessed the accident and was not, therefore, competent to give evidence. Nevertheless, the example does illustrate how limited a history is required within this frame. The doctor merely needs to find out which part of the body to look at and, if there is a head injury, whether there was any loss of consciousness. The first is well within the capacity of even relatively small children and parents may not know the answer to the second.

This framing results from three contingencies, two of which are specific to accident services and one of which is more general. Firstly, there is the organizational problem of the screening task that would be involved if every child patient were treated as a prospective case of abuse or neglect and investigated on that basis. As we have already seen, children make up a very large proportion of the patients seen in accident departments. Even if one screened on simple clinical criteria, the studies quoted in the Court Report (1976) suggest that as many as four-fifths of all children's cases have possibly non-accidental causes, including fractures, wounds, dislocations, sprains, lacerations, superficial injuries, foreign bodies in eyes, ears or other orifices, burns, adverse reactions from medical agents or toxic effects from non-medicinal agents.

The framing, however, is not simply a matter of workload. The SHOs we observed in Shire, for instance, could always find time to enlarge their clinical experience by watching the duty registrar carry out an unusual procedure or assisting the resuscitation team, even if other patients were waiting. We must, then, add to the organizational dimension an occupational dimension. SHOs are trainee doctors. Indeed, since accident work is low-status, staffing levels are maintained only by requiring six months' employment as a part of certain specialty trainings. Most of the doctors we saw wanted to be surgeons or to work in closely allied fields of hospital {40} medicine. They were, then, motivated to inspect the patients presented to them in terms of the possibilities for clinical learning, under what we might call a 'rule of clinical priority'. This was compounded, particularly in the Victoria, a high-status teaching hospital, by the intense competition for SHO posts. One of the ways a junior doctor could draw attention to his talents was by picking out patients whose condition would interest his seniors (Jeffery 1979; Dingwall and Murray 1983). The duty rotas for SHOs meant that they would be involved in orthopaedic or general surgical outpatient clinics and in covering relevant wards. These tended to sustain a view of accident work as part of hospital medicine rather than as having any particular relationship with primary care or community services. The clinical orientation is reinforced by the doctors' sense of vulnerability to litigation and the consequent need to produce independent confirmation of a diagnosis, from signs, rather than relying on patients' reports of their symptoms.[4]

Finally, as Strong notes, a bureaucratic framing avoids openly identifying doctors as regulatory agents, despite their position as state employees. The doctor/patient relationship is constructed as a partnership, a collaboration of right-thinking persons against a random, natural enemy. Citizens are assumed to be respectable until proven otherwise.

One of the consequences of the framing, however, is that it becomes very difficult to make allegations of mistreatment. The frame constitutes a set of assumptions which provide for the interpretation of the available data. Where the data are at odds with the framing principles, they are likely to be viewed as 'reality disjunctures'. In discussing these, Pollner (1975) observes that, when we see a fuzzy road sign, we tend to conclude that our eyesight is at fault because our perception of the world is so framed that we *know* that road signs have sharp definition. Similarly, when a doctor or other member of the accident staff sees an injury to a child he or she knows, in some sense, that this *must* be an accident and that a natural explanation can be produced. Conversely, the parent assumes this orientation to the frame on the part of the doctor and is likely to hear a request for an explanation as a possible implication that one cannot be produced and, hence, as some sort of challenge to his or her identity as honest, competent and caring.

As we would predict, if we are correct about the strength of the frame, accident staff found it difficult to answer direct questions about what triggered off an investigation. One consultant referred to his common-sense 'index of suspicion' accumulated over a number of {41} years' experience. A staff nurse talked about 'something that sets one off thinking a child may have been abused. A sister-in-charge claimed '. . . you can tell by looking, just by looking sometimes that things are not right, it's just experience'. Significantly, the less-experienced junior doctors found it hard even to make statements at this level. Is it possible to go further and specify the conditions under which this frame is broken?

Strong himself suggests that certain types of medical encounter are characterized by what he calls a 'charity frame', where patients' moral character is routinely scrutinized as a condition of treatment. As he recognizes, his data are limited to observations of one doctor working in a free clinic in Connecticut used by black and Puerto Rican patients. For her, to be reduced to charitable assistance was to admit to moral failure. She treated patients, then, on a basis of moralization: that clinical attention would be offered only if the patient also accepted attempts to reconstruct his or her moral character. Accidents or illnesses were social events which resulted from irresponsible behaviour. In the UK, where health care is provided as an entitlement of citizenship, the scope for such leverage is much reduced. Nevertheless, as Jeffery (1979) shows, although in different terminology, moralization is demonstrable in accident services, particularly for those with self-inflicted conditions (attempted suicides, drunks) or without access to primary care (vagrants). Plainly, where belief in the essential morality of parents is suspended, it is much easier to treat their possible responsibility for their children's condition as a matter for investigation.

Unfortunately, we have only one observed example from our Shire data of a case where abuse or neglect was seriously considered by the examining doctor. In fact, he remains undecided at the end of the consultation and the bureaucratic frame remains intact. This makes it doubly important, however, both as evidence of the genuine difficulty of deciding, in the absence of a principle of strict liability, and of the nature of the reasoning involved in coming to the eventual disposal decision. Our observations begin at the point where the patient is seen by the SHO. The child is a girl of Asian origin, accompanied by her father. From the record, there is no evidence of previous contacts and her age is given as two-and-a-half. The researcher recognized the address as lying in the immigrant quarter of Midchester, but later questioning established that the SHO did not.

> Dr Whelan (SHO) asks the child what has happened and the father says she doesn't speak English. His own English isn't very good. {42}

SHO: Do you understand English?

FATHER: Yes.

SHO: What happened?

FATHER: I don't know. I wasn't there when it happened.

Dr Whelan examines the child's arm carefully. She seems to have dislocated her elbow.

SHO: When did it happen?

FATHER: I don't know. Maybe yesterday. Yes. When I got home from work she was holding her arm out in a funny way.

Dr Whelan makes no comment on this. The child is crying in a monotone. The doctor moves her arm about but she appears to react no more strongly however hard he twists and turns it. He goes to look at her other arm for comparison but she snatches it away. The child is nice-looking and appears to be well nourished and nicely dressed. The father is silent and makes little attempt to question the child or to hold her affectionately. He has her sitting very much on the edge of his knee. Dr Whelan sends them down to X-ray.

(Later) By this time the little girl, two-and-a-half years old, with a pulled elbow is back. The registrar has come back and he examines the plates with Dr Whelan, and examines the child and tries to manipulate the elbow. The child is very tearful but she is not screaming. It's still this monotonous pitch. The registrar doesn't talk to the father much nor to the little girl. He takes no history of the accident and doesn't appear to have much conversation with anyone other than Dr Whelan. He does explain to the father that he thinks that it's a pulled elbow and not dislocated and that he's trying to manipulate it back into position. The father makes a few soothing remarks to the little girl who has clearly been hurt quite badly by the registrar, although she patiently allows him to do the examination. After some more discussion about the diagnosis in front of the father, Dr Whelan says to the father: 'We are not quite sure what it is but I would like you to come back tomorrow and we'll see how it is.' The time is then 21.45 and the father and the little girl walk out. They have no GP's letter or note. Dr Whelan had also mentioned putting the arm in a sling but they have gone before a nurse does this. Dr Whelan and the registrar go back to the table and Dr Whelan says to the registrar, 'I didn't like it, I didn't like the father's attitude. It's odd you know, there was a delay in, he said he had noticed yesterday when he came home from {43} work. It's a bit funny. I think I'll post a letter to the GP and mention a few things.' The registrar nods and they go on to discuss the diagnosis. The registrar seems to think it's a pulled elbow but he is not sure. He said his manipulation might have helped and the child might be back to normal tomorrow. The nurse comes and asks Dr Whelan where they have got to. They have walked out without the sling.

(Later) I then ask Dr Whelan about the little Indian girl with the elbow. He said, 'The diagnosis is difficult. It could be a pulled elbow or a dislocation.' I asked him how pulled elbows are caused and he said, 'There are only really two ways with a child that age, either it falls and in falling holds on to something and thereby takes the full weight on the arm or else, which is more common, it's done by an adult, say, getting hold of the child's hand and pulling it sharply by sudden jabbing at the arm.' I said, 'Could it be caused by twisting the arm,' and he said, 'No, not an injury like that.' I said to him, 'You seem concerned about the child' and he said, 'Yes, I didn't like the way there was no explanation. This is worrying. He wasn't very articulate but I'd expect more than that. The other thing is that the bonding, well that wasn't good was it? The child whined all the time. Children don't usually do that. They usually bellow when you touch the bad bit and stop but she didn't bellow, she just went on whining. That isn't the usual course of events, nor did the father calm her very well.' He said some more things about being anxious about the amount of affection shown and said that the other problem is he may have been in difficulties with the language and not understanding. Then he said, 'Of course, he was embarrassed (the father) it's this cultural thing. They won't answer questions.' I didn't pursue that at that moment as he was about to be distracted. Having been distracted he then said to me, 'I'll write to the GP rather than giving the patient the letter. That gives him the chance to discuss the injury with the father.'

The SHO, then, cites seven grounds for being suspicious in this case: the lack of explanation of the cause of the accident; the vagueness about when it happened; the delay in presentation; the injury type; the apparent lack of affection between parent and child; the submissiveness of the little girl and her apparent lack of response to painful manipulation; and the lack of information offered by the father.

Let us consider these in more detail. If we begin with the actual injury, the pulled elbow, then we could point out that this is not uncommon in children, to the extent of having a semi-established diagnostic label, 'nursemaid's elbow'. The label arises because the condition was thought to result from impatient nursemaids pulling recalcitrant children across busy streets. On a strict liability basis, {44} this could be considered abusive. There is, however, no evidence to suggest that either doctor is treating the injury as sufficient. The example of a 'normal' consultation which we have already cited shows that there is nothing unusual about vague and partial explanations of the cause of injury and that when information is offered it may well appear to be disregarded. The child's lack of response could be due to shock, from the injury, or an overriding fear of the hospital. The apparently cool relationship might reflect cultural notions of proper conduct. We do not make these points in criticism of the SHO's judgement, but simply to show how, in an alternative frame, all of these 'facts' could be quite differently interpreted. What has prompted the SHO's investigation?

These seven grounds can be grouped into three basic categories of evidence: the injury; the account offered; and the demeanour of parent and child. What Dr Whelan seems to be doing is to locate them in what we might call a structure of mutual corroboration. Are the injury, the explanation and the parties' reaction consistent with each other? While the clinical evidence is necessary, then, it is not sufficient. In part, this does reflect the doctors' own uncertainty in dealing with children. With the exception of those SHOs training for general practice, who might have held a similar post in paediatrics, these doctors were unlikely to have more than the (highly variable) amount of knowledge about children that is covered by basic medical education (cf. GMC 1977). The importance of the social evidence seems to be similarly limited. Little history is taken, as we saw earlier, and we established that the doctor did not recognize any possible significance in the child's address. This is not surprising given the limited amount of background data on the record and the fact that SHOs move on too quickly to acquire much knowledge of the social geography of the catchment area, even if they considered such knowledge worth having at the possible expense of clinical learning. In the Victoria, the only address the SHOs could consistently recognize and use to set framing that was non-bureaucratic from the start was the local gypsy site.

Demeanour, then, would seem to be more important.[5] This is highlighted in the case of suspected abuse cited above by the SHO in opening up the possibility of a non-accidental cause with the registrar:

> 'I don't like it. I didn't like the father's attitude. It's odd you know, there was a delay when he said he had noticed yesterday when he came home from work. It's a bit funny . . .' {45}

The mention of the father's attitude forms the first half of a contrast which makes the delay into something 'a bit funny', rather than, say, reflecting the father's limited competence with the English language. Having identified the father's demeanour as deviant, the SHO could then proceed to link it with a variety of other features which we have shown to be routine and interpret them as supporting evidence. The 'facts' change their character as the identification of the father as morally suspect is assembled. We can, then, see an evaluation against some standard of 'how we would expect a normal parent and child to behave in this department with this injury'. If the encounter is to fall within the applicability of the bureaucratic frame, parents must, *inter alia*, be able to show that they have brought the child promptly, should seem willing to offer an explanation of the child's condition, should display affection to the child and should respond to the doctor's overtones. Together, these document that the parent is honest, competent and caring. The expectations of the child are weaker, but it is at least implied that they should show some reaction to their surroundings and to the doctor and should display predictable responses when pain is caused. By these criteria, the girl and her father are deficient, where the boy and the young man in the first example are not. The father does not volunteer an explanation and the girl does not interact with the examining doctors.

39

We propose that the doctor is led to consider breaking with the bureaucratic frame by the father's failure to offer evidence of his compliance. In this respect, it may be that Strong's account underplays the interactive nature of the framing. The choice of frame is not purely a matter for the doctor so that patients who step out of their allocated identities may free the doctor to challenge their moral character. It is, however, important to note the SHO's uncertainty as an indicator of the strength of the initial framing. He tries very hard to find reasons why the father could still be treated as honest, competent and caring. The man's ethnicity is plainly involved in this, as a possible excuse for his behaviour and his failure to comprehend what is expected of him.

'Of course he was embarrassed. It's this cultural thing. They won't answer questions.'

In the light of our discussions in chapter 4, we would argue that it is the availability of this excuse which allows the doctor to stay in frame and leaves him uncertain about whether or not this is a case of abuse. He, therefore, chooses to dispose of the case by a letter to the {46} child's GP rather than putting it straight into the official non-accidental injury procedure.

Given the limited nature of our data, it is difficult to take this particular analysis much further. Three specific points ought to be made, however. First, it should be stressed that, since the department is recognized to be an unfamiliar and hostile environment for both parents and children, they are allowed considerable latitude in their demeanour compared with other settings. Children, in particular, are only weakly considered to be agents of their own behaviour and, as such, their demeanour is not used as an index of their character. Although their conduct may resemble that of 'bad' patients, they are seldom the object of moralizing (Dingwall and Murray 1983). Parents, on the other hand, are likely to be held to account for their own demeanour to a greater degree, although a certain amount of distress is acceptable and even expectable.

An excessive display of concern, though, and this is our second point, can also cast doubt on a parent's character. Dingwall and Murray (1983) present an example of this in relation to a minor, accidental, injury to a teenage boy who was a frequent attender at the department for trivial complaints. Both the boy and his mother were visibly treated as morally suspect. Jeffery (1979) reports similar data on adults presenting with trivial injuries, although, as he observes, the strength of the bureaucratic frame tends to exclude moral challenges from the surface of these encounters, restricting it to record entries or subsequent conversations between staff. Even here, certain sorts of justifications or excuses may be used to reconstitute the moral character of over-anxious parents. Phrases like 'it's

THE PROTECTION OF CHILDREN

only a little scratch but it could leave an unsightly scar for a girl to carry' were employed by doctors to reestablish the responsibility of parents who brought in children with trivial complaints, provided that they showed contrition for being so bothersome.[6]

Finally, we must note how these problems are likely to be compounded in areas like County and Borough, where there is more reliance on overseas doctors. Their unfamiliarity with British society and behaviour may deprive them of the ability to use even the crude standards of physical condition, social background, and interpersonal conduct that indigenous doctors employ (cf. Hughes 1980a). One overseas registrar summed up the problem for us:

> 'It's not the same standard in (Middle Eastern Country, CSLS) you know . . . You must remember that cultures of this sort love their children. They would sacrifice themselves for their children but they {47} are aggressive too. This is the same in my country. It doesn't bother them to hit a child but they will tell you they love them and they do (. . .) In my country you don't see things like this (child abuse CSLS) or at least if you see it, you can't afford to take notice of it. We can't have a standard that you have here. The hospitals would be packed. There are just too many.'

We should, perhaps, stress that this is not intended as an aspersion on the clinical competence of overseas doctors, but simply as an indication of the problems they may encounter in considering a particular case in the light of their experience of a very different culture, where, for instance, child survival may be uncertain, let alone the quality of the child's life.

CHILD HEALTH CLINICS

It would be tedious merely to recapitulate our analysis of accident departments in a different context. However, we do think some discussion of child health clinics is justified, partly in order to substantiate our claims to the generalizability of our analysis and partly because we have said relatively little so far about neglect. This omission is not an oversight on our part. As Holter and Friedman (1968) showed in their study of identification in US emergency room services, neglect is simply not present as a conceptual category in accident work. This is just as true in England. We never saw any attempt even to weigh or measure a child, let alone carry out any sort of development testing, although the clinical evidence which might be revealed could bear on the consistency of the child's condition with the offered explanations. The doctors are not trained for this task and, under the rule of clinical priority, define their concern as accidental events rather than the general health or welfare of their patients.

41

One of the key settings where children's health and development are surveyed is the child health clinic. These are the responsibility of the AHA community medical services. Clinics vary greatly in their premises and organization, but their functions are similar. Well children are brought in for developmental testing, immunizations or for their parents, almost invariably their mothers, to ask advice on any problems of management. One or more health visitors will always be present, but if any immunizations are being carried out, a doctor must also be in attendance, for medico-legal reasons. {48} That doctor will usually carry out some, if not all, of the examinations specified in the Area's programme of developmental testing. Clinic doctors may be full-time employees of the health authority, but are more likely to be sessionally employed, either GPs contracting to provide the service for their own patients or married women doctors seeking part-time work. In theory, they are not supposed to treat or prescribe for sick children, but this restriction was seldom adhered to rigidly in GP-run clinics, and even AHA medical officers might be given access to prescription forms by local arrangement. None of these doctors need necessarily have any formal training in child health, although full-time medical officers and younger GPs were unlikely not to have had some preparation for this work. The clinic personnel may also include registered nurses to carry out the actual immunizations and either auxiliary or voluntary workers to weigh children, extract and replace records and sell vitamin drops or welfare foods. In total, we observed 14 clinic sessions in the three study areas.

For the purposes of this chapter, we propose to concentrate on just two parts of the clinic's work: the weighing and developmental testing of children. The first is important because of the significance which is attached to weight charts in case conferences and court proceedings, as we shall show later. The second is the main point of contact between doctors, the licensed interpreters of clinical data, and children. These are the occasions on which clinical evidence is most regularly made available and where the identification of abuse or neglect would occur, if we accepted the 'self-evident' model.

Despite its importance in later decision-making, weighing is actually one of the least significant activities at clinics. Although nominally part of the health visitor's duties, the task is generally delegated to loosely-supervised auxiliary or voluntary workers. On no occasion did we see a health visitor actually weigh a child herself. Relatively little attempt is made to obtain weights with any precision: children are hardly ever stripped; scales are heaved around without much concern for possible effects on their accuracy and voluntary workers, in particular, often seemed very confused by metrication. There are two reasons for this in the health visitors' thinking. Firstly, clinic premises are often draughty and ill-heated. Routine undressing of children may be seen by both parents and health visitors as an unkind and intrusive act. Like the implicit moral challenge of asking for explanations of injuries in an accident department, a request to strip a child may be heard to imply an allegation which threatens the bureaucratic framing of clinic interaction. {49} If nothing is discovered this may discourage future visits to the clinic, a dilemma which will become familiar as our presentation unfolds. Not only are weights inaccurate, then, but the opportunity to observe more than a small area of the child's body is foregone. Moreover, health visitors have, in the last decade or so, been strongly influenced by paediatric concerns about overweight babies. Parents are thought to regard weight as a good indicator of a child's general condition and to suppose that the bigger the child, the better. By playing down the significance of weight, and its routine measurement, health visitors have been trying to re-educate parents on the undesirability of obesity and to reduce the competition which used to occur from week to week at clinic sessions over the extent of weight gain, a strategy which has met with rather limited success in the face of pressure from clients and voluntary workers. If weighing is defined as relatively unimportant, its delegation can be used to free health visitors for what they do define as important – talking to parents.

Once taken, weights are entered on to a card held by the parents and on to a record held at the clinic. In fact, this latter most usually takes the form of a chart which shows the normal statistical distribution of weight for particular ages, plotting the mean curve and the third and 97th centiles. This means that 94 per cent of children have a weight for age between these two limits. We are most concerned here with the three per cent who fall under the lower curve. In the course of our fieldwork, we encountered a number of people who were prepared to argue, on a strict liability basis, that any child whose weight was below this limit was, self-evidently, neglected. Even if we were to place any great confidence in the weight record, this would be a fallacious argument. The distribution of weight for age is normal in a statistical sense. However perfect the society and its child-rearing conditions, some children must fall below that centile as a matter of constitutional chance. (Just as 50 per cent of adults must be overweight!) A statistically infrequent weight for age relationship may, for instance, represent an inherited characteristic or a metabolic disorder as much as neglectful treatment. Once again the physical signs do no more than provide a possible ground for further investigations of the child's social environment and his or her parents' moral character. As in the accident departments there is a preference for natural explanations, locating the cause of the low weight in a domain of events which are not, or only weakly, subject to human control. Indeed, where parental character seems unimpeachable, as in the 'case of the martinet officer', to be discussed in chapter 4, {50} the attempt to naturalize the cause of the observed signs may be both protracted and exhaustive.

Most developmental testing is done by the clinic doctors, although health visitors may share this work in some areas. The testing programme is supposed to be done to a schedule recommended by the local Specialist in Community Medicine (Child Health) which is usually derived, ultimately, from the descriptions of developmental progress in 'Mary Sheridan', a pamphlet issued by the Department of Health (DHSS 1975). The following example is taken from our observations at a clinic provided in a general practice under contract to the AHA. The doctor is a relatively young man who has been through a specialty training for general practice and was considered by the experienced clinic health visitor to have more than average knowledge of, and interest in, child development.

> (. . .) the next patient comes in with her baby for a developmental check (. . .) He asked her to strip the baby, who was about six months old (. . .) The baby screamed most of the time. He approached her in a fairly threatening manner and forced her to lie on her back while he listened to her heart and chest, making her scream even louder. He also felt for her liver and kidneys and must have pressed quite hard because new screams were let out, (. . .) He shook a rattle near one ear and crumpled up some paper near the other one. He said to me, 'They're very rough these checks you know, very rough indeed.' (. . .) He then asked the mother about vaccines and it appeared she was missing the triple vaccine. By this time the mother had re-dressed the child and the doctor had to make her undress her all over again so he could put the vaccination in her leg. The wails and screams reached a crescendo. (. . .) When the mother and child left, he said to me, 'They're very rough these checks you know. I don't really do much, not really. I look for the major things, heart, lungs, hearing, vision etc., but they are very rough. If they're obviously having problems I send them off to the specialist. I don't do anything much really. The health visitors keep an eye on their development and if they're worried they refer them to me, but I usually send them on to a specialist straight away. They're not very good these checks, you know. I mean they are very rough and there is not very much you can do if the child is screaming.'

This was, obviously, a rather unfortunate consultation and we are not claiming that it was typical of all those we observed. In particular, the doctor may have been unlucky in encountering a rather tired or hungry baby. Nevertheless, data like this do enable us to bring out the key points on developmental testing.

Firstly, there is the degree to which doctors are trained for this {51} task. By chance, one of the research team had attended a class held the previous day for new health visitors by an experienced full-time community physician on the topic of developmental examinations. This doctor had stressed the desirability of examining children in their mother's lap, if possible, of winning their confidence before handling them, of completing the agenda before having the child dressed and the like. On such criteria this supposedly more than averagely competent GP had obviously made a number of rather elementary mistakes which we could only conclude reflected on his preparation for this work.

Secondly, as this doctor himself recognized, the tests are a rather imprecise activity. They are performed under widely varying conditions and there seemed to be no provision for continuing standardization or monitoring. The doctors' standards, especially in the absence of systematic training, owed more to their personal experience than to any agreed definition.[7] Some of the reasons for this will be explored further in chapter 5.

Thirdly, and to some extent this underlies both of the previous points, assessments are seen to be a rather low-grade use of medical time. From a clinical perspective, they are understandably boring. Most abnormalities are picked up by the neonatal examination in hospital. What is missed at that stage is so dispersed in the population that clinic doctors see a very large number of children for every one where they discover a condition of any significance for which medicine has anything to offer. Where deviations are identified, one has the same problem as with weight charts: some children are naturally slower to develop than others. Again, it is a question of putting the clinical assessment alongside social and moral data. As in the accident departments, however, these data are not uniformly available, most of the doctors are poorly equipped to interpret them and the setting is considered sufficiently strange for a wide variety of conduct to be accepted. These limitations are not exactly the same for each doctor: AHA-employed staff may have greater clinical expertise or commitment but less sophisticated knowledge of the social geography of the clinic catchment, while GPs may know their patients but be less interested in the testing. Moreover, a GP who is familiar with the child and his or her parents may find the charge of neglect or abuse a matter of such enormity as to be unable to contemplate it, a point which we discuss in more detail later. Nevertheless, the cumulative impact is to lead the doctor away from finding the sort of subtle inconsistencies which may provoke an investigative approach to the child's condition.[8] {52}

THE CONSEQUENCES OF A CLINICAL FOCUS

It seems clear, then, that concentrating on clinical evidence to the exclusion of social evidence or a consideration of parental character will tend towards minimizing identification rates, unless a strict liability approach is adopted. If such a decision rule were implemented, however, both accident and child health services would overflow with identifications. The fact that they are not effectively substantiates our argument that agency staff are using non-clinical criteria to sift children and define those who may be in need of protective action. These criteria must be analysed in detail if we are to understand the decision-making that is going on. A definitive judgement on whether this merely constitutes inadequate practice should be postponed until that account is completed. For the present, though, we can point out the way in which such an emphasis on moral character and parental responsibility may be characteristic of the form taken by social regulation in a liberal democracy. In some sense, it may be possible to criticize the practices we are describing only from an (explicit or implicit) rejection of the values which they embody.

Nevertheless, it is arguable that, even within the present normative framework, identification rates could be increased by a more effective use of the social data which are available in either setting, in accident departments to ambulance staff (cf. Hughes 1980b), to receptionists (cf. Gibson 1977) and, in some places, to nurses; and in child health clinics to health visitors. The sort of changes which could result can be seen in Holter and Friedman's (1968) study. They took a sample of all children under six ($N =$ 87) presenting at an American emergency room in a two-week period. Cases were allocated by cause between the categories accident, repeat accident and abuse, using relatively conservative criteria and, apparently, excluding lacerations and ingestions, either of which might be non-accidental. These cases were then followed up with a home visit from a public health nurse and the classification reconsidered. The first category fell from 74 to 41 per cent, with the others increasing from 18 to 38 and eight to nine per cent, respectively. Moreover the nurses' follow-up led, as we noted earlier, to the addition of a category for 'neglect', which accounted for 11 per cent of the cases.

As we shall show in chapters 5 and 6, there are important pressures against this sort of integration. It is notable, even here, that it was only in exceptional circumstances that this seemed to be possible, {53} namely where the usual hierarchy of doctors and nurses had been undercut by other structural features. More concretely, both County and Borough relied heavily on low-status overseas doctors, whose particular difficulties in assessing children have already been discussed. In both areas, the nursing staff were locally recruited and highly experienced. Some of them had worked in the department for as long as twenty years, while at the Victoria in Shire a staff nurse who had been there two years was described to us as long-serving. The SHOs in Shire, as we have seen, were predominantly indigenous and high-status. Whereas the Victoria was run on traditional lines, with a marked subordination of non-medical staff and highly formalized communications, comparable with the similar teaching hospital described by Gibson (1977), the nurses in County and Borough had had their status enhanced as a check on the SHOs. The inquiry into the death of Paul Steven Brown (1980: para. 154) in the Wirral, an area comparable to Borough, remarked that 'The diagnosis (of abuse CSLS) is most often made by very experienced nursing staff.'[9] This was institutionally recognized in our two areas: County nurses had an independent access to the on-call paediatric consultant at all times and Borough nurses had a right to admit children overnight on their own authority for review on the morning consultants' round. Both areas, however, reported considerable, and continuing, resistance from junior doctors which was overcome only by the authority of the consultant-in-charge of the accident services. Given all the problems which attach to true incidence rates in this field, which we shall discuss later, it seems impossible to quantify the effects of these changes. It seems quite feasible, however, to argue that the highest-status hospital in our study was less likely to identify cases of abuse than the two units in run-of-the-mill district general hospitals.

The fragmentation of responsibility for child health clinics makes similar innovations harder to suggest. They are much more variable in character than accident units, depending upon the relative knowledge, experience and motivation of the staff involved. In some clinics, with particularly committed doctors who defined their involvement as part of a continuing personal responsibility for the care of their patients, assessments were taken very seriously and there was careful discussion between staff about the children who were seen at any particular session. These were not typical of the clinics which we saw, where assessments often seemed to be treated as something for the doctors to do while providing legal cover for nurses carrying out injections. This has led us, at least, to consider {54} whether health visitors should take over all assessments and, indeed, how necessary medical cover really is. When health visitors do assessments, they regard this as high-status work which they take very seriously. It has the additional virtue of demonstrating to parents the full repertory of their skills and knowledge which is otherwise seldom visible and, thereby, legitimating their claims to some expertise in the health and welfare of children. Obviously, extra training would be needed, for instance, in listening to heart and lung sounds, but this is not necessarily an insuperable problem given the degree to which modern audio-visual teaching methods can accelerate the acquisition of clinical experience.[10]

If these non-clinical types of evidence are playing such an important part in the process of identification, then we must obviously explore their character in some detail. Are they merely unexamined biases and prejudices or do they too have consistent roots in the organization of agencies and their staff within a particular framework of social and moral values? This is the task which we now set ourselves.

3

The Child as a Social Object

The insufficiency of clinical evidence for the identification of children in need of protection was established in the previous chapter. Physical signs or symptoms could be interpreted as evidence of abuse or neglect only by an (implicit or explicit) reference to the child's social circumstances. We did not, however, examine these references in any great detail: indeed the very limitations of accident services and child health clinics in this respect allowed us to create natural experiments where we could test our model of decision-making. If we are to understand how that model works, though, our next step must be an exploration of the way in which front-line workers do make use of social evidence. In the process, we can also assess the theoretical possibility that such evidence might itself be self-sufficient. Our data will be drawn mainly from our work with health visitors and social workers. Both occupations are licensed interpreters of social evidence and have ample opportunity to collect it.[1] At the same time, social workers, in particular, have rather restricted access to clinical evidence. Health visitors have more access, but their licence to interpret this kind of evidence is, as we shall see, rather problematic.

LAY SOCIAL THEORIES

In the course of this discussion, we shall underline the front-line workers' use of concepts of 'normal' family life as a way of identifying deviance and, hence, considering the possibility of abuse or neglect. These concepts form part of 'lay social theories', ideas about the nature of society held by non-specialists (i.e. people other than social scientists). It may, therefore, be helpful if we begin by summarizing the general sociological literature on this process.[2]

If we recall our initial quotation from Waller (p. 2), this stated that {56} the existence of a social problem depended upon a prior value judgement. One of the points which more recent commentators have brought out is that the same is true of the existence of normal events. When we

49

define some event, person or act as deviant, we are necessarily presupposing some idea of what would count as normal and that it is relevant to draw attention to its absence. Normality *and* deviance, then, are both outcomes of an interaction between what is available to be observed and the framework of ideas within which observations are actually made.

This body of knowledge is a lay social theory. It is our common-sense, practical guide which we can consult to make sense of everyday occurrences and to formulate appropriate responses. Incorporated within it are ideas about the typical sorts of people and situations we may reasonably expect to come across and the relevant ways in which we should act. Of course, such knowledge must have a provisional character. It still has to be elaborated and developed to fit the specific features of any particular occasion as that occasion itself unfolds. Nevertheless, by referring to that stock of knowledge we can produce actions which others will be able to recognize as normal and, similarly, decide whether the actions of others should be so regarded. The elements of lay social theories are unevenly distributed: some are shared by quite large numbers of people, like the citizens of a nation, while others are limited to comparatively small groups, like families. Each of us combines these elements in a particular fashion, depending upon the social groupings in which we have acquired membership. Social theories are both descriptive and prescriptive, specifying not only how people *do* act but also how they *ought* to act. A failure to comply with these prescriptions on any occasion may lead to the other parties questioning one's competence as a social actor and challenging one's right to be regarded as a member of relevant groupings.

One example of the use of such knowledge can be found in Sacks's (1972) discussion of the way in which police officers on patrol identify suspicious characters. He argues that the officers learn to treat their beat as a 'territory of normal appearances'. Slight variations from expectable behaviour for the time and place furnish grounds for further inquiry. It is such practices, for instance, which allow officers to decide whether an attractive woman arriving at a flat by taxi is just that or is a call-girl visiting a client. Conversely, criminals will seek to fit their actions as closely as possible to those which are expectable in the neighbourhood at that time in order to evade detection. {57}

The tasks for both health visitors and social workers are rather similar, and they also can be seen to operate with a model of normal appearances grounded in the social ecology of the area. The importance of this, particularly for health visitors, can be seen in the orientation programmes which are drawn up for new employees to acquaint them not merely with local agency contacts but with the social organization of their clientele. This is somewhat less critical for social workers, who will often receive some briefing on a client from a referral. Nevertheless, both groups must be sensitive to variations from their conceptions of normality as a warrant to undertake further investigations. Conversely, those attempting to deceive either agency will model themselves as closely as possible to their idea of expectable conduct.

Health visitors' and social workers' conceptions of normal family life have two principal dimensions, one relating to the material and the other to the interpersonal environment created within particular households. These are not altogether independent but are frequently treated as if they were, in that a 'good' finding on one may compensate for a 'bad' finding on the other or that the findings on each may be used as mutual corroboration. Logical consistency is not a necessary feature of lay theories. It does, however, pose a problem for the organization of our discussion. We have elected to treat these two dimensions separately, but the reader should recognize the element of artifice in this decision.[3]

THE MATERIAL ENVIRONMENT

This part of the social evidence may itself be further divided into a number of subsidiary categories. These include the physical condition of the home (the state of the property and its furnishings) and the physical condition of the occupants (the state of their clothing and self-care), although we have space to discuss only the former in the present text. In some sense, these data may be considered to be 'harder' than the observations of the interpersonal environment. They are more publicly available and their evaluation requires no specific training or esoteric knowledge. At the same time, the framework of interpretation incorporated within particular occupational licences may discount their significance.

Appraisal begins from the immediate location of the property and the observations made at the point where it is first seen. The address forms part of the worker's knowledge of her area as a territory of {58} normal appearances. She can search that knowledge to form a set of expectations about the condition of properties having that address, which she can then use as a standard against which to compare this particular dwelling. These two examples are from home visits with Shire health visitors.

When we get out to (the military base) the first family we go to see are the Chaucers. HV doesn't expect her to be in because there is a note on the midwife's discharge form that she was planning to go north to visit a dying parent. She was breast-feeding, which HV says is peculiar for the (service). There is a lot of pressure against it from both families and their friends. She remarks on the fact that the garden has been done. This again is unusual and she regards it as a mark up.

'Mr Plowman is a steady chap. There has been a lot of improvement at the house since he came. They all like him and seem happy with him . . . they are a rough sort of type but they have lifted themselves out of the mud a bit . . . . I think we'll put up the roof here . . .' (We have been leaving the sun roof open but HV plainly does not consider that appropriate outside this row of council houses). The family prove to be out. HV waves at the well-tended garden, it's nice to see them lifting their standards though.'

It is important to note what these observations are doing. The address is not defined as a matter in which clients have much choice, especially, as here, for service families or council tenants. What is done with the house once allocated, however, is a matter within the client's control. This, then, can be used as evidence on the moral character of the client. In both of these instances, the families have risen in the worker's esteem by virtue of their attempts to improve unpromising dwellings. Similar inferences can be drawn from the general standard of housekeeping.

Conversely, a decline in material standards may also serve as a ground for questioning a client's responsibility. This is a typical example from a social worker's visit to a Borough family whose three children had been received into care on numerous occasions in the past.

SW warned me to light a cigarette and keep smoking it in the house. The house is a tip, we go in the back door but in fact there is no back door. The garden is a mess of mattresses and rubbish, bits of metal, cars and coal . . .(. . .) The kitchen consists of one cooker with a few stinking pans and a sink. There are no table or chairs and no cupboards. The place is black. It looked like a house where there has {59} been a fire and never cleaned up. The stench is pretty strong, not helped by a couple of dogs . . . . The living room has no wall-paper or paint on the walls, there are only two chairs . . . . The curtains are drawn and the whole effect is dingy, smelly and very sparse. The SW told me these are the only children she knows who enjoy coming into care . . . . The children thought the foster homes were palaces but this is something of a conflict as the children are shown life need not be like it is in their home and this is having effects . . . . Both parents have had previous marriages to people in the area and she has visited both sets, who live in smart and tidy conditions. Mrs Reagan admitted that she was not the sort of housekeeper she is now that she was then. SW feels the state of the home indicates Mrs Reagan is psychiatrically disturbed to a fairly high level . . . . Unlike some other working-class families which lived in similarly impoverished surroundings there was no emotional warmth to compensate for the lack of physical amenity.

The social worker organizes her account to show that Mrs Reagan is capable of better things, and then uses the decline in her standards to justify defining her as 'psychiatrically disturbed'. If Mrs Reagan were fully responsible for her own actions, she would clean the place up. The fact that she has not is evidence of her own incompetence as a social actor. Several other points can be noted in this extract. First, it is noticeable that responsibility for the condition of the household is imputed to the children's mother. Hers is the primary obligation in this area. At a second level, however, her failure can be used to question Mr Reagan's character, in that he, too, is capable of something better but has not exerted himself to ensure that his wife is successful in meeting the worker's standard. In a passage not reproduced here, the social worker actually goes on to develop such an attack by reference to Mr Reagan's alleged habit of drinking away his money in a club at lunchtime rather than spending it on the home. The responsibility of men for their women is a common theme in our data. Finally, we can note again the attempt to find an excuse for the parents. Just as in the accident department, the emerging moral challenge is appraised to see whether it is possible to defeat it, in this case by finding evidence of emotional warmth.

This extract also introduces the idea of change as significant. The worker's judgement is made by invoking a standard of 'what we could typically expect from this couple.' It is their failure to match this that exposes them to attack. Compare it, for example, with the following extract from a visit with a Shire social worker to a gipsy couple to discuss the progress of their eleven-year-old ESN child at {60} his special school:

> After lunch, we go off to visit two families. The first is a gipsy family called MacFie. They live in a caravan that's inside a barn on the Richborough Estate in Aulworth. It's a most fantastic barn with beautiful proportions and beams and stuck inside it is this grotty caravan. There are lots of animals about, dogs and cats, etc. There is also furniture and clothing piled up in the barn. We go into the caravan which had a smell which was quite indescribable and suffocating to my nostrils. SW appeared not to notice. Inside was Ida MacFie who I would imagine was about fifty years of age, although in many ways she looked older. She was filthy and stank. She had been plucking turkeys and her hair was full of feathers. The hair looked rather unwashed too. Jake MacFie was drunk. SW told me that he gets merry on cider. He was dressed in a three-piece suit with some filthy jacket on and some equally filthy cap. He was lying on one of the beds drinking cider although he made a token gesture of hiding it when SW walked in the door (. . .) We finally leave after about forty minutes. I'm tremendously relieved to be out in the fresh air.

The social worker's only comment was that the conditions were no worse than usual and not all that bad anyway.

It was possible, though, to, as it were, go off the scale at the other end. Families could be too fastidious. This is a Shire health visitor talking to her nursing officer:

> HV tells NO that one of the GPs had been on the phone to her this morning. There was this little boy who had fallen down the stairs and

you know how it is that the man is always right and this is one that is always in his mind as an NAI. It isn't in my mind at all . . .'. NO: 'So how did it happen . . .?' HV explains that this nine-year-old boy was climbing over a stairgate at the top of the house and slipped, falling down the flight of polished wooden stairs. The house is very tidy and the GP thinks it's obsessional (. . .) The GP has always thought this about this family but I haven't . . . the mother does worry about nothing and she is perhaps a bit obsessive in that and asks questions *ad infinitum*, but I think she just needs a contact . . . he worries about her but I don't except that he makes me more alert because he is always right . . . the children fit in at school, they are clean, tidy, are just average children . . . there is no concern about this child but it has always niggled at me because of their obsessions.' (There is also a lot of stuff about the very formal layout of their front garden with cypresses in triangular beds surrounded by equally spaced begonias and French marigolds). {61}

This extract is useful in bringing out the degree to which many of these issues are a matter of judgement. On the same facts, the health visitor and the GP are able to come to rather different conclusions. We can see, however, the way in which the mother's concern to maintain the house and garden in an immaculate order provides for doubts about her responsibility. Both the GP and the health visitor subscribe to a theory that children need to express themselves through play which necessarily involves some disorganization of the home. The absence of such disorder may be taken as evidence that a child is being deprived of such experiences, with possible adverse effects on his or her development. Since a normal parent would, of course, want to maximize the child's potential, such deprivation can call into question the parent's character, presenting him or her as rigid, inflexible and selfishly intolerant. In the present instance we even have the quasi-psychiatric term 'obsessive'.

Social workers tend not to attach great significance to material standards. This comes out very clearly, for instance, in the report of the inquiry into the death of Malcolm Page (1981), which contrasts the commonsense account of a detective chief inspector detailing the squalid condition of the bedrooms in the Page home, smelling strongly of urine and covered in rotting excrement, with the social services' view that the house was merely somewhat grubby. As the report comments:

> . . . this illustrates . . . a tendancy (*sic*) to adjust expectations downwards to the level at which a family can perform. One way of reading statements about the condition of the house as 'not too bad' is 'not too bad for the Pages'. (p. 50)

In some respects the report is unfairly critical here, as we shall show when we discuss relativism as an excuse in the next chapter. What we want to bring out at this point, though, is the difficulty of impugning the moral character of families whose material conditions are so openly displayed. Where the family co-operates with the frontline worker, he or she is under great pressure to minimize the importance of possibly discrediting observations. Nothing, it seems, is being hidden: there are, therefore, no guilty secrets. Moreover, social workers define their distinctive skills as being in the appraisal of the interpersonal environment, a definition that, as Satyamurti (1981: 164-7) and Smith (1980: 106-10) also show, limits their intervention to those client problems which they have the resources to cope with. Their ability to resolve material difficulties is restricted and these are, {62} in any case, not seen as a matter for specialized knowledge. Indeed, within social services this kind of work is usually done by unqualified auxiliaries operating on a commonsense basis. The Pages, for instance, had a family home help working on their housekeeping standards and a qualified social worker dealing with their child management.

Health visitors do seem to attach greater weight to material conditions, although there is some evidence of a shift away from this in the search for a more distinctive skill base.[4] On the other hand, they are much more reliant on client co-operation than are social workers, since their access to resources as inducements, or statutory powers as threats, to extract compliance, is limited. The problems are brought out in one of our Shire cases, which also illustrates the difficulties of questioning the material front presented by a family. The extract which follows comes from an interview with the health visitor to the Illingworth family about Mandy, a three-and-a-half-year-old girl who was the subject of care proceedings on the proper development ground. The first reference is to this woman's initial visit about eighteen months previously, just after the birth of a younger sibling, Darren.

'(. . .) On the surface things looked all right. Certainly with this baby and Mandy wasn't there that day, I think she'd been sent away to stay with relatives while her mother was in hospital having this baby, and I didn't meet Mandy that day. The baby was clean, the house was clean and everything seemed to be fine. (. . .) There were no marks on her (Mandy) of physical abuse, she was always clean and the house was always clean (. . .) There were several visits that I paid that I wasn't able to see Mandy because this was during the winter so the child wasn't outside anyway, even though I visited in the morning, but I would stay there for some time and I could hear her upstairs, she never made any attempt to come downstairs, and I used to call from the bottom of the stairs, 'Hello Mandy', and she'd shout 'hello', down but she'd never come down and Mrs Illingworth never made any attempt to let me go upstairs. Mrs Illingworth used to say, 'Oh she's helping me doing the housework up there and I'm going back when you've gone', y'know, and she'd left her up there. (Date) In fact I was allowed up to this bedroom having visited for something like eight weeks now and only seen her a couple of times in that time, because I used to visit about every 10 days and I've never told Mrs Illingworth when I was going and I never went on the same day any week and never at the same time, so she never knew when I was coming, and I used to leave my car up the road and walk down and all this business. {63} Because I felt sometimes that Mandy was rushed downstairs and placed for my benefit so I used to appear at the door and I think this is how I managed to find out that she was upstairs so much. But (Date), I was allowed up to the bedroom and there was no covering on the floor at all, no toys in the bedroom, just a bed in the corner of the room with coats thrown on it that the husband was sleeping on probably, although he wasn't in it at that time, but he used to sleep there because Mrs Illingworth used to sleep downstairs with Darren, and Mandy was just sort of stamping her feet on the wooden floor. There were no toys in there and she was just standing there, there was no heating upstairs and it was quite cold and she'd got very little on her. But she seemed happy enough, she played peep-bo round the bed with me, but she was shut in this room, she wasn't bolted in and she made no attempt to come out, she wasn't locked in, she could've reached the handle but she made no attempt to come out at all.

Mrs Illingworth was presenting a carefully maintained front downstairs while Mandy was spending most of her time in a bare, unheated bedroom. Although Mandy 'seemed happy enough', the health visitor draws on a theory of normal child behaviour to discount this for the benefit of the interviewer. A genuinely happy child might be found in this bedroom as part of a game but would attempt to come out and greet a familiar visitor.

Nevertheless, the health visitor has also shown what a hard time she had getting to this conclusion. Earlier in the interview, she had explained that her concern had been aroused only following an anonymous report to the general practitioner, to whom she was attached, that Mandy was being put to bed in the early afternoon and left for eighteen to twenty hours without food. Following this tip-off, she began to vary her routine of visiting children in the mornings and old people in the afternoons and to call at varying times of day. This sharp division in the routine is unusual, but health visitors' unannounced visiting allows the concealment of deliberate investigations. Health visitors, for instance, tend to avoid visiting at known mealtimes but may 'inadvertently' do so to check a child's diet. In areas, like Borough, which still maintain a front parlour/back kitchen distinction, health visitors will go to the back door to ensure that they are admitted to the part of the house where the living is done. Even with such subterfuges, access is limited by the voluntary relationship. Indeed, one can argue that it is only by virtue of that voluntariness that unannounced, random surveillance is made acceptable. The health visitor's choice of phrase, 'I was allowed up to the bedroom . . .' is revealing. Her licence to enter the house is {64} exchanged for the right of the occupants to determine what she may inspect and to restrict the inferences she may draw.

This point is worth emphasizing because health and social work agencies are commonly criticized for failing to probe superficially adequate material environments. These two press stories are typical:

> Little Malcolm Page's last few months were sheer hell – a hell of shocking neglect, filth and suffering. Hidden away in an upstairs bedroom by his parents, he slowly wasted away in sub-zero temperatures. (. . .) experienced health visitor, Mrs C____ W____ called on the family. She wanted to see how the baby and his brothers and sisters were progressing. She got a hostile reception from Mrs Page who was finding it difficult to cope with the children. Mrs Page refused to let the health visitor see Malcolm despite repeated pleas. In the end Mrs W____ took the only course of action open to her. She called in the social services. (. . .) Despite Mrs Page's harsh attitude, the young social worker tried again and again to see the baby. In the months before his tragic death, she called at the house forty-eight times. Sadly, she didn't get much further than chatting to Mrs Page because Malcolm was kept hidden away upstairs (. . .)[5]
>
> *Daily Mirror* 16.1.1980

> B____ social services was criticised for allegedly failing to spot warning signs. The judge commented that officials visiting the G____ family never seemed to progress further than the carefully-tidied hall and sitting room. Asked whether such superficial cleaning could lull a social worker's suspicions, (the Director) says: in cases where, if you like, there are visible signs of improved parenting, the house is clean and tidy, yes, it is quite possible.'
>
> *Guardian* 15.12.1980

Without firm evidence of deviant conduct, both health visitors and social workers must rely on client co-operation. At the same time, if co-operation is forthcoming, that provides for the family's moral character to be so framed as to inhibit the reading of evidence in a discrediting fashion. Too investigative an approach can jeopardize access before yielding sufficient data to justify recasting the family's character in a way which may permit identifications to be made.

We should, perhaps, reiterate that families enjoyed considerable latitude, not least because of the range of possible excuses for poor conditions, and that these judgements were not one-off matters. The normal house is one whose standard of housekeeping varies within certain limits. The fieldworker calling unannounced, more common in health visiting than social work, expects to find a certain amount {65} of untidiness and dirt as an inevitable correlate of the presence of children. The observation of an absence of disorder on any particular occasion may be discounted by reference to a temporal cycle of household cleaning. A chance visitor is as likely to come upon a just-cleaned as an about-to-be-cleaned house.

Nevertheless, a consistently uncared-for home may be used as a ground for inferring either that parents have an uncaring attitude to their whole environment, including their children, or that parents are diverting their resources of time, energy and money into their own pleasures rather than investing in their family. Either of these can be used to discredit them. In the second case, this is an obvious inference; the first trades on an ambivalence about mental states. If depression is seen as a social rather than a natural phenomenon, then it may become viewed as a form of self-indulgence. The same conclusion, as we have seen, can be reached about the over-cared-for home. The relative dearth of challenges in such circumstances is not a straightforward case of class bias, but reflects the difficulty, in all classes, of under-cutting a surface compliance with the liberal standards which are being applied. Even where squalid conditions are manifest, they may be discounted in the light of a compliant demeanour on the part of parents.

THE INTERPERSONAL ENVIRONMENT

The second dimension of the social evidence relates to the conduct of household adults as displayed in their relationships with each other, with their children and with the community at large. To an even greater degree than the material conditions, these are seen to be matters which lie within individuals' control and, hence, even more reliable indicators of their essential character. Once again, a great range of matters may be the subject of comment and we have had to make a rather arbitrary selection. Three examples will be discussed: family size and spacing; adult/adult relationships; and adult/child relationships.

Both health visitors and, to a lesser degree, social workers use a rather sophisticated model of rational planning to optimize family size and birth intervals as their normative standard. Fertility regulation is evidence of individual and family functioning, indicating the degree to which people are taking responsibility for their own life-chances and recognizing a mutual version of domestic relationships. {66} Failure to control reproduction may cause physical damage to mothers and overstrain the household's economic resources. Attempts by either party to prevent the other's compliance cast doubt upon their respect for liberal values. In either case, inferences may be drawn about the parents' moral character. Again the issues of selfishness or thoughtlessness arise. Children's interests, in the matching of family size to family resources, in a spacing which permits an appropriate amount of individualized adult attention and in the health of their principal caretaker, are being jeopardized by adult irresponsibility.

We can illustrate this through the sorts of comment which are made about large or closely spaced families. This example is a Shire health visitor talking about an Asian woman:

> She has got eight children under ten, a boy, six girls, and another boy. Now she has had this second boy she has at last been allowed by her mother to have family planning. (Health visitor) likes her. Although there are a lot of children it's not a particularly deprived household. There is a lot of love and things going for the children.

This extract was selected because of the way it also brings out the search for mitigating factors. The health visitor seems to be aware that a simple statement, to the effect that this woman has eight small children, is hearable as some kind of moral attack. She goes on immediately to discount this, partly by a reference to cultural norms, 'a second boy . . . allowed by her own mother', of the kind we saw in the accident department, and partly by a reference to 'a lot of love', a feature we have already remarked on in this chapter. In effect, she is telling the observer how to interpret the fact of family size in the light of the character of the parents.

The model of rational planning is not, it should be said, inherently conservative. This extract comes from a Shire social worker viewing the case from the perspective of a committed and active feminist:

> Mrs Genn has five children and has had nineteen pregnancies . . . This lady is 29. Of the five children, two are in care and attend special schools for the maladjusted . . . Her own mother was an alcoholic and Mrs Genn brought up the children of her family from the time she was 12. She has always had babies to look after and she has never worked. The social worker is trying to encourage her to get a job when Duane goes to nursery school as she will have time on her hands. SW feels this will give her an outlet beyond the home and will also reduce the possibility of her adding another child to her overcrowded home. {67}

The observer is invited to read the facts of the case as an example of how women's lives are destroyed by poor family planning. Here we have Mrs Genn as a victim of circumstances – her own mother an alcoholic, bringing up her siblings and so on – who now has a chance to realize herself in work. It does not seem to us that the net result is very different from more traditional concerns to limit the reproduction of the poor, although, of course, the reasons are not identical. There is still an implicit use of the virtues of work and of the rational ordering of private affairs as standards for the assessment of clients.

The threshold for charges of deviant family size came at different points in the three authorities. In Shire such charges could begin after the fourth child, while in Borough and County families of up to six children were accepted as normal, a finding which also raises implications for the use of cultural norms to mitigate allegations of deviance. Nevertheless, in all three areas, such demographic facts furnished a ground for inquiring into the moral character of parents. All front-line workers treated pregnancy as a social act, where motives were available to be found. This applied even if clients considered pregnancy to be a natural (i.e. unintended) event.[6] Such a disjuncture provides for 'illegitimate' motives to be imputed for conception where none are avowed. Motive imputations commonly encountered in this study included the desire to save a failing marriage, an attempt to constrain a wandering spouse or a way of cementing a new cohabitation. If clients could be seen to be motivated by such factors, their whole moral character might be opened for investigation. These same general arguments apply to any family which may be regarded as demographically deviant: for instance, where there is a marked discrepancy between the ages of the adult partners.

A second area of interpersonal conduct which is examined is the relationship between the adult members of a household. In general, little importance is attached to whether this relationship is legally recognized or not. Marriage, of itself, is insignificant compared with the quality of the observed conduct. On the other hand, the normative standard does embody traditional marital values. It might be summarized as depicting a household which was a secure, stable, sexually exclusive, internally harmonious unit of law-abiding and responsible citizens. Failure on such counts opens up the possibility of discrediting the public appearance to reveal a different essential character. Thus, fieldworkers draw attention to matters like violence between adults, small-scale crime, prostitution, petty theft or {68} social security fraud, unemployment, indulgence in drink or drugs which, once established, furnish a legitimate basis for scrutinizing the parties involved. These are not all equally important: of those features listed, most weight would be placed on domestic violence and the use of drugs. The first is pretty well self-explanatory. Clear evidence of wife-battering, for instance, proves that violence not only can but does occur in this household. There is always a danger that children will get in the way, even if they are not actually targets. The reaction to recreational drug use is interesting. Health visitors tend to be more hostile, but social workers also get alarmed about children in drug-using households. In our view, this reaction reflects the drug-user's supposed impairment of responsibility. The actions of such people are, consequently, unstable and unpredictable. Their appearance cannot be trusted. This view does not extend to habitual drunkards, although, both pharmacologically and sociologically, the outcomes are not much different.[7]

Even with known drug-users, however, we can still demonstrate the institutionalized preference for the most optimistic version of observable conduct. These extracts are from fieldwork with Shire social services and concern a single woman, living with her small child on a caravan site.

SW then says that Bernadette's mother, and the health visitor had confirmed this, that she thinks Bernadette is taking drugs. Bernadette apparently used to be quite involved in the drug scene and was squatting in London. Her mother thinks that she is smoking pot again. SW says she thinks it may be sour grapes by mum. She is very irritated that SW has organized Bernadette and her child to move out of the house (. . .)

(On the visit) Bernadette was a nice girl, very articulate and intelligent, aged, I would say, in her late twenties. Not long after we had been there it occurred to me that she might be high and as the visit progressed she seemed to get more and more agitated, wringing her hands together, rubbing her thighs and generally making nervous movements. She wandered about back and forwards, fiddling and fingering things and moving her fingers and making some rather weird noises and some distorted comments. (. . .) As we go I say to SW, 'I think she was high, don't you?' SW said, 'Yes, I thought so. I'm glad that you confirm what I am feeling.' (. . .)

The social worker initially discounts the allegation that Bernadette is using drugs. As we show later, health visitors' reports are treated as {69} suspect until verified. In this case, the only corroboration comes from the client's mother, whose motives can be discredited by turning this breach of family loyalty back as evidence of her own moral deficiencies. During the visit, the researcher independently forms a view of the client's mental state, that she is high, and puts this to the social worker. The phrasing of the social worker's response seems to indicate a distrust of her own perceptions which should recall our earlier references to the idea of reality disjunctures. She does not, for instance, choose to reply along the lines of, 'Oh you noticed too, did you', which we might have taken as evidence that the woman's state was so obvious as to be beyond question. It was obvious enough to the participant observer on a commonsense basis which was, presumably, also available to the social worker. Acting in her occupational capacity, however, she seems to be displaying a preference for finding any alternative explanation.

Once a household does move away from the front-line workers' model of acceptable conduct, however, its moral character can be openly questioned. A good instance of this is in our notes of a Shire social worker's handling of the case of a child, Kevin Malone. His parents had been divorced shortly before and Kevin and his sister made the subjects of matrimonial care orders.[8] Both children had, however, been in care for some time previously. This case came up when the social worker was notified that seven-year-old Kevin had set fire to his foster home. The point here is not so much the details of the case as the way in which Mrs Malone is talked about.

The first extract comes from the social worker's telephone briefing of an assessment centre to which Kevin is being transferred.

'Kevin is a sturdy boy who has had a disturbed life. Mrs Malone, his mother, farmed the children out, sometimes looking after them herself for a few weeks but even when they have been placed out she has always seen them daily and interfered wherever possible. His mother removed the children after she thought they had been hit by a previous foster-parent that they had been with for sixteen months and then placed them with the Connollys, who are a splendid couple (. . .) Kevin is showing a classic disturbed child syndrome as a result of episodes caused by contact with his mother.'

Later in the week the social worker was interviewed by Mrs Malone's solicitor. The following extract comes from that meeting.

SW: I have been trying very hard to see it from the children's point of view . . . I checked the story of their first five years and you've probably seen that report too. {70}

SOLR: They were rather shunted around.

SW: Mrs Malone must appear the person who pulls up Kevin's roots every time he puts them down. He has never really had them properly before and he feels very threatened (. . .) Mrs Malone is an emotional and disturbed lady. We can weather it but it only needs one episode like the occasion when she attacked Mrs Connolly in front of the children for that to have an effect.

SOLR: She and Mrs Connolly met in the summer. Was that reasonably amicable?

SW: I would say that it was restrained rather than amicable. Mrs Malone was trying very hard to give the children a lovely time . . . usually her job takes a great deal of priority in her life . . . for that ten days the children took priority and it all went well (. . .)

This was a case that caused a great deal of concern, and Kevin seemed an extremely disturbed child who was said by a consultant psychiatrist to be on the verge of an irreversible psychosis.

Plainly, we could use this analysis for ironical effect, as we suggested in our discussion of the accident department. The same facts could be used to portray Mrs Malone as a victim of the oppression of women, torn between her children and her work and making what she can of inadequate substitute child-care facilities. Kevin's condition could then become a quirk of nature, an endogenous mental disorder which might arise in anyone. Again, though, this would deflect the reader from our concern with how the social worker is organizing her interpretation into a plausible and preferred version of events.

What is of interest is the way the social worker assembles Kevin's condition as the end-product of a series of causal events. Like pregnancy, mental illness is located as a social phenomenon with a human cause rather than belonging to the inaccessible world of nature. However, Kevin's responsibility for his actions is limited by his incompetent status as a child. The search for a cause then shifts to the adults socially and legally associated with him, his parents. As we have already noted, that search goes first to his mother. She has failed to give him the necessary security or to accord his needs the necessary priority, at whatever cost to her own desires. In passages not reproduced here the charges go on to Mr Malone, who is depicted as a weak and ineffectual man who was, and still is, intimidated by his ex-wife. His failure undercuts both his own character and {71} that of his wife, by strengthening the view of her as a selfish, domineering and uncaring woman. Against this version of the Malones, we are given the contrast of Mrs Connolly, mother of a large Catholic family, who has cheerfully taken on two highly distressed children. Her home is a model of warm, open, boundless affection. Whom would any reasonable person trust?

The Malones' divorce is too recent to affect the main issue, which is that conformity to the pattern of a conventional nuclear family does not prevent charges of deviance. Conversely, departures from that standard do not necessarily invite charges. We can consider this through a discussion of single-parent households. These can result from a number of circumstances – death, divorce, separation or illegitimacy. Any of these may reflect upon the parent who has care of the children, but need not. Generally, the first three tend to work to the credit of the parent with the children, since this parent controls information about their erstwhile spouse. This is a particular limitation for health visitors, who are much less likely to see both parties than are social workers. Nevertheless, the widowed or divorced have at some time constituted 'normal' nuclear families. Their deviance may be excused by death or justified by the misconduct of the former spouse, neither of which is easily challengeable. The former is generally treated as a chance event with natural causes, the latter may be difficult to overturn without countervailing data on the other party.

Unmarried mothers, however, have never, in this sense, been normal. We might characterize fieldworkers' approaches to them as employing a principle of 'every dog is entitled to one bite'. A single illegitimate child may be accepted either as an accidental or unanticipated outcome of sexual intercourse.[9] The choice between abortion and completion of that pregnancy is not one in which either health visitors or social workers are anxious to become embroiled. Both fieldworkers and management are very sensitive to the apparent public ambivalence about abortion and attempt to define it as a private matter, which does not furnish a basis for evaluation. In practice, however, single parenthood, as both demographically and relationally deviant, is available for moral scrutiny. This extract is from fieldwork with a County health visitor:

HV told us a bit about the fourteen-year-old who was pregnant. She said it's not really surprising. Her mother is living with a young man only a bit older than her daughter. She has an elder sister who has had three terminations and one illegitimate baby and is now living with a chap called Simon who bashes her about. HV said she had to {72} smile as the mother was absolutely furious with the fourteen-year-old. (. . .) It seems the girl will keep the baby although the HV is pressing her to have it terminated. She said, 'I know I shouldn't influence her really but I feel a baby in that household would be a disaster.' The girl has been referred to the hospital for abortion counselling by the GP but the HV continues, 'The doctor says he thinks it's too late, anyway there is no reason, she is a perfectly healthy girl and she knew what she was doing.'

Once again, we can see the difference of interpretation on the same facts. The health visitor excuses the girl's actions by a 'sad tale' rather reminiscent of Mrs Genn's earlier in this chapter. The general practitioner, on the other hand, regards the girl as fully responsible and, hence, not deserving of an abortion. We can also note here the health visitor's awareness of her limited licence in this matter. Her reluctance to 'influence' the girl reflects the tutelary relationship between families and state welfare agencies. The integrity of the family is maintained by such sentiments, although, of course, the girl's unwillingness to accept advice may call into question her own status as a responsible person and legitimate a more investigative approach in subsequent contacts.

This evaluation, by the health visitor, turns on the discrepancy between her model of teenage life and the girl's. Most front-line workers operated with a view of the teenage years as a time for an exploration of the world outside the home, for the pursuit of the teenager's own pleasures and interests before assuming the obligations of parenthood. A young woman who chooses the latter may be thought to be displaying a lack of understanding of this trade-off. When the expectations of youth are contrasted with the expectations of parenthood, fieldworkers find a contradiction which leads them to anticipate subsequent failure, on one count or the other, leading to future trouble for the agency. Failure on the first is less serious in the short term, although it may be thought to represent a long-term problem if the woman comes to feel she has missed out on her time of licence. Failure on the second has fairly self-evident consequences in the short term for the interests of the children. Such judgements are likely to be reinforced if there are further pregnancy episodes, whether or not these lead to abortions. A second or subsequent illegitimate pregnancy may be used as a ground for inferring a general want of care and reconsidering the condition of previous children.

Finally, we come to questions about the relationships between parents and their children. The workers' model of this relationship locates it in the sphere of nature. Love between adults is a social and, {73} hence, changeable phenomenon: the love of parents for children is natural and immutable. Its failure is, then, a particularly grave charge. This, indeed, is at the heart of many of the difficulties in identifying abuse or neglect. If the love of parents for children is an event in nature, instinctive rather than motivated, then those who fail are, in some sense, not members of the same species as the rest of us. If we may use the word in an old-fashioned sense, they are monsters, inhuman creations. Suspect parents, however, are not monstrously formed but are rather banal individuals. An allegation that they have failed to love their children is a matter of such enormity that it can seldom be contemplated in the absence of substantial corroborating evidence which thoroughly undercuts the parents' moral character, as the following examples show.

The first is a case from County which involved a girl declared by her parents to be of the 'wrong' sex, who died twenty-five days after birth from untreated pneumonia. Her parents, apart from failing to seek treatment, had, we were told, manifested no grief or other emotional reaction to the child's death. The front-line workers who knew the family thought that the death was probably the result of deliberate neglect, although the official version was that the parents had been ignorant of the significance of the child's symptoms. We have no evidence which would allow us to choose between these accounts, but we can consider how they were produced.

Many parents express some prenatal preference for a child of a particular sex. Few, however, insist that a child of the 'wrong' sex would be utterly unacceptable. When such a declaration is made the parents' character can be questioned. The sex of a child is beyond voluntary control in the present state of our knowledge. The declaration is, then, irrational since it seeks to control uncontrollable nature. It also challenges the natural status of parental love by asserting that some children are just not lovable.[10] While workers can find cultural justifications for statements of this kind – as we have seen, Asian families are thought to have a particular preference for boys – this area is treated somewhat less relativistically than others. If love is part of the natural order, it is the same for all ethnic groups. In this case, however, no such justification was applicable. The death was a one-off event in an otherwise respectable household. What we see, then, overriding the front-line workers' personal doubts, is an institutionalized preference for an optimistic version of the events, which could have been displaced only by other evidence sufficient to initiate the 'total denunciation' that we discuss later (pp. 147-50 {pp. 162-5 in orig.}). {74}

The point is made even more forcibly in our second example, one of our case histories from Shire, a girl called Jayne Wallace. This child first came to our attention shortly after her eighth birthday. Her mother had married young and had one child, shortly before taking up with her present husband, by whom she had rapidly had two further children, an older sibling and Jayne, and, after an interval, a fourth child. At Jayne's birth, her mother had requested that she be placed for adoption since her present husband had, at that time, temporarily abandoned her, and she could not manage three small children on her own. The birth was normal and Jayne weighed just over 9 lb at delivery. Her mother withdrew the adoption request within four weeks and Jayne was returned to her at the age of three months. Jayne made normal progress, doubling her birth-weight at six months. By 18 months she had only gained another 1 lb 4 oz and was referred for specialist investigation. She was reviewed at 18½ months, 23 months and 32 months. On the last occasion she was admitted to hospital, where she gained 3 lb in one month compared with a gain of 1 lb 4 oz in the previous year. It was firmly stated that her stunted growth and withdrawn nature were due to severe emotional deprivation.

The case was reopened by social services around the time of Jayne's third birthday. A social worker visited three times in two months but could find no cause for concern. Jayne appeared rather small but there were no bruises and she did not appear cowed or withdrawn. Just after Jayne was four, the health visitor and her nursery school began expressing concern about the adequacy of her clothing and diet, and there were incidents of bruising. At four years seven months she was readmitted to hospital and gained 2 lbs in two weeks. During her fifth year, there was concern over her bed-wetting and her parents' response. At six years, there was a further bruising incident which was referred by the health visitor to social services. The latter decided not to visit because of parental hostility. Jayne's weight remained virtually unchanged from the age of six to the age of eight, rising slightly during school terms and dropping in the holidays. From the age of six, too, there were frequent neighbour reports about the discrimination against Jayne by her parents. She was consistently being denied treats, birthday or Christmas presents which were being given to the other children. The first formal case conference was convened when she was seven-and-a-half. The conference we attended was, then, the second. It had before it a proposal from the senior social worker supervising the case that the child should be voluntarily received into care and, failing this, that care {75} proceedings should be taken.

This course of action was agreed to and it was decided to seek a further paediatric assessment. However, at a third case conference, eight months later, it emerged that Jayne had, in fact, been placed in a boarding school without reception into care. No mention was made of the proposed assessment. After seven months at boarding school her weight had reached the twenty-fifth centile despite losses of 6 lb during the Easter holidays and the summer half-term. Consideration was now being given to a voluntary foster placement for the school holidays.

Even at this length, such a summary can give at best a highly truncated account of a complex and long-running case. It is, however, one to which we shall return at a number of points subsequently. Nevertheless, it should be sufficient to draw out a very clear picture of a scapegoated child who has suffered severe emotional and physical damage, probably of a permanent and irreversible character, over a period of nearly ten years. The difficulty facing the agencies, however, is well captured in this conclusion from the senior social worker's paper to the second case conference:

> Those who know Mrs Wallace all describe her as a concerned and caring person in her dealings with the other children. They are well-clothed and well-fed. Medical attention is sought for ailments and the teachers are consulted about their progress at school. The rejection of Jayne therefore almost to the point of denying her existence (the Health Visitor comments that Jayne is never mentioned in conversation in the household unless she brings the subject up) is the more severe in contrast to the treatment of her siblings.
>
> Although this record catalogues a devastating history of deprivation there has never been any firm evidence of physical abuse by the parents nor has Jayne herself manifested signs of disturbance outside the home sufficient to justify a referral to Child Guidance. Indeed she appears to accept her role without protest. In view of the constant refusal of the parents to accept counselling help over Jayne's failure to thrive, no further intervention has hitherto been felt to be possible. Although the child is now eight the Health Visitor, GP, and school remain gravely concerned about her rejection and failure to put on weight. I propose therefore to offer the parents a further opportunity to accept help voluntarily. I would like to explore whether a failure of the parents to accept this could lead to a successful application for a Care Order under Care Proceedings.

If love is natural it is indivisible. All parents, whether natural or step, are required to love all their children equally. The wicked step-parents {76} of fiction are figures in morality tales, negative models for the audience. Parental failure here yields the scapegoated child, the Cinderella who is consistently discriminated against. Real-life Cinderellas, however, seldom seem to be concealed beauties: Jayne Wallace was exhibiting signs which all those involved regarded as indisputable indicators of neglect. Her condition, however, is a one-off event in this household whose material conditions and interpersonal environment are more than adequate for the neighbourhood.

Moreover, the existence of a 'natural' capacity for loving was demonstrable in their treatment of the other children. Given this, no one has yet felt able to break with the voluntary relationship and seek to compel the parents to act otherwise. Without being able to discredit their character in other respects as corroboration, the accusation against their moral nature which would be inherent in care proceedings cannot be sustained.

There are two other features of interest in this case. One is the presence of other children. An attempt at coercive intervention which failed might compromise voluntary access and the surveillance of their condition. The second feature is the impact of staff turnover. Looking at the process of decision-making in this case, it seems clear that, each time a new social worker took over, he or she wiped the slate clean. The preference for optimism, which we noted earlier, meant that each social worker started with a determination to think the best of the family and became disillusioned only after a period of time. No one in the basic grade stayed long enough to move on to a coercive course, in contrast to the health visitors and general practitioners in this case, and to the last senior social worker. The second case conference had its decisions set aside largely by the action of new social workers from Child Guidance services who did not know the full history but who were determined to make an attempt at achieving a non-coercive disposal.

THE SIGNIFICANCE OF SOCIAL DATA

We concluded the previous chapter by suggesting that settings organized around clinical evidence would tend to minimize identification rates. In this chapter, sufficient should have been said to indicate that organizing a setting around social evidence would tend to maximize identification rates. Townsend (1979) found that, of all children under five in the United Kingdom, over a quarter lived in houses which were structurally deficient, about a fifth in houses {77} which lacked one or more basic facilities, a similar proportion in houses which lacked sufficient internal play space, and a tenth in houses which were so structurally deficient as to constitute a health hazard. If these proportions still applied, and there is no reason to suppose substantial change, something over 850,000 children under five could be candidates for care. The same study would suggest that 16 per cent of all children under fourteen were in households with more than four children, almost two million children on present figures, and about 6 per cent of all children under five were in one-parent families, perhaps 200,000 children. Of course, all these statistics are very imperfect indicators of the situations we have analysed, but these figures may give us some indication of the order of magnitude of potential for fieldworker concern. By contrast, in 1977, just over 96,000 children were in care in England, of whom slightly more than 11,000 were under five. An equivalent of strict liability would pose an impossible burden on existing forms of social organization. We would either have a vast extension of coercion removing children from 'unfit' homes or enormous programmes of public expenditure in rehousing, income redistribution and the like, with accompanying supervision of these disbursements. These are equally antithetical to the liberal social order and its organizational mores. Two devices seem to be important in reconciling the population of potential candidates for identification as somehow mistreated with the population actually identified.

The first of these is what we might call the 'division of regulatory labour'. So far we have left this implicit in our discussion of the different types of evidence and the agencies involved. What is striking about this system, however, is its decentralization and differentiation. Only when several different occupations and organizations, each licensed or chartered to deal with different aspects of a child's circumstances, are all convinced of the propriety of interpreting that information in a light unfavourable to the child's parents, do we find the clear definition of mistreatment which precedes attempts to find a basis for compulsory action. In our more facetious moments, we have drawn an analogy with a gaming machine: care proceedings result only when three lemons come up simultaneously. The serious point is that this division between autonomous agencies institutionalizes a set of checks and balances which effectively restrict the identification of mistreatment.

We shall develop this argument further in chapters 5 and 6. For the present, however, we want to remain with the analysis of agency assessments of parents' moral character, which more than anything {78} else seems to cut down the choice of candidates for compulsory intervention. Here, of course, we are picking up the conclusion of the previous chapter, where we showed that the analysis of parental demeanour as evidence of moral character similarly contained the numbers of children who became the subject of detailed investigation. We have shown that the same is true of a wider array of social data which are thought to be manifestations of that essential character, to be matters within the control of parents as displays of their own nature. Throughout, however, we find that these data are perceived within some equivalent of Strong's description of the bureaucratic frame. We can characterize this as an injunction to front-line workers to interpret the available 'facts' as evidence that parents are honest, competent and caring, unless an exhaustive inquiry into their motivation renders this impossible. If parental failure is established, those same 'facts' can be read in a quite different fashion.

The liberal order, it can be argued, is maintained by a comprehensive system of moral inquiry. Such surveillance, however, seems to be sustainable only by its starting assumption that the surveyed are of sound character. A family that cooperates with state agencies and manifests at least a surface compliance with their requirements will not be coerced. What about the family that fails to comply? This forms our theme in the next chapter, where we shall focus in more detail on the scrutiny of parental responsibility.

4

The Rule of Optimism

{79}
The central fact to be explained by any analysis of decision-making in child protection is the rarity of allegations of mistreatment. If we were to test our findings about the clinical and social features of cases used as criteria by agency staff by turning them into operational rules from which we could make predictive statements about decisions in particular cases, we would vastly over-identify by comparison with the decisions actually made.[1] The reconciliation, we have suggested, is accomplished by an additional assessment of parents' moral character as revealed partly through their demeanour and partly by an inspection of those aspects of their life which can be seen to lie within their own control. That assessment, however, is conducted under what we might term a 'rule of optimism', that staff are required, if possible, to think the best of parents. This chapter will attempt to specify the components of that rule.

DEVIANCE AND RESPONSIBILITY

Both sociological and legal scholars have long been interested in the relationship between ascriptions of deviance and moral character. We have already introduced the notion that deviance is a matter of judgement, a charge made by one person against another, rather than an inherent property of certain acts. McHugh (1970) points out that such charges involve two issues. The first is whether some rule, convention or standard has been broken in circumstances where it could have been followed. Did a parent avoidably mistreat a child? This formulation, of course, echoes the words of the Children and Young Persons Act 1969 (p. 8). An affirmative answer involves both the question of fact and the possibility of rule-following. This latter element shades into the second issue, the degree to which the actor is {80} defined as the agent of his or her own behaviour. Did a parent *intend* to mistreat a child in the sense that he or she knew how the child should be treated and chose to act otherwise? McHugh analyses this in terms of the actor's theoretic status, an idea which is very close to Hart's (1968: 227) discussion of 'capacity-responsibility'. By this, Hart means

> the ability to understand what legal rules or morality require, to delib-
> erate and reach decisions concerning those requirements, and to con-
> form to decisions when made (. . .) 'responsible for his actions' in this
> sense refers not to a legal status but to certain complex psychological
> characteristics of persons (. . .)

Hart goes on to make it clear that by 'psychological characteristics', he actually means social ascriptions rather than inner states. An actor's external behaviour is used as evidence for inferences about his or her mental competence. As Blum and McHugh (1971) note, in their very similar account of motive ascription, this process identifies an actor as a person who has a particular moral character. His or her actions are *chosen* from a set of possible actions, a selection which excludes other possible formulations of the sort of person he or she is.

The importance of character has already been hinted at in the way it is used to interpret observed conduct in a prospective-retrospective fashion. This means that past events can be re-analysed to fit the actor's present status, as evidence, for instance, that a parent was 'really' an abuser all along, and to organize the unfolding present as yet further confirmation of the correctness of this ascription.[2]

> Persons dreaded for their brutality are the first ones to be suspected of
> a violent crime; despised persons, of a mean act; and those who arouse
> disgust, of an unclean act. People with bad reputations are accused and
> convicted on the basis of evidence which one would consider insuffi-
> cient if an unfavorable prejudice did not relate them to the crime in ad-
> vance. On the contrary, if the accused has won our favor we demand
> irrefutable proof before we impute to him the crime. (Fauconnet 1928:
> 266 quoted in Heider 1944: 363)

Moral character is, then, central to decision-making in child abuse and neglect, as with any other type of deviance. Its ascription, however, is not a straightforward matter.

If deviance is ascribed rather than inherent, there is necessarily room to resist or negotiate the inclusion of any particular behaviour {81} within this category. Hart (1951: 147-9) suggests two ways in which a defendant may defeat or mitigate a charge: first, by disputing the facts; and, second, by claiming an impairment of what Hart later came to call capacity-responsibility, by the defendant pointing to deficiencies in his or her knowledge and/or will.[3] A third means, which Hart does not cover in his focus on courts and identified deviance, is concealment. In anticipation of a possible charge, deviants may seek to prevent the discovery of their behaviour for what this may allow others to infer about their moral nature. As Duster (1970: 109-10) observes, in another context,

> Whether a drug user is noticed and labeled is thus dependent not upon behavior caused by the drug but upon the degree to which the user can prevent the society from looking for the marks on his arm or administering physical-chemical tests.

The identification of child abuse or neglect is similarly related to the visibility of children and the respective power of parents and surveillance agencies.

We shall take up the techniques of concealment and of disputing facts later. Before doing so, however, we want to look in more detail at Hart's second category, deficiencies of will or knowledge. This has been developed by Scott and Lyman (1968: 46) in their discussion of 'accounts':

> By an account (. . .) we mean a statement made by a social actor to explain unanticipated or untoward behavior – whether that behavior is his own or that of others, and whether the proximate cause for the statement arises from the actor himself or from someone else.

As this quotation suggests, accounts may also be produced by observers and used either to substitute for or to evaluate those offered by actors.

> (. . .) the label of deviant can be attached successfully to an actor only if he was unable to relieve himself of the negative interpretation of his intentions. If he is able to offer an acceptable account (an excuse or justification) for his presumed untoward action, his behavior is no longer deviant. When his account is honored, we may say that his deviance has been neutralized. (Scott and Lyman 1970: 91)

In fact, we think this understates the role of the audience. Child protection agencies may actually relieve parents of the burden of {82} producing accounts by volunteering or imputing acceptable reasons for apparently untoward actions. Given the scale of the screening problem, it is not feasible, within present organizational forms, to do this by the kind of detailed examination of individual cases which Scott and Lyman propose, although, as we shall show, these do emerge once challenges are formulated. What we found, then, were two institutionalized devices – cultural relativism and natural love – which combined to eliminate the overwhelming majority of potential cases by providing justification or excuse and allowing front-line workers to prefer an optimistic reading of client behaviour. These neutralized deviance in advance of any specific challenge.

CULTURAL RELATIVISM

Cultural relativism is an agency *justification*. Justifications concede that, in some sense, the ascription of deviance is correct but that, in practice, the observed conduct is permitted or required by the particular circumstances. In the present instance, this amounts to saying that the mistreatment of a child was somehow unavoidable. The acts complained of are not abusive or neglectful but positive attempts to comply with alternative normative standards that would allow them to be recognized as appropriate parental behaviour.

The term 'cultural relativism' is used here to denote an intellectual position that all cultures are equally valid ways of formulating relationships between human beings and between human beings and the material world, together with the possible political corollary that members of one culture have no right to criticize members of another by importing their own standards of judgement. In this respect it differs from a simple tolerance of diversity. As Bailey and Brake (1975: 10) observe in a widely-quoted social work text:

> The danger of hegemony is that it may result in psychological damage to those who resist it. In this way casework may assist people to resist hegemony and develop pride instead of self-hatred. *A framework of cultural diversity is more illuminating than an uncritical acceptance of the ideology of normal'*. (our emphasis)

The task of social work is not to impose any particular set of values but to facilitate clients in the realization of their own even to the point of resisting or opposing the prevailing forms of social organization. Ideas of this kind had a profound impact on training courses for health and welfare workers in the late sixties and early {83} seventies through such varied sources as labelling theory in sociology and assorted non-directive or non-judgemental approaches to counselling in psychology.[4]

> The prevailing climate of ideas among those who wrote about deviance in the late sixties and seventies – and to a large extent also among social work practitioners – was not merely generously optimistic in its view of human nature but also quite strongly libertarian. The term 'social control' came to be used pejoratively . . . in the sense of 'enforced – and therefore unarguably undesirable – conformity to certain arbitrary norms of behaviour' . . . . Protestations that a given system is dedicated to promoting the welfare of the individual children passing through it tend to be received with some scepticism as long as compulsory powers are exercised in order to bring about changes in behaviour in the direction of greater obedience to laws and social conventions. (Martin et al. 1981: 23)

By the time of our study, such ideas were well-entrenched in the practice of front-line workers. Satyamurti (1981: 132) had found, in 1971-72, that

> Social workers (. . .) did not have a conception of an alternative way of living, of different standards from their own. They operated with a model not of working-class standards or West Indian or Pakistani standards of conduct, but with a middle-class set of standards, *lowered.* (Original emphasis)

With the partial exception of some staff in County, this was no longer the case in any of our three study areas, at least to the extent that workers were prepared to treat that as a legitimate model to use in discussing their own practice with each other or with the research team.

We have already cited two examples of ethnic origin being used to justify deviant conduct in Asians: the child and her father in the accident department (pp. 39-40 {pp. 45-6 in orig.}) and the woman with the large family (p. 59 {p. 66}). The following extracts from a case conference on a West Indian girl who had made allegations of sexual assault against her stepfather are typical of references to this ethnic group:

SSW: So you wouldn't want to take any action on them?

SW: I think we should just want to monitor them. {84}

SSW: Yes, monitor them via the school and the health visitor. I think we have learnt to expect a variety of family situations on the Attlee Estate and to accept them.

(. . .)

SW: . . . her father was very annoyed and beat her with a strap.

SSW: With a strap?

SW: Oh this sort of thing does happen in this community.

(. . .)

SSW: This violence is very difficult to prove and we have to accept that it is just part of West Indian culture.

Lawson (1980: 149) gives another similar example.[5] References of a comparable kind were also made to gipsy families. Such ethnic justifications were recorded in all three study areas, although County had a negligible black population and did seem to be less accepting of its gipsies. Front-line workers there displayed a greater willingness to demand conformity and appeared less reluctant to use compulsory measures in support of such demands.

Within each study area, one could also notice the relevance of the knowledge of social geography which we have also commented upon. Front-line workers' knowledge of their patches as territories of normal appearances incorporated the notion of 'normal for this local culture'. The basis might be geographic, as in the references to service and council estates at the beginning of the previous chapter (pp. 51-2 {p. 58}) or to a specific district like the Attlee Estate, or it might be based on kinship. The 'battering Walshes', to be discussed in chapter 7, exemplified this. That knowledge could, however, incorporate the whole study area. We saw this most explicitly in Borough. This is a health visitor discussing her work:

> Honestly, you go from socialism to the national front in one day in this area. You really do want to tell people to get on with life and stop looking for ways of propping themselves up. The situation is political, though, isn't it? I mean the problems here are social policy ones, they are not medical, they are not health. I know people complain about the welfare state and that sort of thing. I know people sort of say the situation is wrong and the structure's wrong but really what can you do? A million pounds in Borough wouldn't make much difference (. . .) I don't know what you could do here with a million pounds to improve the quality of life. (. . .) It is generation after generation of {85} poor parenting that leads to further poor parenting and so forth (she goes on to talk about the role of women in this community). I mean the girls here wouldn't know what to do with it (women's liberation) if you gave it to them and, anyway, they don't want it. All they think of is getting pregnant and getting married and things that would be prestige to a liberated woman such as her job and no family, these would be a disgrace in this area. To go to work and not have a man would be a terrible thing up here (. . .) I mean what is there for girls to work at? – it's not very stimulating stuff in factories or down mines.

Another health visitor described her objectives:

> I try not to be biased about any particular aspect. I'm given the situation and I'll, you know, try to look at that and digest it and think that this is what I've got and what's been presented to me. I don't particularly figure out, 'what can I do about this?' but 'Right, this is what I've got, let's try and make the best out of what we've got' and that way and by the attitude I've found I've been accepted much better and then I try (. . .) to make the best of that particular given situation. (. . .) I don't think it's right that I should impose my standards which might not be someone else's standards anyway (. . .) it may not be the best situation but I think that if, taking the parents' attitude and their commitments and how they rear the child, you know, (. . .) just take for example the sterilization is adequate and you know that those bottles are as clinically clean as I, you know, that mum is ever going to be able to do then I think at least we've made one step, you know.

Finally, we have a third health visitor responding to a question from one of the research team. She had remarked on the value of an assessment done on one of her families by a specialized unit at a neighbouring teaching hospital. The interviewer asked if this was because of its application of an absolute standard of child competence rather than one which was scaled down to the norm on her patch. This extract is typical of her response to a line of questioning which put the possible desirability of absolute standards to her:

> I felt that the people concerned with this had actually not tried to gear themselves or lower their own standards conducive to the area from which the child had come and that possibly their overall impressions of the child's ability instead of using a standardized set of performance scales and so on, that the child was expected to conform in a different setting. I felt that there was a great need for these people actually to come into the area to do the assessment rather than in a {86} clinical situation, people who were totally divorced from the area because, looking at it from a class point of view, a lot of the workers within these assessment centres tend to be from the upper social classes and are not aware that there are such lower scales in the social class, I mean they say that classes go from one to five, well I've got my own six and seven here and feel that people should adjust themselves accordingly and I felt in that particular case that hadn't been done.

While all these examples happen to have been taken from health visitors, they could readily be matched by comments from staff in any of the other agencies on which we had sufficient data. A similar body of statements could be produced for County and, with somewhat more difficulty, for Shire.[6]

NATURAL LOVE

The other device which may be used to neutralize deviance is the offering of an *excuse* that we have called 'natural love'. Excuses again recognize the deviant nature of the acts in question but withhold moral liability because of impairment of the actor's capacity-responsibility. While justifications appeal to a social framework of interpretation, excuses are located in the realm of nature. They are the moments at which agency is overwhelmed by forces beyond its control, either chance or mysterious inner urges.[7] Excuses, then, are a particularly powerful type of account. If accepted they are likely comprehensively to exculpate the alleged deviant, since he or she was not *capable* of being responsible for the acts complained of. At the same time, their very power creates dangers for social order in a liberal society whose fundamental regulatory strategy rests on the assumption of responsibility for action. There are, then, strict limits to the admissibility of excuses and profound disincentives to relying upon them. For evidence of the limits one has only to think of the extensive legal debate on the principle of *mens rea*, the intention to offend, and the pleas of accident or diminished responsibility. The disincentives flow from the status of excuses as events in nature. If they are a failure of human agency, this may call into question the status of the alleged deviant as a human being. We can see the consequences in the proliferation of controls over those whose capacity for responsible action is, or is thought to be, impaired, most notably the mentally disordered.

This background is important for understanding the force of natural love as an excuse for parental deviance. As we observed earlier, {87} front-line workers distinguished between adult/adult love, a matter of choice which lay within a social framework of explanation, and parent/child love, an instinctual phenomenon, grounded in human nature. As such it has a special, enduring, timeless and culture-free quality. Natural love is, then, a powerful part of the operational framing of front-line work. (cf. Davis and Strong 1976). If it is assumed that all parents love their children as a fact of nature, then it becomes very difficult to read evidence in a way which is inconsistent with this assumption. The challenge, as we have remarked, amounts to an allegation that deviant parents do not share a common humanity with the rest of us.

We have already presented some data which bear upon this point in our discussion of the case of Jayne Wallace in the last chapter. She gave every indication of being a scapegoated child but the agencies involved refrained from intervention at least in part because her parents were able to demonstrate a capacity for loving relationships with the other children. Similar concerns are apparent in the health visitors' responses to the two black eyes described on pages 89-90 {pp. 99-100 in orig.}.

The general issues are well brought out by a case from Borough. This involved four children, aged between four and eleven at the time of our fieldwork. In descending order of age, the children are Annie, Carl, Darren and Tracy. The social services file began some seven years previously, when Carl was admitted to hospital with malnutrition and Annie was referred for psychological assessment due to retarded speech and aggression. There were various tests and social work contacts over a period of about twelve months, and contact then faded out until an NSPCC referral about two years later following neighbour reports about the children being left on their own. Around this time, Carl had two further admissions to hospital for infections and malnutrition. He was placed on the at-risk register. There were various material inputs from social services to help with bedding and rent arrears. Carl remained on the register. Some years later, there is a note that the children's father has been charged with causing actual bodily harm (to another adult). Shortly afterwards, one of the local paediatricians was asked to examine Annie after injuries had been observed on her at school. She claimed that they were caused by her father, but the doctor determined that they were more consistent with her mother's explanation of an accidental fall. By this time, Annie was attending a special school for the subnormal. The paediatrician was provoked to wonder in his report how much her home background was contributing to her apparent retardation. A few months later he saw her again with minor injuries {88} but still considered them to be inconclusive, although cause for suspicion. Shortly afterwards, all four children were received voluntarily into care. The parents were threatened with proceedings and conditions were said to have improved sufficiently to justify the children's return. The paediatrician reviewed them and still felt there was no evidence of abuse. Malnutrition was less likely to occur as the children were now old enough to get food for themselves. He considered that it was a severely disordered family but that there did seem to be signs of love between mother and children. Finally, shortly before our fieldwork, Carl came to school with burns to his hair and to his stomach. He was again seen by the paediatrician, who considered the injuries suspicious but insufficient to warrant a place of safety order in a family so well-known to social services. The subsequent case conference report had not yet reached the file, but did not dispute this conclusion.

The social worker involved with this case had intended to take her accompanying researcher to see the family but they proved to be out. She did, however, discuss the household:

SW says that they have been pressurized a lot to move these kids from various other agencies but there is a strong bond of affection between them and their mother and she queries whether it would be right to whip the kids out when the only ground for doing so is their moral judgement, (. . .) She wasn't much involved in this case herself now and most of the visiting was being done by the social work assistant. It was rather difficult but she felt the oldest boy had quite a good future in front of him with a bit of help from them and would probably have been benefited by being taken out of the family into care but SW thought that he also enjoyed feeling superior to his mother. She was thinking of trying to get him into the cubs because he was a bright active child. He enjoyed reading a good deal and they had provided him with a lot of books, although there were difficulties because the other children tended to tear them up. (. . .) SW said that one of the reasons for leaving the oldest boy at home was the degree to which the school were making a big effort with him. They have been sending books home and helping him to find somewhere to keep them safe from the other children. The father was quite intelligent which was where the boy got it from but he had just not got any idea about what a home should be like and his role as a father. SW said that she had tried to sit down and talk to him about this but he wouldn't get involved in the discussion. She felt that frankly in a more demanding area, and she regards her own as comparatively undemanding by Borough's standards, the family would have been

shelved until a crisis came up when the children would have been received {89} into care. She still felt very unsure about whether they
shouldn't really be waiting to let the children come into care at an appropriate point.

This case is typical of those which lie on the borderline of intervention. Of
the 27 cases in our Shire sample, for instance, 15 had broadly similar
histories, 10 coming to court and five being dealt with in other ways. One
has a situation where children are suffering a run of minor injuries which
are not demonstrably inconsistent with parental accounts, are displaying a
degree of developmental retardation and are living in poor material circumstances, but where there appears to be a certain positive emotional
relationship between parents and children. Often, the parents were seen as
having very limited capacities themselves, but were able to fulfil this basic
test of loving their children. Where this occurred, it seemed that social
workers were prepared to go to considerable lengths to resist the removal
of children.[8]

THE CONSEQUENCES OF NEUTRALIZATION

It is the operation of these two techniques which results in what we have
called the 'rule of optimism'. Singly or together they provide, on the one
hand, for a highly elastic approach to parental deviance and, on the other,
for the charge of deviance to be a matter of such gravity that workers are
understandably inhibited from making it. Cultural relativism has no
internal limit to its theorizing. It is indefinitely extendable, so that any
small group or articulate individual can find their own theories being
elevated to the status of a culture and turned into a justification. What may
seem like eccentricities or perversions are elevated into valid cultural
statements. Front-line workers are led either to an open acceptance of the
client's justifications, if called for, or to concluding that the fault lies
within them, for failing sufficiently to empathize with the alleged deviant.
Tout comprendre, c'est tout pardonner. Even if the question of deviance
does arise, the enormity of the implications must give the workers pause.
When parental love is defined as a natural fact any challenge constitutes
its objects as deficient in their humanity.

These neutralizations lock into the bureaucratic framing of agen-
cy/client encounters and underpin the reading of parental behaviour as
honest, competent and caring. As such they solve two particular problems
for front-line workers. The first is a latter-day equivalent of the problem of
theodicy, the persistence of failure. {90} As Pearson (1975b: 36) observes
for social workers:

Professional ideology preaches the redemption of social ills: all men (. . .) can be reached by the exercise of the principle of 'acceptance' (. . .) Social-work departments are instead experienced as a mad rush, a helter-skelter of crisis and troubled lives (. . .) Meanwhile the social worker is left with a headache – a personal problem which is also a political problem, namely, how to act on the ideals of social work in a less than ideal world.

Rosenfeld and Newberger (1977: 2087) echo these sentiments in their remarks about health care workers:

Fused with Utopian notions about the power of love and genuine concern, the compassionate model may also demoralize professionals when the treatment relationship proves hopeless. One may take it as a personal failure to love sufficiently or appropriately.

In this respect cultural relativism and natural love are also accounts which front-line workers can use to bridge the gap between their own ideals and the realities of their practice, that their impact can be no more than marginal in a liberal society. This limitation is perceived to result from an acceptance of the principle that rewards in a society should be distributed in proportion to economic or social contributions rather than on the basis of needs, with the consequent endorsement of the legitimacy of inequality, and from the constraints on coercive attempts to influence individual conduct. These two devices allow the front-line workers, despite substantial evidence to the contrary, to reconstitute families as having some integrity and personal worth through which some gains can be made, however slight.

This was most apparent in Borough, where the palpable material deprivation of many households raised most acute questions of enforcement and, of course, of the organizational problem of the scale of its target population. The following extracts are from interviews with a senior social worker and a social worker in that area:

SSW: (. . .) one of the dangers that I'm always aware of – one of the things that worries me very much is that, in a sense, our sort of standards of what is appropriate intervention, or when an intervention is appropriate and when it isn't – reflects the area. And whether, in fact, it ought to more reflect outside concerns or an outside set of values. In a sense, what I'm saying is that perhaps our set of values become consistent with the area, but become very much at variance from the sort of external set of standards. I think {91} that's what happens to social workers generally, doesn't it? That's why people throw up their hands in horror, when one goes wrong. (. . .) You know, the sort of stuff that's routine to us, is absolutely horrifying to other people who are outside. (. . .) You know, I mean, because these days most people are comparatively affluent – most people don't have much contact with people who, sort of, murder children, or neglect their children, or, for whatever reason, because they've got damaged personalities or whatever. Most people don't have that much contact with it. You know, and yet, our day-to-day bread-and-butter work is with people who do these things, who are damaged themselves, who have many, many problems, don't manage their finances. But . . . And it's so difficult, it's so easy in a sense, for us to get that out of proportion.

SW: I think my own attitude is, well, in this particular case, um, I was probably more aware of all the different problems that are placed on me in, sort of, decision-making, in that sort of way, of riding rough over people's lives. So, I would; I don't know. But, I mean, perhaps I'm just very well aware of the, er, dangers of going into a situation and saying, you know, with a very crude assessment, 'that is a grotty family, there is no possibility for a change, therefore, the child will be better off in a different environment, and that's it – let's begin over there'.

The second problem is related to the constraints on regulation in a liberal order. In dealing with child abuse and neglect, the bulk of the task is uninvited surveillance. This is quite different from, for instance, dealing with welfare payments where there is a supplicant relationship. The latter, as Zimmerman (1969) has shown, is marked by an investigative treatment of clients where their moral character is assumed to be discredited by the act of application and, hence, to be suspected until proven otherwise. One of the most important points to grasp seems to be the *weakness* of surveillance agencies, especially those which penetrate private spheres of action. Indeed, strong agencies are often regarded as a mark of an illiberal state. The liberal compromise, that the family will be laid open for inspection provided that the state undertakes to make the best of what its agents find, is enshrined in these two devices. State agents will not find proven deviance, as opposed to questionable diversity, unless presented with quite overwhelming evidence. Parents may have problems or treat their children in ways other than those preferred by the front-line worker: they are *not,* however, so bad as to be conceived of as abusive or neglectful. {92}

Under what kinds of circumstances could allegations ever be made, then? We identified two types of event which consistently seemed to precipitate a more investigative treatment of a family: withdrawal of parental compliance and failure of agency containment.[9]

PARENTAL INCORRIGIBILITY

By parental incorrigibility, we do not mean to imply that the nature of the child's alleged mistreatment is of a chronic or continuing kind, but that the parents have repudiated the legitimacy of agency involvement. The provocative effects of such actions have been documented in studies of agencies as disparate as the Oakland police department (Piliavin and Briar

1964), the Boston juvenile court (Emerson 1969) and the English water pollution inspectorate (Hawkins 1983) and are also remarked upon by Newberger and Bourne (1978). Conversely, as long as parents maintained at least a surface co-operation they were less likely to be the object of compulsory action. The Shire social services' Principal Adviser (Child Care) commented on the case of Jayne Wallace (pp. 66-68 {pp. 74-6}):

> (. . .) it is not an offence to discriminate against a child, not to buy it presents or not to take an interest in it at school. It seems to me that the parents know just how far to go and have succeeded up to now in doing that.

Bacon and Farquhar (1982) report a very similar case with an emotionally disturbed and incontinent five-year-old boy who was subject to rejection by his family. While a case conference agreed that he met all the criteria for inclusion on the local child abuse register, it was agreed not to include the child because of the parents' superficial compliance with agency involvement.[10] The point is, however, best demonstrated by considering a case from County described by the local authority's solicitor as 'typical, it's one of a class'. This example relates to two children, John and Luke Dawson, aged two years and five months respectively. Their mother is severely subnormal and may be mentally disordered and their father was thought to be of low average intelligence.

The following extracts come from the care proceedings on these children. The Dawsons have been visited two to three times a week for the previous nine months by a family aide from social services, {93} providing homecraft instruction, as well as by a senior social worker and a health visitor. In examination by the local authority solicitor, the senior social worker gave an account of her final joint visit with the family aide. We begin by quoting after it had been established that Luke was in his cot with a bottle propped up in his mouth. The solicitor asked what followed.

SSW: We suggested that she picked up the baby. She was very unwilling to do that. Each of us suggested it in turn for over a period of about 20 minutes. Eventually she did this and then plonked the baby down onto the table. She took him out and put talc and a clean nappy on the bottom without cleaning it.

LAS: How quick was her response to your suggestion?

SSW: It took quite a long time. Some 20 or 30 minutes.

LAS: Can you tell the court what John was doing?

SSW: This was when he woke up. I saw that he had a rash below his knees. While he was asleep he both wetted and soiled himself. He kept crying and pulling at his pants and was obviously uncomfortable. Mrs Dawson didn't respond. The family aide went and got a nappy. Mrs Dawson again powdered his bottom and put a nappy on over the soil.

LAS: Can you tell us a bit more about this rash?

SSW: It was very bad and quite extensive. It looked like nappy rash to me.

LAS: You said it extended as far as his knees?

SSW: It was confined to the nappy area as far as his waist, down to his knees and round at the front.

LAS: Can you tell us anything more about John on this visit?

SSW: He related well to the family aide. He went to her handbag to look for some sweets. He stayed around her throughout the visit.

LAS: Is there anything else about John?

SSW: He still doesn't speak. He just sat silently again. On one occasion he deliberately banged his head on the floor and resumed rocking. {94}

LAS: Is that something you have got experience of?

SSW: Yes.

LAS: What would rocking generally indicate?

SSW: It's a way of dealing with frustration. It's a very withdrawn type of response. It's something children do as opposed to being comforted.

We have quoted this at length partly because we want to underline our contentions about the elasticity of front-line workers' standards. As long as the Dawsons exhibited a minimal compliance, they were prepared to excuse this treatment of the children by recognizing the parents' 'natural love'. Although both parents had limited capacities, they were exercising these to the full. It was not, therefore, possible to find them culpable of neglect even though both children were patently suffering. What did lead them into court was the parents' withdrawal of cooperation and demand that agencies respect the privacy of their home and their parental liberties.[11] At this point the Dawsons immediately became vulnerable to coercive action. Indeed, one of our Shire cases presented this quite baldly. Shirley Austen, aged fourteen months, had been admitted to hospital diagnosed as failing to thrive. Her parents had broken off social work contact three months previously and refused two invitations to renew it. The senior social worker supervising the case asked bluntly at the case conference: 'Do they realize that their refusal may have the consequences of legal action?'

The importance of parental opposition is twofold. Firstly, it undercuts the parents' moral character within the liberal compromise that trades the rule of optimism against co-operation with surveillance agencies. By 'standing on their rights' they are indicating that some feature of their character may be discreditable. This could affect middle-class families as much as working-class. The Conrads, one of our Shire cases, were an auditor for an international company and his wife who had two children under five. Mr Conrad was frequently absent from home for long periods, during which his wife made heavy demands on both health and social work services. She had been under treatment since childhood for what was diagnosed as a personality disorder. Her difficulties had been excused over a long period, although the view had grown that she was a manipulative woman.[12] As we have observed, mental illness, especially in its minor forms, seems open to being regarded as intentional or at least {95} intentionally exploited. Attempts to restrict services to Mrs Conrad had led to her threatening to harm the children, and they were eventually made the subjects of a place of safety order. The following extract is from a subsequent letter to her over the signature of a Senior Social Worker acting as Area Director:

> You will remember from our discussion on the telephone and when I visited you on that day you told me that you were afraid you might damage the children, and that on the previous day you had in fact kicked Charlotte 'all over' when she was lying on the floor, and that you were afraid this sort of thing might happen again if something was not done. You will also be aware of this department's general concern over the past months. In particular, recently, when you found it difficult to cope in your husband's absence and resorted to taking overdoses of medication which have resulted in your urgent admission to hospital. We consider, as has been explained to you, that this sort of happening has adversely affected the children.
>
> We have attempted to resolve a recent incident by informally taking the children into care under Section 1 of the Children Act 1948, and would have preferred that they remain in care, at least until your husband's return, but you will recall that, as was your right under that agreement, you demanded their return to you. The decision to take a place of safety order was made in order to remove from you the responsibility which you appeared unable to bear at the moment for their proper care (. . .)

The analysis of this letter allows us to show how Mrs Conrad's character is progressively discredited and the place of safety order made inevitable. It begins by locating the responsibility for this intervention with Mrs Conrad herself. She has asked for help and put herself into a supplicant position where her character can properly be scrutinized. The writer then alludes to her self-poisoning and dismisses it as a possible excuse by setting it into a social frame. It has been explained to her that this is adversely affecting the children, which any responsible person would regard as a serious concern, and yet she has done nothing about it. The letter goes on to refer to an attempt at negotiating a resolution by arranging a voluntary reception into care. Most analyses of dispute resolution stress a preference for avoiding litigation. The department has acted reasonably in attempting this and been rebuffed. The end of that sentence is particularly interesting: '. . . as was your right . . . you demanded . . .' This is a further aspersion on Mrs Conrad's character. A person with nothing discreditable about them would have no reason to insist on {96} the letter of their legal rights, let alone *demand* them. This is the new element in the situation which finally stigmatizes Mrs Conrad as a potentially abusive parent and legitimates the allegations against her.[13]

The second consequence of parental opposition is that it knocks away one of the possible libertarian arguments. If, as we are arguing, agencies share the prevailing liberal value of minimum intervention, then they too are susceptible to arguments that voluntary measures should be given a further chance, a feature that was evident in the Jayne Wallace case, for instance. Where parents actively reject help, though, agencies can argue against their critics that they had no choice but to take compulsory measures. Parental incorrigibility is an account for agencies to use in bridging the gap between external standards and actual practice. It should perhaps be stressed that 'compulsory measures', here, does not necessarily imply a desire to remove a child, although, as the law stands, this may be the only power which is available.

FAILURE OF CONTAINMENT

The other precipitating factor which we identified was what we have called 'failure of containment'. By this, we mean the degree to which knowledge of a family's circumstances had spread beyond a small group of front-line workers. This could occur in two ways: either the parents presented the child to agencies outside the primary group whose concern then fed back to the front-line workers, or the primary group members concluded that their own resources, whether organizational or personal, were exhausted. The first of these seems most applicable in analysing those cases which were actually identified in accident services and effectively referred back or where neighbours or kin alerted the police or NSPCC about known but hitherto contained cases. In the other type of case there is literally no-where else to go. The parents involved have, metaphorically, exhausted their social credit with the community and local agencies. We can bring out the point in this extract from an interview with Mrs Conrad's health visitor:

I felt that she was using these children as pawns, y'know in her game, in inverted commas I use the word game and I felt that she'd had several psychiatrists, social workers, she was now on, well she certainly had Mrs Harrison going, the other health visitor, and she'd had {97} two temporary ones in between and then myself for two years and the way she used to play (GP) along (. . .) I mean there were as many as ten phone calls in as many days, and I mean the majority of them were made by him. They had terribly unrealistic demands on people, I mean, y'know they just felt that everyone was sitting there just waiting for them (. . .) (the social worker) one of the first things she did was to organize a rota of neighbours, y'know, some to collect the children for different things and some to make her hot chocolate at night and whatever have you. But you see, she did exactly with them as she did with the professional workers, y'see, it was manipulation (. . .) and they all got exhausted (. . .)

Once this point is reached there is nowhere left to go, except to agencies whose staff are more insulated from the rule of optimism. Parental character is subject to harsher judgement and allegations of mistreatment are more readily made, whether or not the parents can also be depicted as incorrigible.

We find this particularly helpful in understanding why what seems to be a disproportionate number of abuse cases, as opposed to those of neglect, result in coercive intervention. We are highly suspicious, for reasons to be discussed shortly, of many of the statistics which purport to measure the true prevalence of children in need of protection. Nevertheless, in all three areas, staff identified neglect as more prevalent than abuse to a degree which was not reflected in the proportion of cases considered for or resulting in legal action. The key difference is that abusive treatment of children is more likely to result in children being referred for specialist investigation. Frontline workers are mostly generalists and subject to interpersonal pressures to apply the rule of optimism in excusing or justifying conduct. Specialists are partly insulated from these by the referral system and can afford to treat parental protestations more sceptically.

In practical terms, failure of containment seems to be more important as a trigger for compulsory intervention. It was clearly implicated in 18 of the 27 cases in our Shire series.[14] The reasons for this will be discussed more fully in the next three chapters but, briefly, seem to relate to the increasing risk of criticism for ineffectiveness which agencies run once a case actually gets documented as a matter for concern. Parental compliance may be most important in precipitating the involvement of other agencies, in a search for one capable of establishing a voluntary relationship with the family. The further this search extends, the more agencies are drawn in and the less contained the case becomes. {98}

THE DISTRIBUTION OF ALLEGATIONS

It is, then, the theorizing of front-line workers that gives a particular shape to the pattern of allegations which arise in child protection as parents are sorted into the reputable and the disreputable. This is not a simple class distribution.

Certainly, under the rule of optimism, the families most difficult to cast in an adverse light, in order to suspect mistreatment, were middle- and upper-class. The case of the martinet officer in County, to which we have referred previously (p. 43 {p. 49}) is a good example of this, although not strictly a front-line worker's account. These extracts are from our interview with the consultant paediatrician in the case:

(The child) had been under (my colleague) for twelve months, um, be- cause of developmental problems, so thought. And eventually (he) sent him to the assessment centre and I happened to see him (. . .) I exam- ined the child who was rather short, stocky odd-looking child, short legs, short arms and fixed expression, um, couldn't really make a diag- nosis at all for the first afternoon anyway. And I say (the father was) a very agreeable chap, he came not his wife. (. . .) So we saw him again. On the second time he went into details and scraping the bottom of the barrel sort of said, 'Well I think lead poisoning' or something like that, you see. And so, some remark and he said, 'Yes, well, he's eaten about 50 per cent of the paint off his cot but it's a Mothercare cot so it shouldn't be poisonous.' So, immediately, 50 per cent, Well, what's he doing all that time in his cot? you see, and we went into the care of this child. And eventually to cut a long story short, I gathered that he was a great disciplinarian, and that his father had been a disciplinarian that he also was a (serving officer) wanted everything to be absolutely spot on and perfect and he wanted his child to be spot on and perfect and when he said, 'Come' the child comes and when he said, 'Sit' the child sits, you see. So we X-rayed that child and every damn joint was dis- rupted, that's why he had such short arms and short legs, nobody had thought about that, not seen it. And he said, 'Well I haven't injured the child', there were no marks on the child but I say every bone had peri- osity in every joint, so this child is going to be permanently short and incurable. Um, and we had him in the hospital and he came to see it you see, and he said we were ruining this child, we were ruining this child, 'You're letting it do as it likes', the child began to develop in the ward you see, run around and pick up toys and when he said, 'Come', it didn't come so quickly and he felt insulted so he took his own case to court. And in the court he really believed he said, you know, 'They are ruining my child because {99} before I said you sit there and don't move and he sat there and did not move, and now it won't take any no- tice of me.'[15]

We can see, even in this brief account, the long search for any explanation of the child's disorder that did not involve an allegation of abusive treatment and the essentially adventitious nature of the ultimate diagnosis. The father's social status insulated him from the possibility of moral challenge. Comparable cases could be found in our health visitor data. Thus, in Shire, another case described to us related to a child whose father was a senior academic and mother a successful barrister. The child had been looked after by a succession of foreign au pairs and had severely delayed language development. Her parents had refused to accept speech therapy and the rural district in which they lived had no nursery or playgroup facilities, even had the parents been willing to consider them. Although the health visitor was concerned for the child's welfare, she was nevertheless quite definite that it was not a matter for onward referral to an agency with greater coercive power.

On the other hand, these difficulties are not confined to these classes. As we have already seen, front-line workers have a broad acceptance of diverse parental conduct. The Illingworth case, which we have already mentioned (pp. 55-6 {pp. 62-3}), is a good example. The health visitor had not thought anything of Mandy's development until she received a tip-off. Even then it took a relatively long period of investigation to discredit the tidy appearance of the house and to redefine the child as in need of protective intervention of some kind. The same principle is evident in these extracts from our observation of two visits to 'respectable' working-class households with different health visitors. On both occasions, the researcher has observed black eyes on babies under one year old which the health visitor had not commented on in the course of the visit.

> (. . .) I thought I noticed the child had a black eye. The mother seemed quite pleased with the baby and said that she had been sleeping which had been a great relief to them, although the mother herself looked simply ghastly with large rings around her eyes. We didn't stay long at this house and in the car I said to HV had she seen the black eye. She seemed extremely embarrassed and put her hands over her face and said, 'No, I didn't. I really hadn't noticed.' She seemed very anxious about this and I tried to reassure her. (. . .) We discussed possible explanations (. . .) She then remarked, 'I think we are all getting too jumpy about this (child abuse). I'm sure (client) wouldn't bash her baby and if she did she would come and tell me about it.' (. . .) {100}

This baby had a fairly large and extremely obvious black eye. From what I could gather the health visitor made no comment to the mother about it nor did the nursing auxiliary (who was helping with a routine domiciliary hearing test) (. . .) HV went off to speak to another mother (in the same house) (. . .) While HV was doing this, the nursing auxiliary was talking to this other mum and saying things like, 'Amy's at a very difficult age.' The mother said to her, 'I nearly strangled her last night.' I pricked up my ears rather and then the mother said to the nursing auxiliary, 'I expect you are wondering how she got her black eye.' The nursing auxiliary didn't really take much notice and the mother says, 'It was my fault.' The nursing auxiliary continued to sort of coo and chuckle at the baby (. . .) The mother went on to talk about something else. Once we were in the car I asked HV if she had said anything about the black eye to the mother. She said not. She thought some explanation would be given and she didn't think that this was a bashed baby. The nursing auxiliary made no reference to the fact that the mother had tried to speak to her about it and we let the subject drop. HV, however, referred to this later and again the next day. (next day) HV once again brought up the child with the black eye. It seems to be preying on her mind that she didn't ask this mother about it and she tried to explain to me again why she didn't think that this mother would batter her child.

Should questions arise about their care of children, 'respectable' parents could resist agency intervention to a greater degree, if there were no other evidence to corroborate the implied deficiency in their character. Although they might be differentially vulnerable to an unfavourable assessment if further evidence did emerge, the chances of finding such data would be much reduced by the greater restrictions on surveillance. This could operate even with mentally incompetent parents. One Shire case, the Carrs, concerned a four-month-old baby of a retarded woman and her husband who had suffered brain damage in a road accident. The compensation Mr Carr had received for his injuries meant that, unlike most such families, they enjoyed a good material standard of living. Their apparent success enabled them to resist the high level of surveillance that the health visitor attempted to maintain as a result of neighbour reports of Mrs Carr's neglectful treatment of the baby. In the absence of first-hand data, more directive intervention seemed impossible, although this was regarded as a risky case for the agency.

Where parents can afford to purchase primary health or welfare services, they can achieve a greater degree of control by virtue of the financial relationship. This is, however, of infinitesimal significance in {101} England. Even upper-middle-class children seem to be largely dependent on the National Health Service. What this does do, though, is to shift power towards the doctor, as a duly licensed expert, in that parents' attempts to dispute his or her proposed findings may simply confirm their incorrigibility. It is here that the wealth or sophistication of parents becomes more important in buying or pressing for a second opinion from another licensed specialist.

We have already noted the effect of the agency justification of cultural relativism on ethnic biases in identification.[16] There may also be gender effects at work. Our data on these are, unfortunately, limited. However, two kinds of effect seem to be discernible. The first is that a violent man may sufficiently intimidate other members of his household to conceal child mistreatment. The second is that a violent man may sufficiently intimidate the (predominantly female), front-line staff in health visiting and social work to prevent them from discovering mistreatment. Perhaps the most notorious example of this was revealed by the inquiry into the death of Stephen Menheniott (1979), whose father appeared to have instilled fear into not only his immediate family but the greater part of the small, remote island community where he lived. We observed at least one similar example where a woman social worker was so alarmed by the violent record of a man whose son had been referred through a school-teacher as possibly mistreated that she failed to investigate the report except by telephone calls to the family's health visitor and general practitioner, despite a case conference decision that she should visit the household.

One further effect which may be worth mentioning is that recent research has indicated a possible long-term decline in compliance among the poorest section of the working class. Blaxter and Paterson (1982) followed up a sample of women in social classes IV and V who had had babies in Aberdeen in 1952 to compare their child-rearing experience with that of their daughters. They report a markedly less deferential approach to health care services among the younger group and a greater tendency to demand 'rights', both of which might tend to increase vulnerability to allegations of mistreatment.[17]

The rule of optimism, then, would seem to filter moral character in such a way as to hold back some, upper-, middle-, and 'respectable' working-class parents, members of ethnic minorities and mentally incompetent parents while leaving women and the 'rough' indigenous working class as the group proportionately most vulnerable to compulsory measures. This effect is achieved by tests which are not {102} class-biased in any simple and overt sense but which various social groups are differentially able to meet.

Once allegations are formulated, parents can, of course, adopt various defensive strategies against them. To some extent, these may even be anticipated by agency staff and incorporated into their general array of justifications and excuses. We shall, however, look at these in more detail when we come to analyse court hearings, since these are the settings where such accounts are most visibly displayed. For the present, however, we need to consider just what it is that differentiates this moral evaluation from an *ad hoc* assembly of frontline workers' prejudices. To do this, we must examine the organizational contexts within which their decisions are made.

5

The Division of Regulatory Labour

{103}
We concluded the previous chapter with a question: just what is it that legitimates the moral evaluations made by front-line workers? This chapter argues that the answer is to be found in an analysis of the moral accountability of those workers to the society at large through the organizations and occupations to which they belong. To some extent, then, our focus will shift from the *culture* of decision making to its *structure,* both within and between agencies. The occupations and agencies involved with child protection in England are marked by the operation of two classic organizational forms – professions and bureaucracies – and a third, modern, hybrid – bureau-professions. We shall demonstrate that each has its own implications for the accountability and power of front-line workers but, more importantly, we shall establish that the differences between them represent a further constraint on intervention through what we have called the division of regulatory labour.

THE PROFESSIONAL MODEL

At the heart of social order in modern societies lies the problem of trust.[1] With an advanced division of labour and of knowledge, people are unable adequately to evaluate the quality of many of the services which they must, of necessity, purchase. The monopolistic licences afforded to the professions reflect a bargain that members will regulate the quality of each other's services by use of their privileged access to the relevant specialized knowledge. Clients can rely on licensed practitioners in areas as vital to them as their life and health, the integrity of their persons and possessions and their prospects of eternal salvation. The establishment of a monopoly does not, however, guarantee a clientele. Like other service occupations, {104} then, professions have developed a marketing strategy based on the individualization of practice. Clients are promised personally-tailored treatment by discreet, sensitive and virtuous fellow-citizens. This promise has implications, both for the efficacy of outside regulation and for the nature of the professional/client relationship, which impinge directly on the identification of child mistreatment.

Strong and Horobin (1978) suggest that doctor/patient relationships may be best understood in terms of the classical market. This, as it was formulated in the nineteenth century, depicted the relationship as a private contract between individuals which was substantially impervious to state intervention (except in so far as the state guaranteed the conditions for the formation of contracts in general). Individual patients were, like economic man, assumed to be perfectly rational and knowledgeable and to act in such a way as to maximize their self-interest. They *chose* to use the service, deciding when they needed help, whom to consult and whether to follow the proferred advice – purchasing assistance in achieving their own objectives. One of the consequences, Strong and Horobin argue, was the development of an accommodative attitude to patients by doctors, so that the relationship is marked by moral neutrality and surface courtesy. Moral accountability was established by the workings of the market. While this was not necessarily true of charitable practice, it became established as the model to which all patients might properly aspire. The nationalization of health services translated this aspiration into an entitlement of citizenship, so that the 'bureaucratic frame' characterizes most doctor/patient encounters (cf. Stimson and Webb 1975, Byrne and Long 1976, Strong 1979a), except with otherwise disvalued patients like drunks in accident departments (Jeffery 1979) or drug addicts in dependency clinics (Stimson 1978).[2]

Mutatis mutandis, these arguments seem equally applicable to lawyers, although the empirical evidence is much thinner.[3] Duman's (1979, 1981, 1982) writings on the English legal profession in the eighteenth and nineteenth centuries bring out the influence of 'gentlemanly' values in a way which is consistent with Strong and Horobin's general thesis, although his immediate concerns are different. The only contemporary observational data are in Cain's (1979) study of solicitor/client interaction, where she notes the lawyers' role as what she calls conceptive ideologists, translating clients' problems into legal language to achieve client-defined outcomes. Again, this is in line with the idea of a rather accommodative relationship although her sample is very small.

We have already pointed to the importance of bureaucratic framing {105} from our observations of doctors and children in accident departments. We did not have directly comparable data on solicitors and their clients, although, in interviews, several of our private practice informants hinted at its relevance:

ANDREW: (. . .) having heard the evidence of Dr Matthews and knowing what instructions had been given by the Dickens's, I mean, I immediately felt that the Dickens's were not telling me the whole truth, *of course I shouldn't really say that but there it is* (. . .)

HARRIS: (. . .) You've got to understand the problem and give assistance. *It takes experience to disagree with someone without them storming off . . . that does need practice* (. . .) (our emphases)

This topic will be taken up again when we consider the task of representation. In both medicine and law, the same difficulties arise when the ostensible client (i.e. the actual or metaphorical purchaser of the professional's services) is not the immediate beneficiary. The interests of children can easily become obscured by the interests of adults in such a context to a degree which minimizes the possibilities of identifying mistreatment.

This is reinforced by the absence of any counter-pressures from the professionals' moral accountability. The promise of personalized discretion is enshrined in the preferred form of work organization, a collegial model based on loose federations of autonomous practitioners. Patients or clients are assured that they are receiving a uniquely-designed service from practitioners who are all equally competent, although each may have specialized skills and experience which render them complementary rather than interchangeable. In the process, colleague control is significantly attenuated, and it is only in the most exceptional circumstances that professionals will explicitly attempt to constrain their fellows' behaviour.[4] Even where professionals are employed in public agencies, their privileged access to esoteric knowledge gives them a counter-weight to this implied accountability. Doctors can indulge in so-called 'shroud-waving', appealing to clinical expertise to threaten lay members of health authorities with the life-or-death implications of policy decisions. Solicitors have a similar power as interpreters of the statutes under which local authorities operate. Failure to comply with these may render councillors liable to surcharge and personal bankruptcy. Even as state employees, then, professionals are not state agents and retain much of the autonomy characteristic of what is seen as {106} the 'natural' mode of fee-for-service independent practice. As a consequence, a great premium is placed on the professional's conscience as a determinant of the service provision, with all the consequent problems of equity and territorial justice which this implies.

THE BUREAUCRATIC MODEL

Sociologists have traditionally tended to see professions and bureaucracies as antithetical forms of work organization. As Benson (1973) and Davies (1983) have pointed out, however, the empirical support for this thesis is rather weak. Professions and bureaucracies, in their modern forms, appear to be historically contemporary developments. Both are marked by public claims to rely upon demonstrated achievement in assessing the worth of members, to treat all clients equally, to limit their activities to specific areas of licensed competence, to refrain from moralizing and to be oriented to general community interests. 'The dominant norms are concepts of straight-forward duty without regard to personal considerations. Everyone is subject to formal equality of treatment; that is everyone in the same empirical situation' (Weber 1947: 340). By implication at least the 'bureaucratic' framing of encounters with clients is as true of bureaucracies as of professions.

Weber (1947: 329-411) argued that bureaucracy was the organizational counterpart of the rational-legal mode of authority. This provides for the legitimacy of a social order to be founded on an impersonal and impersonally-applied set of normative rules. His account, however, is rather elliptical about the source of these rules. We would argue that it is only by attending to this that one can meaningfully discriminate professions from bureaucracies. Professions are, in effect, licensed to create their own normative order – in jurisprudence, clinical science or theology. Bureaucracies operate within rules created by others.

The question of moral accountability is central to an understanding of public bureaucracies, since they are the executive arm of whatever passes for the supreme legislative embodiment of the general will. Clients, then, are dealing with office-holders as representatives of an agency rather than with personalized service-providers. Moreover, those office-holders are themselves under pressure to ensure that their actions fall within the organization's charter. This implies the existence of systems of management, supervision and review, linking service delivery with political objectives. {107}

This is a point of great importance to the analysis of social work in England. Much of its occupational theory and rhetoric have, explicitly or implicitly, been borrowed from the USA, where there is a large area of private practice social work organized on a professional model. Nevertheless, most English social work is channelled through departments of local government which have been, from their inception, executive arms of the state. There may, of course, be many failings in this process. Local government is a relatively imperfect instrument by the theoretical ideals of representative democracies. Bureaucratic employees can, and do, develop interests, associations and aspirations of their own which cut across their public moral accountability. None of these, though, should blind us to the importance of bureaucratic forms in any society with collectively funded public services.[5] Social services departments form a part of the 'great chain of command' from voters to government to state action.

96

BUREAU-PROFESSIONAL ORGANIZATIONS

Professions and bureaucracies are, of course, ideal types, sociological abstractions from empirical observations. Like the absolute vacuum of physics we should not expect to encounter these pure forms on any particular occasion. Indeed, there are considerable variations within professions between those who are engaged in fee-for-service practice and those who are employees, whether of the state or of private enterprise. Similarly, there are significant differences between public and private sector bureaucracies. In order to understand health visiting, though, it is necessary to define a hybrid form. We have adopted Parry and Parry's (1979: 43) term, 'bureau-profession', for this purpose. They introduce it in a discussion of local authority social work.

> (The new social services departments represented) a blending of elements of professionalism and bureaucratic organization. Neither autonomous professionalism nor purely bureaucratic hierarchies emerged from the reorganization. Instead, the new departments were a conflation of both elements, manifesting something of the strains and complexities which such a mixture involves. This mode of organization which had already developed in other important departments of state provision – such as education and health – is a hybrid, which we shall refer to as bureau-professionalism (. . .) Bureau-professionalism has thus offered a chance to create a unified social work profession {108} but within a 'humanized' bureaucratic structure. By this method the social work elite hoped to establish a position of definite, if limited, professional control (. . .)

What we see here is the possibility of tension which justifies the distinction between occupational licences and organizational charters. It is the position that arises when an organized service occupation has achieved a degree of state licensing, short of monopoly, but giving some influence over entry, standards of practice and discipline. At the same time, the state or corporate private enterprises are monopsonistic or oligopsonistic customers for the occupation's services, establishing hierarchical bureaucracies whose charters are under lay control. The occupation's claims to autonomy may be at odds with the managerial direction which is an essential part of the chain of moral accountability which legitimates the organization's activities. In effect, then, bureau-professions attempt to reconcile internally the personalization of professional services with the public moral accountability of bureaucracies.

Nursing is a rather better example of this type than is social work, in England, at least. It has a stronger and more autonomous system of licensure. Certain segments, particularly midwifery and health visiting, have a long-recognized measure of independent clinical practice. The occupation has also come to derive many of its aspirations from its proximity to the professional example set by medicine. At the same time, the Nightingale model of hospital nursing was established on bureaucratic principles, borrowed from the army, whose character has been refined and developed by the 'new managerialism' of the Salmon and Mayston reorganizations in the 1960s (Carpenter 1977, 1978).[6]

ACCOUNTABILITY IN HEALTH VISITING AND SOCIAL WORK

Formally, both health visitors and social workers are employees of public bodies, health authorities and local authorities, respectively. Their work offers very similar supervisory problems, consisting as it does largely of talking to other people in semi-private settings. Quality cannot be controlled by the inspection of a tangible product, as in manufacturing, nor even by continuing observation of the interaction, as was possible in Nightingale-style hospital wards, for instance. There are, however, marked contrasts in the solutions which have emerged within each occupation to these common problems. {109}

Health visitors have a strong concern with establishing the professional character of their work (Dingwall 1977a, 1980). One of the consequences is a deep attachment to the principle of autonomy in front-line practice. Where community nurse managers had themselves been committed health visitors, they had been exposed to and acquired this model of organization. When it came to monitoring their subordinates' practice, then, they found themselves treading a narrow line.

NO: It's very difficult. I am responsible as the nursing officer and to the area health authority for their policy but it is a question of helping them to come to their own professional decision about at-risk families. It is their professional decision. Do we intervene enough on that? (. . .) Just how much flexibility can you have with something that's supposed to be a policy?

Although social work literature and, we suspect, training also make comparable claims, there was no evidence in our study that these had an equivalent impact on fieldwork in area teams.[7] Managers and supervisors, then, had a much more explicitly bureaucratic model of their relationship with basic-grade staff. This area director describes the feelings of his senior social workers about the introduction of a so-called 'career grade' for experienced fieldworkers:

AD: I know that some seniors are very worried about not knowing what would go on if there is less supervision once somebody is promoted onto the career grade. It's an issue that we are going to have to sort out (. . .) How far can people be allowed to be responsible for their own actions? As you probably realize some of these cases are political dynamite.

The contrast between 'allowing people to be responsible' and 'helping them to come to their own professional decision' is an illuminating one. The practical differences come through very clearly in supervisors' use of the five sources of information available to them on front-line work: direct observation, agency records, reports from clients, reports from other agencies and supervision interviews.

We have discussed these in more detail elsewhere (Dingwall 1982a), where we show that nursing officers have fewer chances to observe field-workers' practice and rely more on quantitative work returns; that health visitors keep personally rather than organizationally available records; that there are few occasions on which reports from clients or other agencies are available; and that {110} supervision-type interviews are seldom conducted and, where they do occur, are significantly constrained by the professionalist assumptions of both nursing officers and health visitors. By comparison with senior social workers, nursing officers seem unable or unwilling to exercise bureaucratic authority to override front-line workers' judgements, even where these are thought to be mistaken.

Although apparently bureaucratic in structure, then, the organization of community nursing services leaves health visitors on a very loose rein. Supervision depends on the degree to which individual nursing officers can establish a personal, charismatic authority on the basis of their own practical experience. Moreover, as we have shown elsewhere (Dingwall 1980), health visitors have a substantial countervailing power in their ability to play nursing officers off against general practitioners. Unlike senior social workers, nursing officers have few independent ways of identifying potential cases of mistreatment which they could use to monitor their subordinates' decision-making. Nursing officers are obliged to trust their health visitors' judgement. The problem for the latter, of course, is that, as we have shown, it is by no means easy to decide at what point an identification is sufficiently definite to justify referral. Furthermore, referral upwards is at odds with the tradition of fieldworker autonomy. It not only dilutes the health visitor's personal control of the case but, more importantly, may compromise her own status as a competent practitioner.

The principal determinants of service quality in health visiting are the individual conscience and skills of the front-line worker. This shares the strength of the professional model in its scope for devotion, imagination and innovation: it may also lead to a lack of equity and territorial justice. Since there is no effective check on health visitors' judgements, there is no opportunity to counter the type of reasoning described in the previous chapters, with its inherent tendency to minimize the number of identified cases.

The situation would seem to be rather different in social work. As the quotation from the area director on page 98 {p. 109} showed, managers who are in a line of accountability to popularly elected representatives are necessarily preoccupied with the adequacy of their information about subordinates' work. Most important actions in relation to children required the Area Director's consent. Even out of office hours, they would be consulted if there was a possibility of a child coming into care, either voluntarily or by means of a place of safety order.[8] These pressures for accountability were increasingly being translated into elaborate formal review systems, extending a model {111} originally devised for handling fostering and adoption work.[9] The political pressures can be further illustrated by contrasting the managerial treatment of other client groups. One does not, for instance, find such an elaborated system of case conferences and reviews in respect of the elderly. Their welfare is a matter for *ad hoc* lower-level negotiations and their care placements are more conspicuously a matter of where a vacancy happens to arise. The main exceptions are projects under joint funding, where there are specific accounting issues, and projects which are thought to be politically sensitive, like self-managed group homes for mentally handicapped adults. While it might be argued, then, that the Area Director's involvement reflected financial pressures and the need to regulate the use of departmental resources, we see it as more related to the political defensibility of agency practice and their assessment of the hazardousness of allowing responsibility to rest at a lower level. We shall return to this discussion when we look at inter-agency review systems in the next chapter.

For the present, we want to draw out the consequences for internal practice. First, there is the way in which a multi-client agency becomes skewed towards one particular group, children. This may, of course, be a politically desired objective, but it should be clearly recognized that other groups will be fitted around child-care work rather than receiving services in proportion to a separate judgement of their needs. Second, while the review system tends to downgrade supervisors' authority, and, to some degree, to erode their role, it brings managers very directly into the scrutiny of particular cases and of the adequacy of supervision.[10] This can create problems for basic-grade staff in establishing where the exact line of bureaucratic authority runs, but does involve managers in service quality to a degree unknown in health visiting.[11] All of this might be thought to press social work towards intervention and to favour the identification of mistreatment. There is, however, a further limitation which counteracts this, namely the nature of the agency/client relationship.

ORGANIZATIONAL CONCEPTIONS OF CLIENTS

We have already mentioned the differences between law, medicine, and health visiting, on the one hand, and social work, on the other, in their conceptualization of the worker/client relationship. Within the professional model this is depicted as a personal contract between individuals. The occupations, their working practices and {112} their information systems are organized to embody this principle. In the bureaucratic setting, clients are dealing with an office-holder. It is a relationship with an organization rather than an individual.

The intake process is a good point to bring this out. Doctors take on patient as a once-for-all event primarily as a matter of personal judgement. Health visitors are administratively notified of new births or transfers into their district, again as a once-for-all event. In both cases, there is an implicit assumption that the relationship will continue until the client decides otherwise or becomes ineligible, usually by virtue of death. Only exceptionally will such workers close off relationships on their own initiative. Contact with solicitors is more episodic but is still client-controlled. People may talk about 'their' solicitor even if the last contact was conveying a house ten years ago. In all three cases, client problems and objectives are substantially accepted. The professional's role is as the means to those ends, rather than involving explicit challenges to their propriety, a role which is evident in the 'bureaucratic' framing of encounters with clients.

In contrast, social workers acquire their clients through a process of organizational selection. As Smith (1980) notes, this is a complex process but one whose efficiency is crucial to the smooth running of the agency. It happens frequently, not least because of the episodic nature of agency/client relationships, and service provision cannot begin until the case has been bureaucratically evaluated. The disbursement of public resources requires procedures which produce a defensible documentation of the commitment or denial of services. This, as Smith also found, is achieved by a high degree of routinization, a refined division of labour and a dependence upon written material. Once sufficient data have been collected to assign a case to an organizationally-recognized category, inquiries cease. That initial coding substantially determines subsequent case management.

This process organizationally limits the possibilities of recognizing children as clients with specific needs. It is designed to handle adult applications for assistance and to investigate the legitimacy of their claims. Since, however, the legitimacy of the application is, *a priori*, problematic, anything an adult says in the course of an intake interview may be treated as persuasive or manipulative rather than as literal. Thus parents who profess abusive feelings or treatment of their children tend to be treated as insincere on the grounds that anyone who can make such admissions is either engaging in manipulative self-discrediting or is able to come to

101

terms with and control their behaviour. Smith points to the way in which psychodynamic theorizing may legitimate either interpretation by distinguishing {113} presenting and underlying needs and discounting the client's capacity for self-assessment. Open professions of mistreatment can be interpreted as mistaken or merely as presenting problems.

The impact of such categorization can be seen in our analysis of intake records over a six-month period for three of the four area team offices studied in Shire. Using the department's own category, 'Children and Families' we sought to establish the age of children in the household, whether they were the subject of the referral and who the referral agent was. We treated references to housing or financial difficulties as adult problems with implications for children unless otherwise indicated. There were 564 referrals logged, of which 30 were untraceable and 61 contained insufficient information to classify. Of the 473 remaining, 54 per cent (258) dealt mainly with adult problems. If we take the 201 households with children under five, 49 per cent (98) were self-referrals and 21 per cent (43), the next largest category, from health visitors. No other source contributed more than 6 per cent of referrals. Of these 201 referrals, however, only 29 per cent (58) were treated by the intake social worker as having the child as subject. Here, the proportions are almost exactly reversed, with only 17 per cent (10) self-referrals and 48 per cent (28) referrals from health visitors. The only other significant group of referrals were 10 per cent (6) from medical social workers. This indicates the sort of premium which may be placed on relations with other agencies to pre-define problems as child-care matters rather than expecting to discover them in the course of an intake interview. As such, it also supports the assertion which has commonly been made that health visitors tend to focus rather more on the condition of any particular child, while social workers are more oriented to analysing the child's conditions within the general social, cultural and economic circumstances of his or her family. This may lead health visitors to be perceived as adopting a less contextual definition of mistreatment which yields a larger number of possible cases. We shall return to this point later in the present chapter. For the present, however, we want to explore the process of pre-definition as it takes place in the course of inter-agency referrals.

Informal referrals

The informal referral network, what front-line workers call 'the grapevine', is a system of personal relationships which are only minimally influenced by agency structures. Typically, these referrals are communicated in a rather indirect fashion. Cases are mentioned in {114} conversations or meetings ostensibly taking place for other purposes, often in the form of anecdotes or *en passant* references as specific examples of general points.

Communication of this kind has been extensively documented in health care settings (e.g. Glaser and Strauss 1965, Mauksch 1966, Stein 1967, McIntosh 1977). It has conventionally been interpreted as a device by which a subordinate group seeks to influence the actions of a superordinate group without directly challenging the latter's status by overt requests to take action. As such, it is a style of interaction with which doctors and nurses are familiar. In the light of the present data, it may be a mistake to make too much of the status dimension. Indirect negotiation may be more closely related to dealings between professional or professionalist occupations with contiguous spheres of responsibility, where either may wish to draw a matter to the other's attention but without impinging on the other's personal discretion or implying criticism of their judgement. Whichever is the case, though, the fact remains that informal communications are a familiar feature of professional or bureau-professional work in health care.[12] In this instance, anxieties can be voiced or suspicions tested without having explicitly to formulate a case as one of mistreatment. Other parties are free to pick up the hints, to file them mentally for future reference or to ignore them, as matters falling within their own domain, without openly rejecting the expressed concern and impugning their colleagues' competence.

When applied to contacts between health and social services, especially in primary care, however, important difficulties can arise from the clash of professional and bureaucratic models. Doctors and health visitors assume that communication with an individual social worker will lead to action, neglecting the highly formalized intake system. Unless the social worker as an office-holder receives an officially-channelled communication, departmental action cannot be mobilized. If a case is not already 'open', it has no organizational existence. An open record may have informally-communicated information added, but new records cannot be created or old ones reopened without a formal request. In these latter cases, there is no way in which material can be stored to influence duty officers' responses to formal referrals, to client self-referrals or to other informal communications. Moreover, an informal report, even on an open case, cannot always generate a reason for a call. As we stressed earlier, social workers rarely call unannounced and, if they do, find themselves required to produce justifications for this. This is of particular importance in following up allegations of mistreatment where {115} a premature revelation of that reason for calling may destroy the opportunity for collecting relevant data, data which, as we have shown, will tend to be interpreted in a way which leads to a negative conclusion in most instances. If the referral agent does not provide a reason for a call, social services are likely to be impotent. The other party may, however, have chosen an informal approach, precisely because they do not want to be identified as the originator of a social work investigation. Documentation becomes critical in establishing the precarious legitimacy of such inquiries by exposing them to the possibility of a subsequent public accounting.

On the social services' part, social workers often fail to recognize the structural limitations on information-sharing in professionally-modelled organizations. General practitioners and health visitors do not pool information on a common record, for instance.[13] Indeed, much of their knowledge about patients or clients may not be written down at all, but held in their heads as a token of the personalized nature of that relationship. Only exceptionally will this individual contract be broken and information disseminated more widely. Thus, while the system is highly receptive to informal information, since cases are always 'open', information flows out of and even within the health service are limited. A social worker who talks only to a health visitor or only to a general practitioner may not realize that he or she has neither exhausted the information available in a primary care team nor alerted all its members to survey a particular family.

Informal referrals, then, are more important to an understanding of action in health than in social services. They provide for a tentative exploration of possible cases without committing a front-line worker to an identification in advance of the accumulation of relevant evidence. In general, however, they do not create a record and, as such, do not provide a basis for social work action. Their role in the analysis of mistreatment is in crystallizing a conviction that 'something ought to be done' which then provides for breaches of the professional/client relationship in formal referrals to social services.

Formal referrals

The formal referral is a contact, most typically a letter describing the circumstances of a case, which leaves a permanent organizational trace. It involves an attempt by the referral agent to extract some resource from the recipient or, failing that, to create documentary evidence of the *recipient's* responsibility for denying the resources. {116}

Once again, the professional/bureaucratic split introduces tensions. General practitioners and health visitors do not consider that a referral terminates their general duty towards its subject. The professional's duty to his or her client is personal and continuing. In medicine, this is reflected by the nature of referrals as matters between named individuals rather than office-holders and by the expectation of formal acknowledgement and feedback. A consultant is just that: someone brought in to advise on special problems within the overall relationship of general practitioner to patient. When dealing with social services, therefore, general practitioners are often frustrated by their inability to locate and relate to one particular person to whom they can delegate their continuing obligations. As Hallett and Stevenson (1980: 49) observe:

> ... each time contact is made with a particular team, the referral is likely to be dealt with by one of a number of changing duty officers, leading to the complaint, often made by doctors, that 'you never get the same person twice'.

The involvement of social workers is more episodic. As substitutable office-holders, their responsibility is bureaucratically limited.

When social services receive a referral, then, their initial response is to assume that the other party wants to close the case. This means, for instance, that feedback, a point of some contention with health service workers (Bruce 1980: 83-4), is seen as an unnecessary generation of paperwork. For general practitioners and health visitors, however, referral is something of a last resort, a breach of their traditional relationships with clients in acknowledging that other help is necessary, but a resort which does not abolish their continuing professional responsibility. For the recipient duty social worker, though, referral, as we have seen, is merely a first step in a process which establishes the organizational acceptability of the case by formally legitimating agency involvement and adjudicating on the priority of the case against other claims on time or resources. The referral agent sees only the individual case: the intake workers must balance that need against actual or potential competitors for scarce resources, a problem that seldom faces general practitioners, in particular, whose budgets are not cash-limited. Two specific consequences are worth pointing out. First, the majority of referrals are unlikely to seem particularly important to social workers, although, as a matter of last resort, they may seem very urgent to referral agents. This can be simply illustrated by a graph, figure 2, taking health visitors' and {117} social workers' experience of family standards as an example. If we assume a statistically normal distribution and take X as the mode for health visitors and the point at two standard deviations, 2σ, as the cut-off for concern, we can see that this will give social workers a modal referral at $X_1 = -2\sigma$ and a cut-off at -2_s, which lies to the left of the health visitors'. The difference between the two points represents 'inappropriate referrals' from the social workers' point of view. The logic of this is that health visitors will always be concerned about more families than social workers will accept as appropriate for intervention. This discrepancy is particularly important given the health visitors' greater access to clinical data on a child, both by virtue of their training and their location within the flow of medical information.[14] They may be playing clinical and social evidence off against each other in a way which social workers find difficult to appreciate, with their different mix of skills and experience. The net effect is a pressure against identification of abuse or neglect until either social or clinical evidence becomes so gross that it crosses a threshold higher than health visitors alone would set. Second, the allocation process inevitably slows down social services' responses to referrals, contributing to the complaints frequently expressed in the literature on health service/social service interaction (e.g. Goldberg and Neill 1972, Theophilus 1973, Mead 1974, Bruce 1980, Huntington 1981). Referral agents may be frustrated by the contrasting definitions of a case's priority, so that it is held for an allocation meeting several days later rather than responded to instantly. This is particularly true in many cases of neglect or minor injury where there is no clinical emergency but where the professional who has geared him or herself up to breach the conventional framing of relations with clients finds an apparently lackadaisical response.

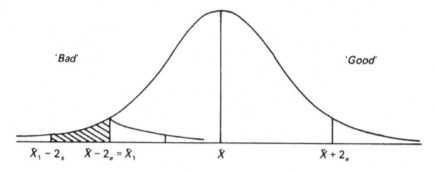

Figure 2 Health visitors' and social workers' experience of family standards

The physical availability of resources is only a global constraint. Social services departments are locked into a complex network of {118} exchange relationships with other agencies. As Handler (1973: 85) commented on their predecessors:

> This constraint not only limited what the Children's Departments could do for their clients but also served to modify the programs of the Children's Departments to the extent that they wanted to develop and maintain continuing relationships with these other agencies. The power and influence of the department was increased only to the extent that the Children's Department could be of help to these other agencies.

In particular cases, then, the differential response to referrals is better explained by the willingness of social services to accept responsibility for rejecting them. Denying a medical referral is, in general, seen as potentially more hazardous than denying a health visitor's referral. Several factors come into this. First, rightly or wrongly, social workers in all the areas we studied thought doctors had escaped their share of culpability in a number of public inquiries into child deaths (cf. Hallett and Stevenson 1980: 56).

Medical referrals, then, excited a response in order to document that they had been taken seriously, in the event of future trouble. A number of issues about the relative power and status of the two occupations are, obviously, implicated here. Second, and partly consequent on these status issues, social workers were keen to encourage medical referrals as a legitimation of their own distinctive skills. Third, medical referrals were comparatively rare. Our analysis of Shire referral logs showed that they contributed 6 per cent (30) of all 'Children and Families' cases (473) compared with 17 per cent (80) from health visitors. Where a child under five was the subject (58 cases), doctors contributed less than 2 per cent (one) of referrals compared with 48 per cent (28) from health visitors.[15] This tended to mean that the cases were regarded as being more serious and, indeed, social workers frequently lamented the apparent delay, as they saw it, in bringing them in.[16]

Health visitors' referrals pose much less of a threat, confer less status on the recipient and are more frequent. In respect of children and families, they seem to relate mainly to three types of service: material assistance, at-risk registration or 'intensive casework'. The reduction in social service budgets means that the first of these is unlikely to be available, although even in more affluent times, as Satyamurti (1981: 167-79) shows, social workers were reluctant, either as a matter of politics or of philosophy, to become involved in such work. At-risk registration puts a case into an organizational {119} category second only to 'statutory cases', i.e. those imposed on the department by court orders which can be closed only by the rescission or lapse of the order. They have an inescapable claim on departmental attention. Quite apart from the libertarian issues, access to this category is jealously guarded precisely because of this priority, which would become meaningless if too many cases shared it.[17] This leaves 'intensive casework', which is cited by both occupations as the distinctive skill of social workers. If one looks at the nature of the activity, however, it is difficult to identify any consistent qualitative differences in field-worker/client interaction between health visitors and social workers.[18]

This receives some tacit recognition in agency practice. When social services receive a third-party allegation of child mistreatment, their first move, especially if the family is unknown, is often to contact the relevant health visitor and ask her to make preliminary inquiries. The practice reflects the fact remarked upon earlier, that investigations can be more easily concealed within health visiting routine. Once mistreatment has been identified, it is not uncommon for health visitors and social workers to alternate visits and report to each other. While the latter might resemble the use of auxiliaries by either party, the assessment task would usually be reserved for qualified and experienced social workers. Health visitor evaluations may be treated cautiously but the two occupations do seem to be, at least to some degree, substitutable.[19] The only advantage might be if social workers made longer or more frequent contacts, but it is by no means obvious that this is the case, although our study was not designed to test this systematically.[20]

Both Hallett and Stevenson (1980: 31) and Bruce (1980: 90-1) also report health visitors' perceptions of the reluctance of social workers to accept their referrals. This does seem to be both genuine and explicable in terms of the limitations on material resources and the absence of distinctive forms of interpersonal support. Moreover, if a referral is denied, the health visitors' professional sense of responsibility will leave them involved with the prospective client. Should the situation deteriorate, the intake staff can reasonably expect the referral to come back. The health visitors' attempts to circumvent this by creating informal channels to 'fix' the intake review founder on the bureaucratic obstacles already discussed.[21]

While formal referrals are the levers of social work action, there are still formidable hurdles both within the intake process and within the professional culture. A general practitioner or a health visitor must break through the constraints of their traditional conceptions {120} of their duty to patients or clients, go on record as having done so and, ideally, set up a reason for a social work visit. Even if this is accomplished, swift action is by no means inevitable. Once accepted, however, the case has moved a long way towards a confirmation of its essential character. The organizing principles of social services departments are such as to constitute a substantial barrier at intake but then to increase the likelihood of defining a child's condition as indicative of mistreatment. Cases are likely to be finely sifted but the survivors are vigorously pursued.

THE IMPACT OF PUBLIC ACCOUNTABILITY

We have stressed the importance of moral accountability as a determinant of organizational form. Professions, bureaucracies and bureau-professions all represent different solutions to the problem of regulation in a liberal society. As we noted, the accountability of professions is primarily to the market, to individual clients. This duty is overridden only in exceptional circumstances which relate to general interests in the preservation of the possible conditions for the market. Doctors are statutorily required to report births, deaths and certain infectious diseases to a designated medical officer of the local health authority. Lawyers have an obligation as 'officers of the court' to ensure that clients do not adopt unscrupulous means of achieving legal objectives. There is obvious scope for difficulties to arise where the purchaser and the beneficiary of the services are not the same person, as in the case of children. Who is then the client? Moreover, in child protection, as in the protection of the socially incompetent in general, professionals may find themselves pressed into a much wider role of state service. Rather than minimally limiting the possibilities for disease, crime and deceit, they may be asked to promote public ends at odds with the goals of patients or clients. Finally, of course, professions are essentially responsive services. Depending as they do on client-initiated contact, their ability to contribute to surveillance is limited.[22]

While professional intervention may be preferred as an individually initiated regulatory act, it is inadequate for the fine tuning of the fragile liberal order. This is the specific contribution of bureaucracies and bureau-professions. By establishing governing charters under the control of the public or their elected representatives, state intrusion into citizen's homes may be legitimated. The chain of moral accountability is the essential corollary of the preservation of {121} liberal ideals. Inasmuch as it is broken or eroded, surveillance becomes oppressive rather than facilitative, coercive rather than regulatory. Thus front-line workers in child protection are answerable to supervisors and managers for their proposed identifications of child mistreatment, and action can be initiated only with appropriate confirmation and authorization. While the professional has only to square his or her conscience, the bureaucrat or bureau-professional must attend to a line of external constraint.

The practical effect, however, may not be all that different. As we have shown, the organization of individual agencies facilitates the operation of the rule of optimism by creating conditions where it is difficult to substitute alternative versions for that offered by the front-line worker. This is achieved either by the weakness of supervision in the bureau-professional case or by the bureaucratization of intake. There is, though, a further dimension of some importance.

Many analysts (e.g. Emerson 1969, Morris and Giller 1979, Donzelot 1980) of diverse persuasions have emphasized the homogeneity of the agencies which are involved in the regulation of juveniles and their families. While there may be some validity in this with respect to juvenile offenders, the main source of empirical documentation for the thesis, it seems highly misleading to apply it to child protection as Morris et al. (1980) have done. What is far more striking in England, at least, is the differentiation. As Handler (1973: 157) observed:

> . . . the really effective limits on the powers of the Children's Departments were imposed by the other agencies that the departments had to deal with in order to carry out their program. These agencies had their own views as to how to treat clients and would cooperate with the Children's Departments only to the extent that common action fit their needs as well.

Giovannoni and Becerra (1979: 229-30) make a similar point from their Los Angeles data.

> There is some evidence that the use of multiple definers – the community, the social workers and the courts – results in an interdependence in the kinds of criteria utilized by each set of definers . . . In a sense this kind of definitional process reflects an adjustment to the sometimes conflicting interests that inhere in problems of mistreatments – the interests of the parents, the children and the community.

Each agency concerned with child mistreatment is licensed to operate over only a small part of the total body of relevant evidence. {122} For doctors, lawyers and, to a degree, health visitors, this is an individual matter, whereas for social workers it is an agency matter. Only when all of these groups are convinced of the propriety of interpreting their information in a light unfavourable to parents do we find compulsory action. This division of regulatory labour between autonomous agencies institutionalizes further restrictions on the identification of mistreatment and, hence, on compulsory action. What are the effects on the arenas where co-ordinated action seems indicated?

6

Sovereignty and Association: Coordinating Intervention

{123}

Each of the agencies analysed in the previous chapter is licensed to interpret particular parts of the evidence available about a child who is a possible victim of mistreatment. In practice, their joint consent is a necessary prerequisite of any coercive action. Yet, as we have seen, they are based on radically different principles of organization. How are these to be reconciled? This question can be addressed at two levels. In the present chapter, we shall study the construction of a framework for inter-agency relations by high-level discussions in Area Review Committees. The next chapter moves to the more localized arena of case conferences.

AREA REVIEW COMMITTEES

Area Review Committees (ARCs) are rather strange bodies: they have no statutory existence and no resources of their own. Yet their position in the interstices between health and welfare services and the weight given to them, in terms of the bureaucratic standing of their members, is matched only by the joint funding arrangements created to manage the complex and politically sensitive transfer of resources from health to personal social services.

The term 'Area Review Committee' first came into national currency following the 1974 DHSS Memorandum, LASSL (74)13/CMO(74)8, on Non-Accidental Injury to Children. Inter alia, this 'strongly recommended . . . urgent joint action' by local authorities and health authorities to establish such committees as policy-making bodies for the management of non-accidental injury cases. These committees should meet at least three or four times each year and their duties would be to: (a) advise on the formulation of local practice and procedures to be followed in the detailed management {124} of cases; (b) approve written instructions defining the duties of all personnel concerned with any aspect of these cases; (c) review

111

the work of case conferences in the area; (d) provide education and training programmes to heighten awareness of the problems; (e) collect information about the work being done in the area; (f) collaborate with adjacent Area Review Committees; (g) advise on the need for inquiries into cases which appear to have gone wrong and from which lessons could be learnt; (h) provide a forum for consultation between all involved in the management of the problem; (i) draw up procedures for ensuring continuity of care when the family moves to another area; (j) consider ways of making it known to the general public that e.g. health visitors, teachers, social workers, the NSPCC and police may be informed about children thought to be ill-treated; (k) prepare a report for 1974. All relevant agencies should be represented at a senior level, usually the chief of the service or his or her immediate deputy.[1]

This guidance was reinforced at a one-day conference in 1974 held a few months after the publication of the Memorandum and attended by both the then Secretary of State for Social Services, Mrs Barbara Castle, and her Parliamentary Under-Secretary (Health), Dr David Owen. The proceedings were subsequently published (DHSS 1975). Another circular, LASSL (76)2/CMO(76)3, was issued early in 1976, summarizing the replies to the request for information on local practice in the 1974 circular. One hundred and two Area Review Committees had been set up, covering the whole of England. By and large, membership closely reflected the earlier suggestions. The DHSS reiterated its advice on a quarterly meeting schedule, on the need to integrate and centralize register systems and to develop procedural guidance. Model register forms and procedure documents were appended. Most recently, in 1980, a further circular, LASSL (80)4/HN(80)20, has been issued. This is intended to achieve a greater degree of uniformity in the criteria for registration and in the administration of local child abuse registers.

An extremely interesting feature of these documents, however, is the persistent mention of specific difficulties in the operation of ARCs. J. W. Freeman, then Director of Social Services for Leeds, was commissioned to present a paper on Area Review Committees to the 1974 conference. While he stressed their role in policy-making and the development of joint responsibility between health and social services, he identified five problems: an overriding responsibility for seeing that action is taken to protect children.

1. the failure to nominate a co-ordinator or designated officer with {125} an overriding responsibility for seeing that action is taken to protect children.

> We all know the difficulties in the situation; the doctor's reluctance to give evidence because it would disturb the patient/doctor relationship;

the difficulties of social workers when they know that often the statements will not stand up in court, because they are based on suspicions. Somehow we have got to overcome these difficulties through deepening our knowledge and understanding of the problem. I am sure if somebody is designated to do this work, the expertise will be acquired which will be extremely important in helping us to treat the problem more effectively. (DHSS 1975: 30)

2. The need for an effective and uniform reporting system for suspected cases. The obstacle here was seen to be differences over definitions of abuse and over the boundaries of professional confidence.

3. The development of standardized, accessible registers of suspect cases.

4. The need for additional specialized resources in diagnosis and intervention, possibly provided by local agreements between social services departments and the NSPCC.

5. The need to balance representation on ARCs so that they did not become 'top heavy with medicals'.

Similar themes recur in the 1976 circular. The DHSS were concerned about the health service dominance which might result if, as occurred in some areas, social service representation was restricted to the department's director. The question of resources was not taken up but the issues of confidentiality and shared authority implied by Mr Freeman's other points were dealt with, or, to be more exact, the problems were stated and the resolution left open. The following are the key paragraphs:

25. The safety of the child must in all circumstances be of paramount importance and must override all other considerations. It is nonetheless undeniable that there will be occasions when the need to protect a child will conflict with the wish to preserve a relationship of trust with another party, and that the problems posed by confidentiality admit of no easy solution, although it is important to work towards solving them. Any decision about the release of information is normally one for professional judgement but the factors which ought to be taken into account in reaching such a decision are the 'need to know' and the consequent restriction of information to those directly concerned with the family and who have the duty legitimately to perform a {126} service on its behalf; and the importance of taking action in a child's best interests in the light of all relevant facts. It would be helpful if the passing of information between the caring professions were regarded and treated as analogous to that passed in confidence within a single discipline. Whenever possible however an adult's agreement should be sought to the sharing of information about him with professionals from a different discipline.

30. It is acknowledged that the decision of a case conference cannot be binding on the respresentatives of bodies with statutory powers and duties in relation to children and that, where a consensus view cannot be reached, any participant may, after consultation with senior officers, find himself constrained to take action contrary to that recommended by other members of a case conference. Where this occurs, we urge that the other members be notified of a proposed action and the reasons for disagreement, before such action is taken, unless an emergency demands otherwise.

The bold statement of principle at the beginning of paragraph 25 is immediately qualified and hedged so that the only specific recommendation is that the adult consent should be sought to the sharing of information. Once again we find the constraining influence of parental liberties. Similarly, para. 30 leaves open the possibility of unilateral action and fails to address Mr Freeman's call for coordinated authority. Beyond these references, ARCs had drawn attention to related difficulties over the involvement of both police and general practitioners in child protection work.

The 1980 circular is similarly devoid of positive guidance, although both issues surface again. Confidentiality is dismissed as a matter for 'local guidelines . . . agreed by the ARC'. Although the circular makes an optional recommendation that a 'senior officer with considerable experience in the field of child abuse' should be appointed custodian of the child abuse register, it stresses equally that this 'in no way reduces the responsibilities of individual agencies and professional officers'. The point is underlined by a footnote to para. 4.3:

> Registration is essentially an agreement between agencies to coordinate their efforts in respect of a particular family, and it is, therefore, considered appropriate that the decision to register should be a joint one. Decisions relating to the exercise of statutory duties remain, of course, the responsibility of the agency concerned.

While it is clear that, in some respects, DHSS guidance has become more positive since 1974, it is by no means apparent that {127} this has touched some of the more difficult and contentious areas. Moreover, many of these problems go back for at least thirty years. Area Review Committees are essentially the heirs to the Coordinating Committees set up in the early 1950s under a joint circular, Home Office 157/50/Ministry of Health 78/50/Ministry of Education 225/50, to secure the cooperation of all local statutory and voluntary agencies concerned with the welfare of children and . . . to discuss 'significant cases of child neglect and all cases of ill-treatment' (Packman 1975: 53). As Packman's account shows, these committees proved a microcosm of the various national struggles for control of child welfare policy between social work, health visiting, medical and legal interests. These battles were fought through a series of government committees and debates on the 1963 and 1969 Children and Young Persons Acts (Dingwall et al. 1982). The same disagreements over agency sovereignty persist within the cadre of advisers employed by the DHSS from the various professions.

While great weight has been placed on local organizational initiatives, then, it seems much more plausible to argue that this represents a failure by central government to resolve the problems which Area Review Committees grapple with. It would, however, be too simplistic to argue that this is simply a result of personal rivalries or occupational imperialism. There are quite fundamental disagreements over the purposes of inter-agency co-ordination which reflect the divisions analysed in the previous chapter and which derive from the different experiences of the staff involved. We can explore these by considering the *ad hoc* solutions devised by each of the three localities in our study.

THE SHIRE EXPERIENCE

The three areas in our study had developed quite different patterns of inter-agency organization. We propose to begin with an analysis of the ARC in Shire, which exemplifies the fundamental obstacles to close liaison between such different bodies. The circumstances which have permitted County and Borough to overcome these, and which may make them less typical of majority experience, will be discussed later in this chapter.

Shire ARC'S core membership can be seen from table 1, together with their attendance record at ten meetings which we observed. The exact boundaries of the membership were difficult to ascertain as a {128} number of agencies might duplicate representation for a period or particular individuals attend on a more or less regular basis for specific agenda items. Nevertheless, table 2 shows that about half of those eligible to attend, or be represented, did so on any given occasion. Our analysis will, necessarily, be somewhat selective, given the availability of space, but we have chosen to concentrate on {129} two topics which were of considerable importance to the ARC over this period. Both of these relate to its duties as set out in the 1974 DHSS circular. The first was to do with 'inquiries into cases which appear to have gone wrong' (para. 12 g) and the second was the ARC's attempt to revise its procedures book and register criteria (para. 12 a–e).

TABLE 1 ATTENDANCE AT TEN MEETINGS OF THE
SHIRE AREA REVIEW COMMITTEE 1977-80*

Members eligible to attend	Number of meetings attended
Divisional Nursing Officer (Community)	10
Deputy Director, Social Services Department⎫ Magistrate Police Administrative Services (Solicitor)⎭	9
Senior MSW (Paediatric) Senior MSW (Maternity) Assistant Director, Social Services Department⎭	8
Nursing Officer (Accident and Emergency) General Practitioner Assistant Chief Probation Officer Consultant Psychiatrist Special Adviser or EWO, Education Department⎭	7
NSPCC	6
Area Director, Social Services Department Specialist in Community Medicine (Child Health)⎭	5
Field Social Worker⎫ Justices Clerk ⎭	4
Consultant (Paediatrics)	3
Senior Nursing Officer (Maternity)	2
Specialist in Community Medicine (Local Authority Liaison) Consultant (Accident and Emergency) Consultant (Obstetrics and Gynaecology)⎭	1

* Each member has been counted for a personal attendance or the attendance of
a nominated deputy.

TABLE 2   TOTAL NUMBERS ATTENDING SHIRE AREA
REVIEW COMMITTEE 1977-80*

Meeting date	Attendance
Autumn 1977	16
Winter 1977	19
Spring 1978	11
Summer 1978	15
Autumn 1978	14
Winter 1979	14
Spring 1979	13
Spring 1980	12
Autumn 1980	11
Spring 1981	13
MEAN	14

* The potential attendance fluctuated between 21 and 26 members over
this period, so that the mean attendance is just over 50 per cent.

Inquiries

The DHSS has not issued any formal guidance to ARCs beyond the role
envisaged for them in advising on the need for inquiries set out in the 1974
circular. In a letter to ARC chairmen of October 1977, however, the Department expressed interest in the investigative systems which some ARCs
had developed and indicated that a standard procedural framework was
under consideration. A draft outline accompanying the letter proposed the
formation of a standing multi-disciplinary ARC subcommittee which
would receive reports from individual agencies, consider their collective
implications and recommend further action. Copies of the subcommittee's
reports to the ARC would be forwarded to the Department. While departmental thinking now seems to have changed on this point, as a result of
the disagreements mentioned earlier, this letter has not been withdrawn.
{130} In practice, local investigations have taken the place of the full-dress
DHSS inquiry on the Maria Colwell (1974) or Susan Auckland (1975)
model. The Wayne Brewer report (1977) was commissioned by the local
ARC and those on the deaths of Karen Spencer (1978), Simon Peacock
(1978), Lester Chapman (1979), Carly Taylor (1980), Maria Mehmedagi

(1981), Malcolm Page (1981), Christopher Pinder/Daniel Frankland (1981) and Richard Fraser (1982) were all set up by joint agreement between local authorities and Area Health Authorities.[2] Although it is not clear whether the relevant ARCs were formally involved in all of these, the principle is similar. The major exception, the Paul Steven Brown inquiry (1980), was set up only after two controversial local inquiries and some twelve months of local authority and parliamentary pressure on the DHSS. The inquiry members themselves felt that such investigations 'should not come to be regarded as the normal method of investigating the circumstances which have led to serious injury to a child' (para. 247) and recommended that, in future, they should be conducted by a neutral person or team under the auspices of the local ARC (para. 249a). The ARC, in other words, should superintend inquiries rather than merely advise on the possible necessity for them.

The question came up in Shire at the first ARC meeting we attended in autumn 1977, in response to the DHSS letter.

> The chairman notes that they already have an investigating committee of a community physician, an area nurse and the deputy director of social services. There are problems of professional ethics here and of the compellability of witnesses. He thinks that the DHSS concern arises from questions about the authority of the Somerset ARC to conduct the sort of inquiry that was seen in the Wayne Brewer case. In his view the question is whether or not this committee has the right and duty to inquire into individual cases and to require professionals to make reports and give evidence on their actions (. . .) DivNo says that in the past health visitors have tried to co-operate with such inquiries but the professional organizations would regard it as a delicate matter between any informal inquiry which the ARC might carry out and a formal AHA inquiry. AD feels that the problem would be the same for social workers (. . .)[3]

The discussion was dominated by statements of the difficulties of pooling authority and the whole matter was remitted to a working party.

This met a month later and, after more than three hours' discussion, failed to reach agreement. As their report makes clear, {131} sticking points related to the powers of any ARC inquiry to investigate individual or agency actions.

> An investigating group would clearly not have the 'legal' authority to demand an individual to attend a meeting to give 'evidence' of their involvement with a case. If a person was requested to attend they should be given the opportunity to be accompanied and/or represented by a legal, Union, or personal adviser. This would immediately add to the formality of the hearing and the question then would be whether rules of evidence applied and if not what credibility or accountability could be deduced from the evidence. Also what role would the employers or

professional bodies of the individual have in such a case. They could insist that the individual did not make available information, which is technically the property of the employer. If an individual did divulge information without the knowledge of an employer, could this constitute misconduct and be in breach of contract?

It was accepted that voluntary co-operation was the only possible method of obtaining necessary information but various members of the Group candidly remarked that if asked to attend an investigation outside their own agency, they might well refuse.

The discussions at the ARC returned to these questions.

SCM: As far as I've been involved my first step has been to discuss the case with the doctors concerned and I've always made it clear that that discussion is as a member of the ARC. The first stage is to discuss the facts about medical involvement and this may of course be cut short if the doctor does not want the information to go any further. If we had proceeded with this discussion it has been possible to decide then whether or not it's relevant to include the medical evidence in reporting back to the Committee. If that does happen it seems essential to me that the doctor should be a party to the discussion. My involvement has been particularly relevant where different medical departments are involved. It would be quite invidious for one consultant to investigate another, and it is useful to have people like myself who can straddle departments. I understand the anxieties about the procedure on the Committee, but it has worked well so far. I think the difficulty that we're faced with is in knowing what to do with the report once it's prepared.

CPO: I think it's, I find difficulties in accepting this report as it stands. We can't guarantee confidentiality to anyone we talk to. (. . .) There is this sort of implied threat behind it all the time. This Committee does need to know what it's about and not give people {132} false assurances about any information they give them. The Committee is there to investigate and that's the fact of it.

AD: There is this problem that the ARC could pretend that it was a benign and educational body, but it's also composed of people who are employing managers if field staff were likely to be interviewed. We cannot hear confidences and confessions and then ignore the possibility of disciplinary proceedings.

PC: It all strikes me as far too difficult. I don't see for a moment how it can be done. If this is the view of the ARC then I think we should tell the DHSS quite firmly.

LAS: I would say that I would certainly not co-operate because information cannot be given in confidence. There is this danger of an investigating committee becoming a sort of Star Chamber.

DD: Nevertheless, I think this has been useful in sharpening the issue. I think we have to decide whether or not we want to send this report to the

DHSS, or whether we amend it to clarify these points. It's clear that we cannot expect co-operation from anybody.

SCM: It seems to me that it's always open to individual agencies to have discussions and to cooperate on a voluntary basis, and certainly there should be a way of bringing forward the principles involved in the matter without naming a particular case. The crucial thing for this Committee after all is the principles at stake.

DD: As long as the case in question is unidentified. This is a difficulty which arises in item 7 on the agenda. Having carried out an investigation, is it right to circulate our report? Because members of this Committee might draw inferences about responsibility as a result of it. We have promised confidentiality to the people who took part in it, but on the other hand if the Area Review Committee doesn't have the report what's the use of investigating it anyway? Is this really a proper function for an Area Review Committee? . . .)

CHAIRMAN: It all seems to me that the only thing we can agree on is the lack of unanimity. I think we should report that to the DHSS.

ASD: Could we add some paragraphs to this report on our discussion today?

CHAIRMAN: In general, I think the feeling of this Committee is against this sort of inquiry. {133}

PAE: I think we should stress the need for authoritative DHSS guidance on this matter. We've got reasonable liaison here between the agencies involved, it seems to me that that's much more important.

The outcome of such considerations could be seen in the discussion of item 7 on the agenda, mentioned by the Deputy Director of Social Services. This was a report from the three-member investigating committee referred to at the first meeting on their inquiry into the death of a child from hypothermia. The ARC discussion is reproduced in its entirety.

CHAIRMAN: I am in some difficulty now as a result of our discussions on item 5 (see above, CSLS), given the problems of confidentiality which would seem to arise in circulating our report on the death of Michael W. I think we have to have some sort of qualified privilege here.

SCM: For myself I should prefer that the report were not circulated. It seems to me that one important principle has been raised by this case but I think we should say no more about it at present, although perhaps we might bring the principle to the Committee in the absence of any reference to the case at some date in the future. For the present I would prefer not to say anything.

PAE: I think we should state this, that you've taken the appropriate steps and trust you to deal with it between yourselves.

PSY: I would support that.

CHAIRMAN: Well we have taken action and the agencies involved are aware of the lessons to be learnt, and I hope what is relevant has flowed out from this Committee.

PAE: That seems to me to be the right way of going about this.

CPO: I don't think that we should be misled here into regarding this as a question of trust. This Committee delegated a task to a subcommittee and it seems absurd to me that the subcommittee can't report back on its findings.

PAE: I'm still inclined to suggest that we don't discuss this report.

LAS: I agree. We have discussed it quite enough.

CPO: Is this Committee being asked to accept the report then? {134}

PAE: I think we should note it.

AD: Well we can only note that such action has been taken as you (inquiry team, CSLS) saw fit.

After this episode, the whole issue of investigations disappeared from view for the remainder of our fieldwork.

Procedures

The attempt by the ARC to reform its inter-agency procedure handbook had a similar history. When we first began fieldwork the booklet in use was, in essence, a compendium of the procedural guides existing in the individual participating agencies prior to the ARC's establishment. These had been put together, with only slight modifications, by an ARC working party on its initial establishment in 1974/5. Central government had been pressing for rapid action and this was seen as an appropriate interim response. Indeed, Shire was one of the first areas to publish an inter-agency guide. The disadvantage, of course, was that there were few models from elsewhere to use for comparison and that there was less chance for coordination through debate over basic principles than in ARCs which had regarded a joint procedures guide as a less urgent matter. Consequently, Shire ARC had recognized the limitations of its handbook from an early date and envisaged that it would need revision, improvement and consolidation in the light of experience and reflection. This process, however, revealed the difficulty of such a consolidation between the various sovereign agencies.

The first mention of the guide in our field notes comes from the winter 1978 ARC meeting, when a subcommittee presented a paper based on discussions begun early in 1975. This attempted to list social and physical factors which might be indicative of child abuse. After some discussion, it was agreed to postpone a reprint of the procedures book in order that these guidelines could be piloted, revised and incorporated. Later in the same meeting, the ARC decided that a working party should be set up to review case conference procedure and the child abuse register.

The (volunteer) membership of the working party included the Deputy Director, a Principal Adviser and an Area Director from social services, the Divisional Nursing Officer (Community) and the Specialist in Community Medicine (Child Health) from the health services and a police superintendent. Five meetings were held, each {135} lasting two to three hours, over a period of nearly six months, with a full attendance on all but one occasion, when the police representative was absent. The Area Director was elected to the chair. He began by addressing questions related to case conferences.

AD: Well, there seem to be two problems here. There is the question of the frequency of case conferences – should they be matters of routine? – and the question of the function or functions of conferences, and perhaps there is a third problem I can add, that related to the role and skill and executive responsibility of the chairman.

The first two of these points generated a discussion on definitional questions. How did one distinguish a case conference from other sorts of inter-agency encounter? This touched on some sensitive issues, as in this exchange between the Specialist in Community Medicine and the Area Director:

SCM: I think one difference is the formality of the meeting (. . .) They are a meeting of professional workers who are concerned with a problem and as such they should have fairly formal arrangements. (. . .) In medical minds at least there is this difference. Although it sometimes may be counter-productive in that doctors do not always draw the distinction where they ought to. Sometimes it is to their advantage when they are calling a discussion and sometimes it's to their disadvantage when they go to a meeting and are searching for a formality that isn't there. (. . .)

AD: I think that social services officers often feel that because there is no formality on these occasions and no recognised constitution that social workers feel overwhelmed by doctors' assumptions of status in an informal structure and that they don't get a clear mandate from the meeting.

There is an immediate clash between the professional and bureaucratic principles here: the doctors assuming a charismatic authority which spills over to social services' territory and the social workers attempting to establish a set of explicit rules for the conduct of conferences which may be bureaucratically invoked to restrict this. This debate underlay the whole meeting. Could any single agency insist on a case conference being convened?

AD: (. . .) Unless enough people are anxious then we are in practice impotent. Unless people are anxious enough then they won't go out and look for information. There is a point, too, here concerning {136} the police. If there is a case conference involving the police all the time, a big meeting with twenty or so people then we might recognize risk far more often than we do. A BASW working party has recently suggested that a strict application of the DHSS guidelines on risk might well lead to a quarter of all children being on at-risk registers. We have, too, to consider whether an agency can decide on risk unilaterally, whether indeed we could cope with the bulk of cases which would be produced on a stringent interpretation of our guidelines.

DD: Well I think it's a question for a professional worker with a first-hand knowledge of the situation to be able to say, in my judgement I consider that this child is at risk or has suffered non-accidental injury, for this and this reason.' The worker is making an assertion. There's a need for a case conference to be held with others to confirm or deny (. . .)

AD: Are we agreed that another agency should be able to demand a case conference, that no one should refuse to become involved, although they might try and contain the anxiety of the other agency initially.

SCM: Yes. I think if only one person wants action then a conference must be held.

The most interesting part of this sequence is the Area Director's contribution. He raises two points which we have already discussed: the barriers to an investigative treatment of clients and the consequences of a strict liability based on 'objective' criteria; but we want to concentrate on his last point, about the ability of any agency to act unilaterally, which echoes the debates set out in the previous section. An agreement on the right of any agency to require a case conference was reached fairly readily, but the committee had great problems with its status. The concern over police action re-emerged.

PAS: (. . .) I think we have to recognize the right of the police to act on their own judgement.

DD: Likewise the right of the social services department.

PAS: Yes, the difference here is that I would hope that the agencies would communicate here without taking unilateral action (. . .) I think that we can agree before action is taken that we should call a conference though the police can't commit themselves to that. {137}

SCM: No agency can give that assurance.

(...)

AD: So there are these two points here. The level of concern and whether or not there is a dispute. This committee can only recommend. We can't bind others to act in accordance with this.

Although any agency could call for a case conference, it did not seem that they could be required to do so. Nor could they commit their own agency to the principle of consultation prior to action in advance of a case conference.[4]

If nobody was prepared to relinquish their right to independent action prior to a case conference, were they prepared to do so subsequently? This first meeting considered that point in debating the need for a case conference to place a child on the register.

SCM: (. . .) If the conference does not arrive at a consensus decision and the social worker decides not to put the child on the register, would that decision be examined by the social services department? What is the mechanism for the Area Director communicating with others about that?

AD: I think we should cover that in the constitution of the conference. It's difficult to envisage the circumstances where the only representative of the department was the social worker dealing with the case. The conference is a dialogue to attempt to achieve a consensus. I think the real question is when there is conflict over registration between the social services department and others.

SCM: As far as I am concerned, it is the social services department's decision. While theoretically an inter-disciplinary register is a good thing, in practice, while it's held in the social services department or any other agency, there will be individual variation. We have to recognize that. We cannot legislate for another agency. (. . .)

AD: Are you questioning whether Social Services Department should hold the register?

DD: I don't think the register is the responsibility of one agency. It's not an agency thing. SCM is raising the whole question here of what the register is for. I mean all we're doing is sticking a red card in an index box and then the only other mechanism is the six-monthly review, apart from that then there are no benefits obtained than {138} those that exist in relation to anybody who gets in touch with the social services department. No additional communication with other agencies.

AD: Not really. I mean admittedly, they are only on a piece of paper until people use them, but it does bring about a sequence of administrative speeding-ups and a higher level of surveillance in case maintenance than would otherwise be the case. This sort of thing would theoretically be recognized as higher concern anyway by a professional worker. But that's not how organizations work. A red card certainly brings about a higher level of attention in case maintenance, and that is a valuable social services function.

DD: But I would see that only as an intra-agency benefit. I can't see it benefiting other agencies. (. . .)

DIVNO: There is this question of the relationship between our informal register and yours.

SCM: Whatever we do, individual agencies are going to keep their own registers.

DD: Well there is this argument for doing away with the register because it gives a false sense of security without giving any extra service to the client. Unless the index is serving any purpose above that of merely being an index, then it is of questionable value. If too we had an obligation to tell parents about them being placed on the risk register, then that might affect the numbers placed on. (. . .) Should parents be told if the family is on the at-risk register, if they are not told are we doing something rather sinister?

AD: I think this is a red herring.

(. . .)

DD: But I think it's important to raise these considerations in evaluating our actions. Putting children on the register is not just a book-keeping exercise. It is a very serious attack on parents' standards of care.

AD: I am not sure whether these civil liberty questions are really within the mandate of this group (. . .) I think we should try and talk about the tasks and functions of the case conference. The register could be an item for a whole meeting in itself. Are there any other functions that we want to raise? {139}

It certainly appears that none of the agencies is willing to give up its own register in favour of one which is, at least nominally, interdisciplinary. Once again we are particularly interested in the Area Director's comments. Notice, for instance, in his first contribution, how he recognises the bureaucratic nature of the social service participation in the case conference. More importantly, he points to the resource implications for social services. The Deputy Director's comments might seem disingenuous. At area team level, it is clear that accepting a case on to the register does, in principle, involve a special commitment of resources. On the other hand, if registration is made easy, the resources may be so thinly spread as to be imperceptible, leaving the agency vulnerable to criticism for having identified the case and not done sufficient about it. The Deputy Director's remarks need to be seen against the micropolitics of the Shire department. Its bureaucracy contained what some might describe as a weak link in the autonomy which area directors had established. In this particular instance, the Area Director's territory was contributing half the county's at-risk registrations for no obvious demographic reason. The Deputy Director's remarks can be seen as an indirect challenge to his judgement and the final remark on the gravity of the allegations questions the area's adherence to the principles of identification which we have already outlined. Are they working within the charter afforded to social work in a liberal society?

Before leaving this meeting, it is useful to see how the Area Director's last question was answered.

SCM: Well, I would have thought first that it's to provide the assessment of the situation by collating information. And secondly to decide what would be the most appropriate action within the resources available.

AD: I think we might add a third to decide who is going to be responsible for carrying it out. And what about a fourth responsibility for monitoring action? The problem is of course that an inter-agency body doesn't have executive power.

SCM: I think that you should certainly designate someone responsible for following up a decision. Someone who is responsible for monitoring what happens. But it can only be a moral responsibility. A key worker might accept a function that their agency didn't want them to.

SCM: Well I suppose that might happen. {140}

AD: Well, there are these questions about the power of a person in a hierarchical department to commit an agency to something, and also these questions about whether independent practitioners can be monitored.

SCM: I would have thought this was a dual role for the chairman, to monitor decisions. If internal conflict arises then the chairman should know and discuss it with the agency and with the conference members. But I think it's crucial that somebody monitors what happens.

DD: I think the whole question of review ties up with the responsibility of the responsible agency and the inclusion on the at-risk index.

AD: Well I think perhaps we should put some problems on the table here. Suppose the conference agrees that a child should stay in hospital until he is admitted to care and through pressures on beds or something the hospital decides to discharge the child home? Or suppose the conference agrees that prosecuting the parents in a case would be non-therapeutic and the police say we must prosecute in the interest of justice? Or suppose our department says this child must come into care and other people don't agree with that, how does the conference act?

DD: But I think this implies a status to the conference in terms of authority and responsibility, which is difficult to define. The case conference has no responsibility as an entity.

SCM: No.

AD: What is the meaning of monitoring then?

SCM: I would have thought agencies could agree to inform the chairman about their actions, so that at least one person knows what has happened and can communicate with other conference members. I think we should consider whether or not there ought to be a professional chairman.

The Area Director is quite clear about the outstanding problems of authority, but the difficulties are stressed by the Deputy Director and the Specialist in Community Medicine, with their greater experience of inter-agency *Realpolitik*. The case conference cannot intervene in a bureaucratic chain of accountability, nor can it direct an independent practitioner. Its chairman cannot enforce decisions. {141} The issue of chairmanship occupied the greater part of the second meeting, without significant modification of this original position.

The third meeting was mainly devoted to examining the administration of the child abuse register and defining rights of access to it. An interim report was prepared from that meeting and submitted to the ARC. The fourth meeting, then, began by considering the ARCs comments.

AD: There are one or two additional comments that I would like to insert. There is this question about the failure of an agency to comply with the recommendations of the ARC. (. . .) I was wondering if the Area Review Committee should consider recommending a formal recommendation of some form of complaint system or internal report back machinery from those members who also were accidentally members of case conferences.

SCM: I think it gets difficult when you put it as explicitly as that. If the chairman is to be drawn from social services then we could have an informal arrangement where non-social services Area Review Committee members could discuss case conferences with social services Area Review Committee members. I think it would be dangerous to spell it out though. I'm satisfied to hear that most cases are attended. I think that this sort of thing would come better from social services Area Review Committee members speaking informally to chairmen. Otherwise we run into the same difficulty as with sub-group investigations of the ones which went wrong, about confidentiality and agency responsibility.

AD: I think those are going to come up on the monitoring item. I think it is difficult to distinguish this from internal appraisal, but it does seem that we have a minor solution here to some of the problems of inter-agency answerability and diplomacy. Perhaps we could ask the Area Review Committee to use this informal network more actively.

DD: The problems arise, of course, when the informal network goes wrong. For example, where there's division of opinion at a case conference with four or five people on either side with firmly held opposing views. Are we going to say that they should just take a vote and if it's 5 : 4 or 6 : 5 then to say that we'll follow the majority? Or are we to say that it's just one agency one vote or that some agencies have no direct responsibility and therefore they should have no vote? A lot of these problems don't arise until you've got a marginal decision. {142}

AD: This problem about voting and about the status of the decisions is a huge one when agencies are in conflict. I think that was the problem which SCM and the Chief Probation Officer were raising at the committee about the question of adequate obedience in following procedures, and in getting treatment plans on the table. If there are problems with the organization at case conference these can have serious repercussions. So I think we need to ask should the Area Review Committee accept formal complaints, or search for them more. For example, at the level of effectiveness of chairmen, but then we have to ask whether this is diplomatically feasible.

The ARC's discussion had picked up references to the chairmanship issue. Once again we can see the sensitivity of the whole matter. The Area Director's blunt attempts to confront the consequences are discounted by the Specialist in Community Medicine. In Shire, the preference is for informal communication, diplomacy rather than procedure. The Specialist comes to what we would consider a critical point when he underlines the need for a case conference chairman to be backed within his own department and by the ARC. He feels that this may be near, over-optimistically, as it subsequently proves.

The subcommittee's report was placed before the ARC at their meeting in autumn 1978 and accepted. It was resolved that the recommended procedure should be incorporated into a revised procedures booklet, for which the copy date should be the beginning of 1979. However, that same autumn meeting set up a new subcommittee on in-service education and professional practice, with very little overlap in membership. This new subcommittee promptly began reconsidering many of the same issues, particularly those relating to chairmanship and register management. By the end of 1980 the revised procedures booklet had still not been compiled and it was merely hoped that it would appear in the course of 1981.

What both examples show, and we could multiply them, is that the Shire ARC was still dogged by the problems of authority which Mr Freeman had identified in his paper to the DHSS conference in 1974. Each agency defended its own autonomy and resisted any attempts to encroach on this by recognizing a collective responsibility for decision-making or the monitoring of performance. This is not a matter of petty jealousies but of fundamental differences of principle that are inherent in any attempt to forge a common purpose between people with such varying backgrounds and commitments. Who can oversee a professional other than members of the same occupation? Who can control the resources available to a {143} publicly funded and accountable agency except its own members? The effect, however, is to institutionalize tensions within the system that reinforce the bias against intervention. By emphasizing the diversity and independence of its agencies, Shire tends towards a position that restricts intervention and extends parental liberties. Both of our other departments, however, had adopted a rather different trade-off between these two objectives.

EXPERIENCE IN COUNTY AND BOROUGH

The inter-agency liaison system in both County and Borough was marked by the development of powerful subcommittees, referred to here as Standing Panels, which oversaw case management in considerable detail. The ARCs were devalued into largely formal entities, meeting at long intervals to discuss only the most general issues. To all intents and purposes, it was the Standing Panels which determined inter-agency policy.

We would emphasize the word 'determined'. The crucial difference between these authorities and Shire lay in the willingness of participants to pool their authority. Within a small group of chiefs of service or their immediate deputies, the Standing Panels were able to operate with a *de facto* executive power denied in Shire. Each of the representatives from health or social services was, in effect, prepared to place his or her full professional or bureaucratic authority behind any decision and take it back to enforce through the participating agencies. This was not to say that there were no private grumbles or politicking: merely that everyone recognized that their agency interest was bound up with collective responsibility. Both of these features come through in this interview with a senior officer from the County social services department:

RES: I would oppose, I wouldn't agree that the panel had an executive responsibility, and SCM and I've had numerous arguments about this. I can see how he thinks it has, you know, as a former member of the old health department and the then person in social services, you know, we're really back to the preventative child care element in the Council being in the health department and the queen bee health visitor. You know, and in those days pre-'75 you know, if the MOH said do this, you know there was far more tendency to touch their forelock and get on and do it. {144}

TM: In your decisions then is there a sort of implicit understanding (. . .) that the social services department in all cases reserve the right to act as they think fit?

RES: As far as I'm concerned, no one can direct the director, and the director is the head of the department.

TM: Rather like sort of police bit, you know, they reserve the right to prosecute however much the . . .

RES: Yes. I mean it's ridiculous, I mean Dick and I have had numerous sessions about this, you see and I would argue 'Yes, the panel has executive responsibility over social services if it has the same power over nurses, and doctors and probation officers.' I mean you don't call an executive responsibility over doctors, I would hope that anybody would ignore a panel recommendation at that person's peril or at that agency's peril, because it is the combined consideration of senior and pretty experienced members, personnel.

TM: So, I mean you personally would see it as an advisory, guiding body that makes properly considered recommendations but they are recommendations, they're not . . .

RES: I don't see, I don't see how it can possibly be executive because the body itself has no power to compel. Or to discipline.

TM: I mean suppose there was a social worker who appeared to have really messed it up, then if there was any disciplinary action even if it was a sort of word in the ear, or something more substantial, that must be left to the director to decide whether he wished to take that action.

RES: Well I don't think it would even reach the director, I think, within the social work department.

TM: But would the standing panel ever be, would they ever say, 'in our opinion there has been a breach of procedure here and there should be some effort to . . .' you know a sort of couched terms . . .

RES: Oh yes I would have thought that the panel could easily comment, it could easily recommend, and I think this happens. I don't think, I think one is wrong to see it purely in terms of social services. I would have thought, you know, that this would apply to all the services and I think this is something that is becoming much more clear in the last eighteen months or so. (. . .) It's, I think, playing {145} with words very much. The panel doesn't have executive authority, you know. I would challenge this, certainly in the final analysis. Dick Blount is the chairman (. . .) I think we go along with this, but, you know, in the final analysis, I suppose if there's a fair old set to, he talks to our director (. . .) and one would hope that it would filter down with executive, but I strongly, you know I have strong things about that word.

Under the pressure of our questioning, the respondent goes back to the version of agency autonomy which we have chronicled in Shire. At the same time he does, in effect, concede the amount of *de facto* authority which the panel has acquired over a period of years and the influence that this has on the executive action of the various agencies.

Our interviews and fieldwork with lower-level participants in those agencies confirmed this interpretation. The Standing Panels reviewed fieldwork in considerable detail. In one of the authorities, they met weekly as a permanent case conference which was attended by local staff involved with cases of current concern. The other area's Panel met at three- to four-weekly intervals, or more frequently if an urgent case arose. It received written reports from local case conferences whose constitution and powers were specified in detail by the inter-agency procedures. Local conferences were required to take and justify clear decisions for which they were then jointly answerable. If the Panel disagreed, it could overturn a local decision by direction. In both areas these powers were highly visible to field staff, who were aware that they were always likely to be called to account for their stewardship of cases. The Shire fieldworkers, on the other hand, did not see the ARC as a salient feature of their work setting.

Interestingly, the private reservations of senior staff in both County and Borough were largely concealed from their juniors. The latter had no doubts about the executive character of the Panels and the implications for agency autonomy. This extract is typical.

> SW was very unhappy with the panel system and the fact that all sorts of people who knew very little about the case or had a very narrow perspective had voting rights. He felt there was a tendency to play safe, to say, 'We had better do this' or 'we had better do that' rather than seriously considering the well-being of the child. He felt this was partly a legacy of the Wicketts case and you couldn't altogether blame people for it but he got very annoyed when he went along and got some health visitor sticking her hand up when she didn't know the first thing about the situation. He thought that the {146} decision should be left to the social services department, bearing in mind the opinion of other agencies.

Although we could discern the same conflicts and tensions in lower-level contacts like referrals and case conferences in all three areas, their scope was much reduced by the perceived interdependence at a senior level in County and Borough. Fieldworkers had an area of uncertainty about the degree to which their management would automatically protect them against complaints from other agencies as opposed to deferring to fellow Panel members. This created an incentive to minimize local antagonisms, to develop working relationships even with private discontents. The effects of this were, of course, most strongly felt in the more bureaucratized areas, social work and community nursing and, to a lesser degree, hospital and community medicine.

The obvious question is, of course, why our three areas differed in this fashion. Our sample is really too small for a definite answer, but we can make two suggestions which seem consistent with the general sociological literature on organizations. Shire had, as a county, been greatly affected by the reorganization of local government and health services in 1974 and had never had a major inquiry into its handling of a case of child abuse or neglect. One of the other authorities had been virtually unaffected by either reorganization and the other had been the subject of one of the most publicized inquiries. Both of these seem to be relevant factors.

In the first authority, the Standing Panel was, in effect, the direct heir and successor of the Co-ordinating Committee on child care set up in the early fifties. Although the 1974 reorganization had changed people's work bases and titles, more or less the same group of individuals had been working together for nearly fifteen years at the time of our study. Much of that experience was pre-reorganization, pre-Seebohm even, so that the community health and social service integration which had been a feature of this authority had carried through essentially unchanged. At the time of our research, certain strains were emerging with the imminent retirement of key members, and we considered that these did pose a threat to the long-term survival of the system. One of the agencies, in particular, seemed keen to reassert its autonomy in a way which would undermine the pooling of authority.

The other authority had been much affected by reorganization and the Panel members did not have this tradition to build upon. However, it had been harshly dealt with by a public inquiry, from {147} which many of the staff still carried wounds.[5] Indeed, although the link between that inquiry and the authority had not been in our minds when we approached the agencies for research co-operation, many of the staff we encountered had a strong initial sense of threat from our work. Some said openly to us that they thought we had been sent by DHSS as spies to check up on their response to the inquiry's criticisms. We interpret the inter-agency co-operation we observed, then, as a defensive reaction. There was a clear determination that no one should be exposed to such attack a second time. Senior personnel had recognized that they could defend their agencies only at the cost of relinquishing certain traditional prerogatives in order to spread the risks of error. This system seemed to be more stable when we observed it but might, obviously, decay as staff memories faded and people retired.

While we might want to argue, then, that County and Borough had evolved, in their Standing Panels, systems for overcoming interagency tensions, it would seem that these did not rest on secure foundations so much as historical accident. We can point, also, to the effects. Both areas perceived themselves as having high rates of intervention. Moreover, the power of these committees pulled all the agencies towards activities related to child mistreatment. This was particularly marked in one of the areas, where other agencies complained about the narrow focus of NHS services for children. Finally, both areas maintained much more extensive registration systems than Shire, collecting more data on a greater number of adults. One of the areas ran a particularly sophisticated intelligence-gathering system with a collator assembling all reports, suggestions, hints or other indications of possible mistreatment on to a comprehensive filing system in addition to the official at-risk register. Some might criticize this on libertarian grounds but others would argue that it was the necessary prerequisite of effective containment of child mistreatment.

The County and Borough systems, then, framed lower-level activities in a way which pressed towards integration and collaboration, while the Shire system left these substantially intact. Both of them, however, seem to represent rather particular institutional circumstances, so that Shire may well be more typical of the general national approach. In all three areas, though, the ARC can do no more than furnish a context within which local relationships are established.

7

Case Conferences and the Legalization of Mistreatment

{148}
Despite our insistence at the beginning of this book on the importance of the statutory framework for agency practice we have, so far, said little about its relation to case management, except in the broad sense that the various types of agency organization are created by different sorts of charters embodying different forms of moral accountability between practitioners, clients and society. This apparent neglect reflects the nature of everyday practice. Doctors, health visitors and social workers are not law-enforcement officers, permanently and selectively attuned to discovering breaches of statute. They are better characterized as problem-solving agents, for whom the law exists as one possible resource for dealing with social troubles.[1] Most front-line workers have a relatively limited knowledge of the detail of the legal provisions, as opposed to being aware that powers exist which they can look up in books or ask advice on from colleagues.

There is, then, seldom a clear and obvious point at which a case of suspected mistreatment can be said to become legalized. It may be better understood as a growing awareness that voluntary means are failing and something else may have to be done, although this feeling may be precipitated or accelerated by a triggering incident like a serious injury which suddenly involves other agencies or a gross act of parental non-compliance like a request to terminate visits. Wherever this process actually starts, however, its most explicit manifestations are to be found in case conferences.

Such meetings are of great importance in the way they combine features of both formal and informal referrals. Within them, members of the various agencies meet face-to-face. Communication is primarily of an oral nature, allowing great flexibility in contributing and incorporating new pieces of evidence, either to defend a particular allegation of mistreatment or to persuade others of its {149} correctness. At the same time, case conferences are formally recognized occasions, officially minuted and taking place within procedural guidelines established by the Area Review Committees. Their deliberations, therefore, leave a permanent record and identify responsibility for the outcome.[2]

By the time a case reaches this stage, it has already been finely sifted. One or more front-line workers has come to acknowledge that it is a possible case of mistreatment, this possibility has not been excluded by informal investigations or, where appropriate, by bureaucratic superiors and a record has been opened in the social services department. In effect, then, the participants are already approaching an agreement that 'something ought to be done'. The main questions are likely to be 'Just what?' and 'How?'. Participants attempt to answer these through debate over what Frank (1981) contends are the two principal tasks of case conferences: identifying a child as a victim of mistreatment and identifying some person as the agent of that action.[3]

Three outcomes are likely to be available at any conference: to do nothing or to place the child on an at-risk register, both of which may imply continuing work with the family on a voluntary basis and which appear to result from a failure to convert the agencies' identification of mistreatment into a legally acceptable form; or to attempt to obtain statutory powers over the child, either by negotiation, within the framework of the Children Act 1948, or by compulsion, through care proceedings.

All of these decisions have particular implications for social services as the agency with the greatest variety of resources, legal and otherwise, and the most direct line of moral accountability. Case conferences can raise many of the issues of agency sovereignty which we discussed in the previous chapter. Are they consultative or executive? Can agencies be bound by their decisions? In the course of such discussions, cases may be referred to the charters of the various agencies as each seeks to define its own sphere of responsibility.

Our interest here, however, is primarily in the collaborative efforts of participants to test each other's provisional formulations of the case against possible alternatives and against their sense of legal adequacy. In the process, as Frank (1981: 172) comments:

> . . . formulations which therapists could take for granted among themselves must now be treated as problematic: those legally trained require different verifications before they will accept the therapeutic formulation of the situation.[4] {150}

Case conferences are the point at which front-line workers are confronted with the inescapability of translating their judgements into legally acceptable forms if they wish to take compulsory measures.

'SOCIAL' AND 'LEGAL' EVIDENCE

The difference between therapeutic and legal assessments was identified by Wigmore in the first volume of his classic *Treatise on Evidence* (1940: s.4f), where he contrasts the methods which courts employ to establish 'truth' with those adopted by other tribunals and by 'social case-work'. Wigmore draws attention to Richmond's (1917) account of the necessity of 'social', as opposed to 'legal' evidence in the formation of social work judgements:

> Many an item, such as a child's delayed speech, for instance, may have no significance in itself, whereas when considered in connection with late dentition and walking and with convulsions it may become a significant part of evidence as to the child's mentality. (Richmond quoted by Wigmore vol. I: s.4f)

Social evidence thus consists of all or any facts 'as to personal or family history which, taken together, indicate the nature of a given client's social difficulties and the means of their solution'. The crucial difference from legal evidence lies not, Richmond claims, in 'the sort of facts offered, but in the greater degree of probative value required by the law to each separate item'.

Agency staff are drawn to convene case conferences on the basis of social data – a child's material and interpersonal environment and the moral character of his or her parents – as these provide for the interpretations of clinical data – physical signs and symptoms. Their assessments are based on the cumulative probability of independently observed features occurring together (Dingwall 1984). Each of these may be of limited significance or otherwise explicable on its own: their concatenation, however, makes alternative accounts of the child's condition implausible. Many of these observations relate to deviations from a model of normality whose finer details are so woven into a front-line worker's framing of a particular event as to be almost impossible to formulate separately in the manner that the construction of a legally manageable case would require. We have already quoted several examples from accident staff (pp. 35-6 {pp. 40-1}); this is a health visitor: {151}

> So much of what you pick up . . . is just what you feel about a case and not only what you hear, and very often one's feelings are in fact a much better gauge than anything else.

This approach is based on the assumption that clients are *a priori* troubled. Any area of their life may be inspected in the light of this assumption for further evidence to establish the exact nature of the trouble. The evidence is interpreted in the light of what is already established about the person's moral character. Against this, the legal approach requires that the formulation of character comes from the evidence.

> The evidence must formulate the identity of the accused; *it must not be the case that the evidence itself becomes understandable only on the basis of prior knowledge of the accused's guilty identity.* Rules of admissibility of evidence exist to ensure that the sequence of formulation, at least as it takes place inside the court, proceeds from documents to identity. (Frank 1981: 181, our emphasis)

Rules of legal proof operate on a different calculation of probability from those employed by agency staff. Rather than proceeding to 'value every statement equally and then add the items together to find a total', the rules of evidence specify weighting procedures by which the significance of each individual item may be adjusted. Direct evidence is more valued than hearsay which, in turn, is valued more than opinion. This is a refinement rather than a transformation of agency reasoning: as Blackburn (1980: 149) has observed, the rules of evidence are, in large part, 'common sense written carefully'. The greater caution reflects the courts' one-off opportunity to assess a case, rather than the more processual character of health or social work judgements.

Nevertheless, the translation from one type of assessment to another presents considerable practical difficulties, as this extract from an interview with the Conrads' social worker shows:

SW: . . . we assume that they have been subjected to a lot of traumatic and distressing experiences, but how one can assess exactly how disturbed they are, well, you know, it's very difficult to, you know I mean one can only predict that they will be. But if this sort of continued they you know obviously they will be but at the end of the case conference we were talking about things that could be brought out in court and it would be very difficult to say that these children are disturbed. {152}

RD: So there's a contrast between what you feel and what you think you can bring out in court?

SW: Yes there must be. Yes, and I'm sure that anybody going into the Conrad household especially, y'know at a time after Mrs Conrad has taken an overdose or there's something happened, I mean one can't sort of fail to feel for those children and think, y'know, what effect it's having on them. But, you know, that's different to actually measuring it and being able to sort of say in court, you know, that these children are sort of emotionally disturbed.

Mrs Conrad's established character provides for a view of the children as possibly disturbed in ways which may only become evident later, and which may be prevented by present intervention. The problem, however, arises of legitimating compulsory intervention in the absence of currently documentable damage, as the law requires in England.[5] The social worker *knows* for therapeutic purposes that the children are being mistreated, but this is quite different from evidence for legal purposes.

Case conferences can come to take on many of the features of a committal hearing.[6] Each of the agencies sets out its evidence and reasoning for the scrutiny of the others involved. In the process, front-line workers are obliged to switch from their usual stance of speaking *for* clients, under the rule of optimism, to speaking *against* them, treating their conduct as possible evidence for legal action, and back again. Through these successive oscillations, the participants attempt to test the prospects of success in any application for compulsory powers and the risks of potential criticism for non-compulsory interventions.

In order to illuminate these general issues, we propose to analyse one of our Shire conferences as a case study. This one is atypical in only two respects: no local authority solicitor was present, as was customary in Shire, and it was relatively short, enabling us to reproduce the whole of our field notes.

'A BATTERING WALSH'

This case conference was held in the paediatric department of the Victoria Hospital in Midchester. Apart from the observer, the participants were a social worker (SW) and her senior (SSW) from the area team, a health visitor (HV) and her nursing officer (NO), a medical social worker (MSW), two policemen (PC1 and PC2), two {153} consultants (Cons1 and Cons2), a registrar (Reg), a medical student and one of the department's secretaries. The child, Lindy Oates, is eight months old and the adults are her mother, Mrs Hancock, her present cohabitee, Mr Finnegan, and Mary Walsh, who was living in to help with Lindy and three other children following a recent accident to Mrs Hancock. All three were in their middle to late twenties. Since part of our interest is in the production of information about the parties, we shall leave the remainder of the history to emerge as our analysis progresses.

> Prior to the start, the MSW spoke to the SSW asking if there would be anybody present from Administrative Services. Apparently they had not been notified and the MSW says that this was a pity, 'We usually leave it to you.' There was a long wait for the police and for Cons2. When he came, Cons2 pointed out that the chairperson should be the senior social worker. The MSW said that this question was under discussion in the Victoria. Neither of the area team social workers nor the MSW had heard of the recommendation of the ARC about this. Cons1 came in and assumed the chair, inviting the registrar to introduce the case.

Several minor points emerge from this. First, it documents our contention that the absence of a solicitor was unusual, although not so critical as to prevent the conference going ahead. Second, we can see the importance of the doctors, in that the conference cannot begin until they arrive, if they are expected. In other cases, we establish that a 'proper' conference could be held without waiting for the police. Third, the issue of chairmanship, which we looked at in the ARC's discussions, surface again. We can see the clash between the medical model of the conference as an occasion for information to be collected and decisions delegated under a doctor's orchestration and the social services view of the conference as an occasion for them to listen to discussion and take advice in the course of forming *their* decision (cf. Hallett and Stevenson 1980: 91-6). Finally, of course, this passage helps to substantiate our earlier contentions about the limited impact of Shire ARC on front-line workers.

> Reg said that the child came to casualty at 5 pm on (Date). The GP had been called at 4 pm. The boyfriend had come home and said that he had held the child up because it was crying and had discovered a lot of bruises. He didn't know how they had got there and he called the GP. The GP had said that he had been called only because of a cough and a runny nose. The only prior admitted incident was that {154} the child fell off the sofa and had a bruised cheek. The mother was living with a twenty-six-year-old boyfriend called Finnegan but the child was a child of her former boyfriend. The mother had had her hand in plaster because she had broken her wrist after falling on ice. They were living with three other children in the house. There was somebody else living in the house as a kind of help for them who was known to the social services. On examination the baby was crying (-u-). She had a torn upper frenulum in the upper lip which was traumatic in nature and was covered in bruises (Reg holds up a chart). These were on the mouth, the chest and the upper abdomen and they were usually circular. Some of them were recent, only a few hours old but others had been there a few days. No other abnormality had been found and there was no bone injury. The child had been admitted for observation and the excuse they gave was that they wanted to look into the bruises. Later, mum became most concerned to know whether there was any internal bleeding. The child's temperature was fluctuating. Everybody commented how wary the child was when anyone approached the cot. This was not normal. She looked suspicious and afraid and not only at people in white coats and sometimes she cried if anybody tried to touch her.

This is typical of the sort of opening statements made at first case conferences. Where a doctor was present (12 conferences), he or she usually made the first presentation (seven occasions).[7] Even where a doctor was not present, the opening statement still focused on the signs and symptoms exhibited by the child and a proposed interpretation formulating them as evidence of mistreatment. The features of the registrar's account should be familiar from earlier chapters. Clinical evidence (the torn frenu-lum, the bruising) is located within a social context (discrepancies in the history, irregular cohabitation, previous contact with social services) that makes it a possible indicator of mistreatment. By the end, the mother's concern, the fluctuations in the temperature of the child (who did have a respiratory tract infection) and the child's distress in hospital all become further evidence of the correctness of this identification rather than as natural and expectable events. We can note, too, the manufacturing of an 'excuse' to detain the child without having to make an overt allegation, a feature we have previously discussed in relation to health visiting and social work visits.

Such 'facts' were seldom disputed in abuse cases.[8] Debates, as Frank (1981: 174-7) shows, are somewhat more common in conferences dealing with neglect where the clinical data are less clearly defined and depend on the location of cut-offs on a continuous {155} statistical distribution, as with weight or development.[9] Here, there may be rather less certainty on the doctor's part and more scope for intervention by others with some claim to expertise in developmental matters. In the absence of dispute, however, the conference discussions turn to the search for an agent of Lindy's mistreatment.

MSW: This is complicated by the fact that there are three adults in the house. No one knows very much about Finnegan. She (Mrs Hancock) claims that she wants to marry him and that he is wonderful with children. Mary Walsh is a vulnerable person who has been known to the social services and she has been the main caretaker of the child. It's a complicated situation.

SSW: Yes, she was known to us a long time ago but we have had no contact since then.

CONS1: Does the present cohabitee have a police record?

PC1: We don't know.

HV: He is a divorcee with children aged six and four whom he visits. He looks to be in his 20s. He's Irish, he comes from Belfast.

PC1: Could the injuries have been due to a fall from a cot?

REG: No.

SW: I know the priest to whom Mary goes when she is in trouble. I had a phone call on Monday from him saying that Mary has been upset about the baby. Mary's version, and she is a person who tends to drift around with problem families, is that four weeks ago she was worried about the baby's chest but the parents would not call a doctor. She knows that she is under suspicion, and her explanation is that they didn't call the doctor because of the bruises and she thought that the boyfriend used to grip the baby too tightly. When asked who gets up when the baby cries at night, she says it is the boyfriend. She thinks the bruises come from the boy-friend's holding the baby too tightly.

The MSW's opening remarks set the tone for the discussion. She consti-tutes the household as a couple plus another, Mary Walsh. Finnegan and Mrs Hancock are bracketed together by their proposed marriage, and their moral character is further developed by Mrs Hancock's praise of Finne-gan's capacities with children. {156} We think the conference is intended to hear this not merely as a testimonial to Finnegan but also to Mrs Han-cock in that she has chosen to associate herself with him in doing the best for her children. Mary Walsh, however, is discredited by successive refer-ences to her vulnerability and her previous contact with social services, which, taken together, constitute evidence of an uncertain mental state and limited ability to achieve independent action, impairments of respon-sibility. She is also presented as the person with the greatest opportunity to injure the children, given her role as their main caretaker.

The MSW's actions here are very strongly reminiscent of Emerson's (1969: 101-41) discussion of the establishment of moral character in juvenile courts. He points to the way in which this is organized around two basic strategies, denunciations and pitches, for relating a delinquent act to its alleged agent's general social background. A successful denunciation establishes the act as one typically committed by persons of a 'bad' charac-ter and constructs a biography of the actor that indicates such a character. A successful pitch normalizes the act and the biography. Emerson points out that both strategies normally involve reference to the delinquent's family circumstances and the availability of reputable sponsors. In the present case Lindy's mistreatment, the act, is clearly established. The MSW is organizing a pitch for Finnegan and Mrs Hancock and a denuncia-tion of Mary Walsh as the only household member with a spoiled character and, by inference, the only one capable of committing this monstrous act.

This debate runs through the conference as the area team social work-ers attempt to make a pitch for Mary Walsh and the others denounce her. After the MSW's initial proposal, the senior from the area team makes a rather weak attempt to dispute the first two references: her contact with social services was a long time ago and it is therefore wrong to stigmatize her as a current client and as someone who is so vulnerable as to need frequent help. The following utterances generally contribute to the favour-able view of the cohabitee: he has no known police record; he is of mature age; and although divorced, he visits his children. Although the first policeman goes back to testing the formulation of the child as abused, the main thrust continues to be with the adults' characters. Mary Walsh's social worker then comes in with another challenge to the MSW's formulation of the household. She links Mary to her parish priest, as someone who might be thought to have a special competence as a receiver of true statements and might be a candidate for the status of 'reputable sponsor', to assert that Finnegan and Mrs Hancock {157} are colluding to cover up Finnegan's rough handling of the child. At the same time, she retains some distance from Mary, speaking both for and against her, by describing this as her 'version' and by referring to her tendency to drift around with problem families. Mary may not be all *that* reliable. The consultant paediatrician immediately comes in to point to the limitations of this (second-hand) story in accounting for the clinical presentation.

CONS1: That doesn't account for the torn lip.

SW: No . . .

CONS1: It seems as if the torn lip was caused by a blow to the face but (Cons2) is more expert at this.

CONS2: There could have been no other way.

SW: Mary is rather dim but very fond of babies. She says that she has had too much put on her of late. She has always looked after other people's children.

This consultant co-opts his colleague, the acknowledged local expert on abuse, to support him. The latter's reply incorporates the absolutist version of abuse which we discussed in chapter 3 but the social worker does not have a licence to challenge that assertion. Her reply does little more than restore the previous depiction of Mary Walsh as not very competent but generally fond of children.

MSW: What previous contact did you have with the family?

SSW: In November 1973, that was the first time when they came to us as homeless. They were living with Mr Hancock's sister and we gave them temporary accommodation. Later they referred to us for financial difficulties and we gave them a bit of help and there was another contact in March 1976 because of a marital problem. Her husband had left and came back with another woman and tried to turf her out. It finished in the County Court and he was evicted and she remained. It is not clear whether the father of the child came to live with her or not. She had become pregnant and she referred in November 1976 because of Maureen's behaviour. This was put down to the absence of a father and things seemed later to get better.

HV: I saw Mrs Hancock yesterday. She said, 'Have you heard of the baby?' She said that it had been to hospital because of a cold on {158} the chest. She said she didn't know how the bruises had happened. She said that on Friday her boyfriend said that she should call a doctor and that he was cross when this was not done when he had come home. There was no mention of the bruises to the doctor but the doctor noticed it when he came. She said she didn't know how they had happened and said that Mary had babysat the previous day and said that she hadn't broached the subject with Mary because Mary was upset due to the death of an aunt. About the lip she said she thought it was simply teething. She said that Mary had been looking after the child the day before. She also said that it was only occasionally that the children were left in a room with the baby but they were not left alone in the house with them. I asked Mary if she knew how the bruises came and she said no. I asked if she had seen them before and she said that she had seen them on Wednesday. I asked why she hadn't mentioned it and she said she didn't want to cause trouble. I had met them just before the baby was born. Mother/baby interactions always seemed to be good. Mr Oates wasn't living with them at the time. He was divorced and had custody of his own children. They originally had planned to get married when they got a four-bedroomed house. Mrs Hancock came to the clinic in January and then I heard that she had now got a new boyfriend who was Mr Finnegan – I visited her – Lindy looked well and went to both Mrs Hancock and her boyfriend readily and cuddled with them and that was the last I saw of them.

This sequence continues the character work on the three adults. The senior social worker runs over Mrs Hancock's record. She is known to the department but not as a persistent or highly dependent client. The most recent contacts with her have been as the victim of her husband's attempt to prise her out of the matrimonial home and as a self-referral for help with her children's behaviour. We think that this last is intended to be heard as evidence of her caring attitude as a parent. This is compounded by the health visitor's contribution. She depicts Mrs Hancock as worried about the baby's health, as a reliable source of data on her boyfriend's concern and as a kindly woman who had not liked to ask Mary about the bruising on the child because of Mary's recent bereavement. Nevertheless, this still does not seem to be sufficient positively to identify Mary as the culprit.

CONS2: What is the baby's weight?

HV: On the (Date) it was 18lb 5oz.

CONS2: I would like to have a look at the chart. {159}

CONS1: Yes, it's on the treatment chart.

CONS2: I'll get it. It's acutely relevant. (Cons2 goes out).

CONS1: Has anybody else anything to say? (There is a long silence.) I think it appears to be a child who by persons unknown has been subject to repeated assaults over a period of time. The reason why Cons2 is here is that we want him to see the child with a view to admitting the child and the mother perhaps but I would feel that the child should not be allowed to return home when further damage might occur. Cons2 being out of the room at present, we will wait until he gets back. Does anybody feel that they would like the child to go home?

SW: Whoever caused the injury, it's quite clear that the others have colluded with it. Because of the relationship, it is not possible to point the finger.

MSW: Mary might be being used as a scapegoat.

At this point, the issue of further clinical evidence is brought up. Will this help them to decide? The second consultant leaves and the first consultant canvasses the dilemma from the chair. Nobody is yet firmly identified as the agent of the child's condition. He still holds out the possibility that it is the child's mother but whoever has done it, as the social worker and her colleague point out, all the adults may be responsible. If she cannot rescue Mary Walsh, at least the blame can be spread. Notice, too, the way in which the consultant shuts out the possibility of disagreement with his conclusion about returning the child. A view is stated and the obligation placed on the hearers to show why it should not prevail, an exercise which would involve breaching a strong interactional preference for agreement, an act which is capable of discrediting the speaker as a person of sound judgement. By her partial agreement, however, the social worker gets into a position where she can renew her attempts to defend her client.

SW: Mary is leaving this weekend. She has known the baby since it was born and she has looked after the older children when Mrs Hancock had her baby. (. . .) What might happen is that if a child is miserable for four weeks with a cold this could be a trigger.

PC1: What is the timing of the bruises, are they days or weeks? {160}

CONS1: Some are going yellow. The frenulum is very nasty.

PC1: Would it be Wednesday, would that be too long?

CONS1: They would be entirely compatible. It has gone septic.

PC2: Was Mary married?

SW: Yes to Matt Walsh, an inadequate person who drank a lot.

PC2: What's her age?

SW: 28 and she is fairly dim.

PC1: Could the children have been responsible? The eldest is seven.

HV: I don't think that she would leave them along with the baby. Maureen's a tearaway; she has set light to a bedroom.

REG: But they are adult fingertips.

PC2: Has anybody seen them separately?

SW: Not really.

PC2: Mary hasn't been seen about it?

HV: No. She has gone to her GP this morning.

The social worker begins to assemble a less coercive outcome. If, as everybody else seems to be suggesting, Mary Walsh is the culprit, she is moving out anyway. The agent is leaving so it is not necessary to remove the children. Moreover, it seems inappropriate to prosecute her. She has demonstrated affection for the children and been trusted by Mrs Hancock over a long period and these injuries are explicable as a one-off event with a specific trigger, in contrast to the first consultant's formulation. He does not press his version strongly, as the police come in with a series of questions addressed to the legal status of the information so far presented. Another alternative story, that the injuries were caused by the other children, is ruled out. At this point the second consultant returns.

CONS2: Her present weight is 7.815 kilograms. She was 18 lb 5 ozs; how do we convert this? {161}

NO: I have conversion tables. Eighteen, her dressed weight was eight something (kilograms CSLS).

CONS2: So there has been some weight loss but she is not chronically starved. I've seen her. She's shown weight loss and though she is not fully frozen, she is clearly very disturbed.

This is an interesting analysis by the second consultant. Statistically, some weight loss is normal for children in hospital. Indeed, in most neglect cases in our study, weight gain following admission was treated as a highly significant indicator of the probability of failure to thrive being attributable to parental deficiency rather than having an organic cause (cf. Frank 1981: 174-5). Similarly, most children are disturbed on admission. Again, a lack of disturbance, especially the so-called state of 'frozen watchfulness' to which the consultant seems to be referring, is commonly treated as an index of mistreatment. Now that the child has been formulated as a victim, however, both of these observations become further documents of the correctness of that interpretation. The second consultant continues:

CONS2: Is this Mrs Walsh part of the famous Walsh family? There is a sub-culture, of which the Walshes are a part, who have been battering their children for 30 years.

SW: He is the brother of Bridget.

CONS2: That's right, she was a Walsh, she flung her baby across the room in front of me. The first time I actually saw classic baby-battering myself. They all belong to a subculture of batterers. My God, a bloody Walsh, God help us.

SW: But she is a Walsh by marriage only.

CONS2: Oh it doesn't matter. It isn't a question of the genes. Well I am very doubtful of taking them on with any hope for success. (There is some further muttering along these lines).

PC1: Are there any signs of neglect, for example, nappy rash?

HV: No.

CONS2: All this is very recent. A very recent intrusion and we have now an intruder with an ominous name.

PC1: It is one for us? {162}

CONS2: Yes, it is for you gentlemen. When the mother broke her wrist, some-one intervened.

PC1: So long as we have a statement of complaint we can act. Is the baby being taken into care?

This passage is the key to the conference outcome. It opens up the possibility of what Emerson describes as a 'total denunciation', which overrides all possible defences by declaring that the person's character is so irremediably damaged as to eliminate all chance of successful voluntary intervention. By linking Mary Walsh to a known child abuser, her sister-in-law, Bridget, she is tied into a group for whom child mistreatment is a natural way of life. As such, she must be the agent of these particular injuries. Moreover, the actions involved are so intrinsic to her moral nature as a member of this 'sub-culture of batterers' that there is little prospect of changing them without compulsion or punishment.

Nevertheless, Mary Walsh's social worker still attempts to test the analysis in the following sequence:

CONS1: Well we must decide this.

CONS2: It doesn't seem as if the mother neglected her.

SW: But she colluded.

CONS2: Yes, that is a matter for the police.

It should be recalled that Mrs Hancock's wrist has been injured and Mary Walsh was staying to care for the children. The absence of neglect, however, is tied to the children's mother rather than possibly being used as evidence on Mary Walsh's behalf. Again, we have the 'facts' being assembled to support a particular characterization. Debate on this is quickly shut down.

PC1: How long will the child stay here?

CONS1: We could keep her a week.

PC1: That'll give us time to do our business.

SW: Has the mother visited the child? How does the baby react?

REG: She has . . . {163}

MSW: So we should wait to hear from the police and then consult with you.

CONS2: Yes, I will do some research.

SW: Yes, it is relevant. She has looked after children before.

CONS2: I'm not accusing her. The link-up is a necessary piece of knowledge.

MSW: I could find out from the social workers where she looked after children before.

NO: What if the parent wanted to take the child home?

CONS2: You should get a place of safety.

CONS1: Who do we ring?

CONS2: You can get one from the police.

CONS1: So I'll ring the police.

SW: Well we will take this back to (Principal Adviser). From my knowledge of Mrs Hancock, she won't go against the advice of a doctor if it is to keep the child in.

CONS1: Is there anything else?

PC2: I need some personal details of Walsh.

SW: Is there any way of finding out a bit about Martin Finnegan?

PC1: We will (laughter).

The social worker asks about the child's reaction to her mother, points to Mary Walsh's record of satisfactory child caretaking and to their ignorance of Martin Finnegan's past. It should be clear that none of these challenges is picked up. The registrar attempts to deal with the first and is cut off, the second is ignored, and the third, as the conference is breaking up, is treated as a joke. The focus of the encounter has shifted to the two consultants and the police. By the end of the conference the police are already referring to 'Walsh' in the way they would characteristically talk of a suspect. Mary Walsh is to be prosecuted and the children left at home. {164}

The debates in this case conference have underlined the importance of moral character in the identification of child mistreatment. Given that a necessary precondition for the conference is a degree of consensus about the existence of prima facie evidence of mistreatment, the final decision turns on whether the adults involved can be shown to be capable of it. In this case we have a choice of three candidates. Mrs Hancock is Lindy's mother, who naturally loves her. Although she has been a social services client, she is generally independent and resorts to social work help only on appropriate, limited occasions. She defers to authority without being obsequious. Although she has had a number of men in her life – at least three, Mr Hancock, Mr Oates and Mr Finnegan – she is not promiscuous. Rather, in the wake of an unfortunate marriage, she has sought to re-create a stable environment in the interests of her children and to provide a father substitute for them. On the other side is Mary Walsh who is vulnerable, dim, tends to drift around with problem families, formerly married to an inadequate person who drank a lot and who is, moreover, one of the famous battering Walshes. In between is Martin Finnegan, about whom very little is known except that he visits his children, although divorced, and Mrs Hancock will vouch for him.

Given the models of normality discussed previously, it is not hard to see who is going to be identified as the abuser in this situation, an identification which leaves a near-'normal' family unit intact and minimizes the amount of coercion involved. Mrs Hancock's natural love does not have to be attacked. Mary Walsh's conduct can be treated as intentional and punished, removing the threat rather than the children. It is the least socially disruptive outcome. Although the area team social worker attempts to construct an alternative account, this is not consistently pursued and becomes entangled in pleas of mitigation which accept Mary's culpability but attempt to excuse her by reference to her diminished capacity for responsibility. In practice, it would be difficult to challenge this consensus, without calling one's own competence into question. Frank (1981: 179) gives an example of the ridicule which greeted a student public health nurse who displayed her inadequate socialization into the rules of interpretation by preferring a parent's account of the failure to keep a clinic appointment to the 'official' clinic account. The social worker fails to enlist support for her version, even from her supervisor, and backs off. As Emerson (1969: 140-1) notes, where a total denunciation is initiated, sponsors must either be brought into line or discredited. A social worker, or any other agency worker, has a {165} longer-term perspective than the outcome of any particular case. Actions which call their credibility into question on one occasion may jeopardize their ability to succeed on subsequent and more important matters. The result is an emphasis on consensus, as Hilgendorf (1981: 81-2) also found. This is a constraint familiar to sociologists of law in discussing the tension between 'one-shot' and 'repeat' players, occasional and regular participants in the legal process (Galanter 1974).

The outcome of this case conference was Mary Walsh's arrest. Following an admission to the police, she was prosecuted on a charge of occasioning actual bodily harm. Her solicitor successfully defended the action by challenging the validity of her statement and the case was dismissed. About two weeks after this hearing, Lindy Oates was admitted to hospital with two skull fractures, a broken arm and three broken ribs. Her brother had bruising in nineteen separate places. It emerged that Martin Finnegan had, five years previously, been convicted of causing grievous bodily harm to his own daughter. He pleaded guilty to the assaults on Lindy and her brother and was jailed for four years. Mrs Hancock continued to insist on his competence as a stepfather and announced her intention of standing by him.

It must be stressed that, although this case may look like some sort of atrocity story, our purpose in selecting it was to show that the selection of Mary Walsh as the agent of abuse was the predictable outcome of the reasoning processes which permeate the whole system for the identification and management of mistreatment. Once Lindy Oates had been adequately characterized as a victim, Mary seemed to be the person least responsible for her own actions and therefore most likely to have perpetrated the injuries. Moreover, her prosecution left Mrs Hancock's household/family intact and the children out of state care. The decision gives effect to the liberal principles within which child protection operates.

THE LEGALIZATION OF MISTREATMENT

Case conferences are the point at which two alternative approaches to formulating the character of parents confront each other. The health and social workers are bringing forward cases where their judgements have been formulated on an evolutionary basis through a period of observation. For one reason or another these cases have reached the end of the road in terms of voluntary action, although they may yet be diverted along unforeseen paths, as with the intervention {166} of child guidance in the case of Jayne Wallace (p. 67 {p. 76}). For compulsory measures to be authorized, however, these processual assessments must be translated into one-off statements of the present situation. It is like summarizing a film by means of still pictures. Each still may encapsulate a whole sequence within its frame but the action is decoded only by a detailed inspection of every separate element rather than by a viewing of the unfolding narrative.

We stressed earlier, as analysts, that such translation involved differences of degree rather than of quality. Nevertheless, the participants perceive it as a hazardous process. Two institutional factors seem to be important. First, child mistreatment is a point at which agency staff confront most directly the coercive aspects of their regulatory role. All agents feel threatened by the prospect of giving evidence in court and revealing the compulsion behind liberal intervention.

> As social workers recognise the conflict they are naturally unwilling to use lawyers: recourse to law is a failure for their ideology. Law is seen as producing disharmony and standing in the way of the achievement of social work's legitimate goals. (Phillips 1979: 39)

We have already discussed the humane vision of medicine, nursing and social work. The social and cognitive distance which these occupations place between themselves and the law, even when behaving in the quasi-legal fashion of a case conference, operates not merely to maintain the boundaries of their work but also to preserve the integrity of the liberal ideal, a good society achieved by persuasion rather than compulsion. This is, perhaps, illustrated most graphically in the selective perception of the legal process as unpredictable and uncertain when applications are almost invariably granted.[10] Departmental memories preserve the occasional 'failures' rather than the usual 'successes'.

The second factor is, of course, the relationship between health and welfare workers and the lawyers acting on their behalf, most commonly solicitors on the staff of the relevant local authority. As Cain (1979) has argued, the central task for all lawyers is the translation of personalized troubles into legal terms. By our choice of a case conference where no solicitor was present, we effectively precluded any analysis of their contribution in this respect. It cannot, however, be neglected and forms a substantial part of the next chapter as we explore the general issues of representation which arise in such cases and their implications for the lawyers acting on behalf of each potential party to the proceedings.

8

Representing 'The Facts'

{167}
In the previous chapter, we considered how the various agencies involved with child protection began assembling a case, translating their concerns for a child's welfare into a basis for legal action by the local authority. At the court hearing, the authority must publicly justify the view that coercive measures are necessary and submit its case for testing by advocates for the other parties involved. The legal framework for this is apparently straightforward. The authority brings the child before the court, so that the child becomes the respondent party and thereby entitled to Legal Aid. Parents must be given notice of the hearing but are not parties so that their participation is, theoretically, limited to meeting any allegations made against them in the course of the hearing. If the child is not legally represented, his or her parents may conduct the case against the authority's application.[1]

All this, of course, makes sense in the context of the delinquency cases for which the Children and Young Persons Act 1969 was designed. While it was intended to decriminalize the treatment of juvenile offenders by bringing them under a civil jurisdiction, the traditional model of adversarial justice was maintained. Although the terminology changed, the local authority would, in effect, act as a prosecutor and the child as a defendant, represented either by his or her lawyer or by his or her parent. When one looks at child mistreatment, however, the effects are rather odd. The very reason why the case is being brought is that the authority is concerned for the child's welfare at the hands of his or her parents, yet the child is, theoretically, called to answer for that care, while those responsible for providing it have few official opportunities to speak on their own behalf. Whereas delinquency is, first and foremost, an accusation against the child, mistreatment is essentially a charge against parents (Eekelaar et al. 1982). This perception is the key to understanding the {168} roles of the various advocates who may appear in the course of the proceedings and their strategies in court.

THE LOCAL AUTHORITY SOLICITOR

In many respects, the local authority's advocate has the easiest task. Nevertheless, all lawyers experience some tension between their duties to the court and to their clients, which are complicated here by the degree to which the solicitor sees his client as the whole local authority or as the social services department.

The source of this ambivalence can be located in the development of the solicitor's role in English local government. We have argued elsewhere that, prior to the major reorganization in 1974, lawyers traditionally occupied a central co-ordinating position in local authorities as interpreters of the statutes which defined the powers and duties of both elected councillors and other departments (Murray et al. 1983). In the terminology of the present book, we might describe them as 'keepers of the charter', determining, for most practical purposes, what actions are and are not legitimizable. They were, however, partially displaced in the new management structures devised by the Bains Working Group (1972), which promoted corporatist management teams under an administrative chief executive, reducing lawyers to the status of technical advisers. We argued, though, that the nature of local authorities as 'creatures of statute', bodies which can exist and act only within an expressly defined legal framework, still gave solicitors significant countervailing power and that a continuing struggle to preserve their professional dominance could be observed. In the present instance, the outcome of this struggle was reflected in two different models of the relationship between legal and social services departments.[2]

Under the first of these, Model A, the legal department acted primarily as a provider of advocates. The relationship was rather like that of a barristers' chambers receiving a brief from a solicitor who has prepared the evidence and taken the initial legal steps, although the 'solicitor's' role is played here by social services' courts staff. As is often the case for barristers, the legal department might receive short notice of the hearing date, so that the lawyer's power is restricted to dropping cases which are legally unsound rather than advising on the relevance of proceedings or on the assembly of a persuasive body of evidence. Equally, the lawyer is unable to advise on the legal adequacy of cases which social services' staff think are {169} too weak to pursue. This model seems to persist in those authorities where the legal department has retained its traditional status and continues to be dominated by the interpretation of statutes in the service of committees. Staff are fully occupied on this prestigious work and there is no motive to expand advocacy. Indeed, in one of the fifteen authorities for which we have data, all social services cases had been presented by their courts officer, a former probation officer, until his retirement a year previously. In another, an inner-city Metropolitan Borough, the legal department were involved only with contested cases or appeals.

Model B involves the legal department in decision-making at an earlier stage. A solicitor will normally attend all case conferences and pre-conference discussions with social services staff are likely to be encouraged. The legal department will be represented on the Area Review Committee and may well provide its secretariat. Its solicitors are also likely to be closely involved in the drafting or vetting of section 2 resolutions under the Children Act 1948. This seems to be a newer model: Shire had adopted it since 1974, Borough shortly prior to the fieldwork, while County still operated Model A. It seemed to emerge where the legal department was under pressure from the chief executive's department. This involvement bypassed the corporate management structure but maintained a substantial influence over the social services department and took up otherwise slack legal resources. Solicitors assimilated this to their traditional role as guardians of the authority's reputation in a sensitive or contentious area (Murray et al. 1983).

Plainly, Model B should, in theory, provide for more effective reconciliation of therapeutic and legal approaches. The lawyer acquires a degree of familiarity with clinical and social evidence and its acceptability in court which most case conference participants, as irregular attenders, lack. He can advise on alternative legal remedies such as matrimonial injunctions or wardship which may fit the particular case better than care proceedings. With experience, he may be able to test the courses proposed by others. As one remarked, 'the longer one is involved with this type of case the more one tends to consider alternatives and discuss not strictly legal points'. Moreover, the solicitor may, as Cain (1979) suggests for private practitioners, pick up an acute feeling that 'something ought to be done' and search for some means of achieving this objective even if the case is evidentially weak. It must also be said that the solicitors perceived Model B as more efficient. The senior assistant solicitor in Shire had initially been unenthusiastic: 'I don't believe that before we get to court {170} that I really have a constructive role to play', he told us at our first interview. A year later, however, he claimed:

> We've found that by going to case conferences we have been I think substantially able to cut down on work in that we've been able to make decisions at case conferences whether to go ahead. We've been able to very much decide who are going to be witnesses . . . and to come away from the case conference with a clear idea of what was, who was going to do what and what was going to happen.

The problem for Model B, however, is its inconsistency with traditional legal career lines. In Shire it had broken down shortly before our observations started, was painstakingly rebuilt during the course of our research (a junior solicitor being inducted to take over from the senior assistant should the latter leave) and suffered a further set-back when both left almost simultaneously. We interviewed 14 principal or senior assistant solicitors, three assistant solicitors, and one legal executive with a range of experience from one to 10 years, the mode being five. It was clear, however, that much of the advocacy was delegated. In only three of the 15 areas was social services work the preserve of a single, usually senior assistant, solicitor with occasional help as necessary; in three, there was a senior and a junior; in eight, two juniors; and in one, three juniors. This is a rather unstable system. As Hilgendorf (1981: 34) comments:

> Promotion within the local authority involves moving away from purely legal work to managerial jobs either as head of department or serving the committees of the council and ultimately to county secretary or chief executive. The fairly small number of posts available in any one authority means that promotion is usually dependent on moving to another authority. This structure results in a fairly rapid turnover of solicitors providing services to social workers: perhaps an average stay of three years.

It is a widely held belief that a solicitor's prospects in local government are enhanced by a wide mix of work in his early career and, within this, by the acquisition of committee work. This relates partly to the experience of the traditional role as keeper of the authority's charter and partly to the development of sponsors among elected members. Those of our respondents who did enjoy advocacy and would have liked to continue with it perceived this as a deviant and unrealistic aspiration. The tendency, therefore, was for care proceedings and similar work to be passed down to the newest recruit to {171} the department who would, in turn, delegate them at the earliest opportunity. Such a system could work with adequate supervision but, as our comments on professional forms of organization suggest, this is seldom encountered in practice.

These two organizational forms were loosely associated with two different strategies for advocacy. Some lawyers emphasized their duty towards the social services department, as their client, to present their case in as forceful a manner as ethically possible. This is a typical example from one of our interviews.

> Oh I think the interests of the client come first and in care proceedings my client is the local authority. The child is legally represented, he has a solicitor who looks after his interests and I'm not concerned to put forward arguments on his behalf.

Against this, however, other solicitors tended to take the view that a more dispassionate approach was called for, putting facts before the court rather than arguing a particular case, as we can see in this extract from another interview.

> Our starting point . . . was that, yes, it's not a question of winning or losing. We are sharing our concern with the court about a particular child. I have always thought, and I may look at this thing far too simply, that we really go to court because we are concerned about a child so I think I would say that essentially we would go there in the interests of the child and not in the interests of the social services department at all.

The first of these tended to be more common in Model A type authorities and the latter where Model B operated. On the other hand, these do seem to reflect contrasting philosophies which are quite widely spread in legal culture (Murray et al. 1983). To that extent, neither was wholly incompatible with any particular version of solicitor/social worker relationships. The second solicitor quoted, for instance, was a newcomer with Model B views to a Model A authority.

While the organizational pattern might have an impact on the initial handling of cases, the practical differences in advocacy appeared to be limited. Most of the solicitors we interviewed said they routinely gave a child's solicitor full details of their case, either because they felt this merely anticipated the balanced appraisal of the positive and negative aspects of the child's experiences which they {172} expect to present or because they hoped to co-opt the child's representative in support of their application. All of them were subject to the same pressures to put up a good show in court, to preserve the reputation of the authority or to press the social services' case. It was, for instance, the last solicitor quoted above who told a social worker at a case conference:

> We've got to get this over. We've got to take a slant on this and present our evidence in such a way. Your report says that, as time has gone on, family relationships have improved. I'm not going to ask you that.

Finally, of course, both types of solicitor are essentially working with 'facts' supplied by the social services department and already assembled to support a particular version of the events in question, which the lawyer is unlikely to be able to dispute with any prospect of success. Once on the floor of the court the solicitor is effectively constrained to press the case as best he can within conventional forensic techniques, whatever his initial principled stance.

THE CHILD'S SOLICITOR

As we have seen, the respondent party in care proceedings is the child, who will almost invariably be eligible for legal aid out of public funds. In mistreatment cases, however, children are likely to be too young to approach a solicitor on their own behalf and to give meaningful instructions. Children, then, have solicitors appointed for them by their parents or by the local authority or by the court. All of these, however, raise complex issues for the private practitioner who is presented with the case. He must determine who his client is, what that client's interests are and how these may best be expressed. The first two of these are unfamiliar tasks within the conventions of fee-for-service practice where, as Cain (1979) shows, there is usually no doubt whose instructions the solicitor is supposed to follow and what constitutes the most desirable option. Such difficulties are compounded by the inexperience of the solicitors. This is not a matter of the cases being handled by junior partners or assistant solicitors but of their sheer rarity.[3] Even relatively senior members of a firm may never previously have encountered them. In departmentalized practices, they seem to be assigned either to a family department, most of whose work is in divorce, or to a criminal department, because of the {173} amount of advocacy involved. Neither of these offers a particularly appropriate type of expertise.

In Shire, all but one of the solicitors who appeared for the children in our sample had originally been approached by parents.[4] Several of them discovered that legal aid was available exclusively in the child's name only when they applied for it, a situation which was familiar to all our local authority solicitors in talking about private practitioners in their area. Whether at that point or previously, then, the solicitor must decide whether he is going to advise them to find their own solicitor at their own expense. This dilemma is, of course, confounded by the frequent inability of parents to pay for independent representation. A further pressure on the solicitor may derive from his own economic interests in maintaining his firm's reputation with potential clients.

Only two of the solicitors actually took a strong line against the parents and pressed them to seek advice elsewhere. In one the result was that parents were left wholly unrepresented. In the other, the solicitor offered free representation by a partner from another office of his firm but the parents eventually went to a different firm which also gave its services without charge.[5] Two of the solicitors decided to treat the issue of a legal aid certificate in the child's name as a legal fiction and to accept instructions from the parents. The remainder, the majority, attempted with varying degrees of success to take an independent view of the child's interests while simultaneously assisting and advising parents. How did this work in practice?

As we have suggested, one of the basic problems for the child's solicitor is in defining an appropriate outcome for his client. He has to represent someone who is normally too young to give instructions, whom he has never seen and about whom he has no direct knowledge. Only three of the solicitors made systematic independent attempts to collect information: one interviewed neighbours, another visited the child in his short-term foster home and a third, much to the consternation of social services, turned up to a case conference. Most of the solicitors took some sort of soundings from their local authority counterparts. The value of this tended to vary with the degree to which the child's solicitor could persuade the local authority's solicitor of his independence from the parents' viewpoint. This, in turn, was often related to the extent to which the private practitioner was prepared to accept education in the technicalities of these proceedings from the local authority's lawyer, who was, of course, far more familiar with the procedure. In fact, towards the close of our study, Shire adopted a policy of deliberate accessibility, {174} partly in order to save time-wasting in court as the less-experienced private practitioners found out what they were supposed to be doing.

Where information was available, there was no guarantee that the private practitioner would be able to interpret it. A lawyer's training does not equip him to assess evidence of child development, for instance. Much seemed to depend on chance life-experiences, being a parent or having married a social worker or a doctor. Only one of the solicitors had attempted to engage an independent expert to advise him on medical evidence and his efforts had failed, partly through the unwillingness of local doctors to appear against a recognized specialist and partly because the low fee available under legal aid was insufficient to bring anyone from out of the area.

The outcome was that the solicitors tended, willy-nilly, to end up presenting some version of the parents' case. They are generally the most accessible source of data and interpretations. Moreover, by adopting these, even with some underlying scepticism, the solicitor can present himself as independent of the local authority. We can bring this out by looking at the actions of one solicitor appearing for a child in a case where the forensic dispute turned upon whether serious brain injuries to the child had been caused by excessive shaking by the parents or, as the parents alleged, by another child falling on the injured child's head. This extract is from the solicitor's closing address at the court hearing.

> That's the case as far as Mr and Mrs Dickens is concerned, I should make it clear that I am strictly representing Samantha, so if Mr and Mrs Dickens would like to say a few words, they are entitled to do so. The weight of the council's evidence has been that Samantha was possibly ill-treated, possibly on a single occasion, just one single incident.

There's no dispute over the medical facts. Dr Salmon was kind enough to say that the injuries could have resulted from one single squeeze or excessively violent movement. The conclusion you are asked to draw is that the Dickenses were the perpetrators of that act . . . . You've not only got to be satisfied that the injuries occurred but also that Mr and Mrs Dickens caused them deliberately and that it could have been avoided. You are not in a position to feel that Samantha would be best served by being taken into care, but that the council has made out its case. Although you may be unhappy about her treatment, you have got to be satisfied that Mr and Mrs Dickens caused the ill-treatment . . . to do this you must find a connection between them and the injuries. There is no direct evidence that they're directly responsible; there's no first-hand evidence that this is what happened. Mrs Dickens was prepared to admit that something could {175} have happened by accident, but these things are always happening in the home; you must find that the injuries were done deliberately. There is no direct evidence of this. Mr and Mrs Dickens have provided explanations for their own behaviour; you have formed your views on the way they gave their own evidence; you may think that Mrs Dickens is a loving, kind and considerate mother and if you want independent evidence of this (it is) confirmed by Mrs Cox's (the health visitor) evidence that there was no apparent strife. Terry (the other child) appeared well cared for and made good progress. In the end it comes down to whether you feel that these two people before you are of the nature that they could lose control of themselves and deliberately inflict injuries of this nature. Unless you are satisfied of that you ought not to make the order that is being requested. It is a legal decision you've got to make, not an emotional one. If you have reservations in your mind about their child care, that is not relevant. You must be satisfied as a matter of law that the council has made out its case. There is no evidence of a history of ill-treatment against this family apart from this unfortunate incident. I invite you to say that the council has not made out its case.

The solicitor insists on a high standard of proof by the council, reformulates the definitions of the 1969 Act in a stringent fashion – it is not necessary to show that the injuries were *deliberately* inflicted – suggests the acceptance of explanations favourable to the parents where a conflict of evidence exists, stresses their good character and asks the court to ignore evidence of their general quality of child care. He concludes by suggesting that the case has not been adequately proven.[6]

When we interviewed this solicitor some days later, however, this is how he described his position:

> . . . in fact, my view of what the child's interests were was really that having heard all the evidence, that a care order ought to be made, which of course may not tie with what I said to them at the end but you see I deliberately didn't, in saying what I had to say to them at the end, I did not urge them very strongly to come to the opinion that a care order shouldn't be made. I really just tried, perhaps not very successfully, but

tried to indicate the points that they ought to take into account in considering whether a care order ought to be made or whether the council had made out its case. It's a very difficult position because clearly the Dickenses, and that's really why I wanted to make sure throughout the case that the Dickenses asked their own questions and then at the end had their own say, so that they couldn't say later on that I didn't put a strong enough case for them or didn't {176} make certain points to the magistrates which I should have done, I didn't want them to be able to say that because obviously I was not really acting on their behalf. It's a very odd situation to be in, but I think one might possibly, if one had been acting for the Dickenses rather than the child, have attacked the doctor a bit more. I mean I don't quite know exactly how I would go about it, but one could've been a bit more scathing, perhaps, about his opinion and about how long he'd been qualified, I don't know. You know, I didn't think I could but I suppose if one had been acting for the Dickenses one could've tried something of that.

As another solicitor put it, the differences the lawyer sees between acting for the parents and acting for the child may lie not so much in the questions he asks as in the questions he does *not* ask.

As Hilgendorf (1981: 118-9) also reports, both private practice and local authority solicitors thought it was appropriate that the authority's witnesses should have their evidence tested by cross-examination. Indeed, where a solicitor was not appointed, the belief in this principle was so strong in all three study areas that either the local authority or the juvenile court clerk, at the authority's prompting, might invite one to act for the child.[7] The difficulty for the child's solicitor is that he is frequently convinced of the merits of the authority's application. As we have seen, the whole pre-court screening has the effect of sifting out all but the strongest or most desperate cases. Just as the authority usually persuades the court of the merits of its application, so too are the child's lawyers generally brought to see the unavoidable necessity of coercive intervention. This was conceded even by the partners in a metropolitan practice specializing in children's advocacy. Despite adopting a more explicitly adversarial approach with extensive use of independent expert witnesses, they had seldom found the case or the disposition to be unjustifiable at the end of the day.

Nevertheless, none of the private practitioners seemed happy openly to endorse the application. While it does not inevitably follow that the solicitor should conclude by formally opposing the case, as in the Dickens extract, it is easy to see how drawing attention to the legal criteria which must be satisfied can take on the appearance of opposition. The solicitor may know that he is pulling his punches in cross-examination but this is not necessarily obvious to anybody else in the courtroom. His accommodation to the roles available within the particular adversarial framework created by the 1969 Act leads him to appear to argue against his own belief that the authority's application is not in his own client's best interests.[8] It is {177} important that these remarks are not interpreted as critical of the adversarial framework *per se*; what creates the problem is the way in which it opposes the child's interests to the local authority's actions, when, as one local authority solicitor put it, 'If we, as the local authority, were not there in the child's interest what the hell were we doing in court anyway?' Commonsensically, the adversarial contest is between the local authority and the child's parents over whether the quality of care offered by the latter is adequate.

REPRESENTATION OF THE PARENT OR GUARDIAN

This perception of the nature of the contest was reflected throughout our interviews. Local authority solicitors constantly switched their answers to interview questions about children's representation to criticize parents' restricted legal rights and exclusion from legal aid. We have already mentioned the availability of free representation, while in some courts we observed deliberate manipulation of legal aid rules to reimburse solicitors. Alternatively, clerks would sometimes step out of their normal role to cross-examine witnesses on behalf of parents. A minority of parents can, of course, afford to pay their own costs (up to £200 at 1981 prices). In the majority of hearings we observed, however, parents were unrepresented.

The main effect of this was to increase the pressure on the child's advocate. Despite the restricted role which the rules of court theoretically allocate to parents, we did not see a single instance where any parent, represented or not, was ever prevented from asking any question, making any statement or calling any witness he or she chose to – further evidence, of course, for the commonsense perception of the contest. The problem is, though, that parents lack the forensic skills of a solicitor which may prevent them from using these opportunities to the best advantage. Parents became conspicuously angry and frustrated by this, disrupting both the solicitors', the clerks' and the magistrates' desire to construct a sense of justice being done. Where it was the parents who originally approached the child's solicitor he often seemed to retain a feeling of residual loyalty, although they had ceased to be his clients. This might be reflected in him assisting parents to formulate questions by way of cross-examination but had a more significant influence on his own approach. Again, it was a reason for treating the local authority's case with public scepticism. As one child's solicitor commented in an interview, {178}

> Yes, I mean the longer the case went, well not the longer the case went, I don't think that, no, I think as soon as I heard the medical evidence I was convinced that if I really was acting for the child *and doing no*

more I ought really perhaps at that stage to have thrown one's hand in. (emphasis added)

Taken together with the factors discussed earlier, the child's solicitor almost invariably ended up as a *de facto* advocate for the parents.

If we look at what the principal actors were doing, then, as opposed to what the statutes and rules prescribe, we find that these hearings were organized as adversarial confrontations between the local authority and the parents of the allegedly mistreated child. The imperfections arose from the fact that accounting controls on the disbursement of public money meant that legal aid rules could not be broken to give parents professional representation. In all other respects, parents were treated as full parties to the case. However, this does not necessarily constitute an argument for simply adding parents to the list of those eligible for legal aid. There are important questions to be asked about the appropriateness of having three lawyers in court, all paid for out of public funds. We shall return to these in the final chapter, when we seek to evaluate the present state of affairs in the light of these data.

9

Charges and Defences

{179}
The naive observer might assume that, in any case involving child mis-treatment, the central issue in a court hearing must be the actual condition of the child. The reality is somewhat different, as we might predict from the argument of this book. If we define 'the central issue' as the matters which are actually *in dispute* before the court, we find that this has much more to do with the explanation of that condition, specifically the degree to which the child's parents can be formulated as the sort of people who could be capable of bringing such a condition about. A further set of subsidiary arguments may sometimes arise around the child's future in care. None of these, however, is a specifically *legal* argument in the sense that it is a debate about the substantive interpretation of statutes. In this respect care proceedings are typical of lower courts in Anglo-American systems (cf. Silbey 1981; Feeley 1979). Their legal quality derives far more from the rules of argument and evidence which are invoked within them.

> . . . magistrates' courts cases typically require few analytical legal skills. Most often little law is argued; instead the case will normally be argued around questions of *evidence*, even in those cases which are contested. (Mungham and Thomas 1979: 174 original emphasis)

Before scrutinizing the adversarial confrontation, then, it may be profita-ble to survey the impact of the law of evidence on these proceedings in general.

THE RULES OF EVIDENCE

Two constraints were perceived as important by the participants in our study as restrictions on their ability to press their case in care proceedings. {180} These related to the rules on hearsay and on the admissibility of expert evidence.

Civil proceedings in magistrates' courts were excluded from the gen-eral liberalization of the law relating to hearsay under the Civil Evidence

Act 1968. This means, in theory, that they are still covered by the stricter common law rule that, broadly speaking, only oral evidence given by a person at the proceedings may be admitted as evidence of any fact stated. Statements about what a third party said or wrote cannot be accepted to prove that fact, although they can be used to cast doubt on the credibility or veracity of that person if he or she now appears as a witness and gives inconsistent evidence. The applicability of these basic restrictions to care proceedings has been upheld in recent Divisional Court decisions (e.g. *Humberside County Council* v. *DPR* [1977] and *Shropshire County Council* v. *PJS (A child)* [1975]). This could create difficulties in care proceedings, where much of the relevant data may come from kin or neighbours who are reluctant to appear as witnesses or from agency records whose authors cannot easily be traced.

In practice, however, the courts we observed tended to operate within the spirit of the 1968 reforms rather than the letter of the common law, a practice which has been tacitly encouraged by the Divisional Court. The 1968 Act allowed parties to introduce official records without producing their authors, provided that the latter were under a duty to compile them. We never observed any challenge to the admissibility of such histories. A few of the local authority solicitors we interviewed did report some difficulties as a result of staff turnover:

LAS: The only problems we have had (on evidence) is where there have been trainee social workers. One of the social workers has gone away somewhere and can't in fact give evidence and therefore the only records are that person's notes in the file and notes of conversations which are hearsay. I have had problems like that in one or two cases.

JE: How do you deal with that?

LAS: Well, there are different views taken. I managed to persuade one magistrates' court that these were records compiled by people and that person is now unavailable as in civil proceedings, therefore someone else could read from these records. And one court accepted that and the other court hasn't accepted, so if you do get into that sort of situation then we can have problems with the case. {181}

There seem to be no recorded superior court decisions on this point. The court which refused to accept such evidence was probably, strictly speaking, applying the law correctly.[1] However, it is not clear that widespread dissatisfaction exists and we suspect, in the absence of appeals, that most courts are conceding the moral legitimacy of admitting this kind of material, provided, as in the cases we observed, it is used circumspectly and alongside direct evidence of current allegations. It looks very much as if there is a widespread acceptance of such evidence, although in the cases we saw, it was always introduced with some caution and in the context of direct evidence of currently alleged mistreatment.

More to the point is the elaboration of the common law on hearsay in the *Humberside* case. The main issue was the admissibility of statements by the mother's cohabitee, a *de facto* guardian, that he had ill-treated the child in question. One of the established exceptions to the hearsay rule is that an admission by a party to the proceedings which is against his or her interests can be accepted. The reasoning is straightforward: while we should be careful about accepting secondhand statements, if their author is available in court as a party, he or she has an opportunity to explain them. It was argued in this particular case that the cohabitee's statements were inadmissible because only the local authority and the child were parties. However, as we saw in the previous chapter, the magistrates' courts do tend, in practice, to treat parents as parties, with the sanction of superior court decisions. The same outcome was achieved in this case, albeit by a curious route, when Lord Widgery, CJ, held that the limited common law exception in respect of 'parties' should not apply in care proceedings because they were 'non-adversary, non-party proceedings' and that the restriction 'would produce a nonsense because if there are no parties to the proceedings then the question of whether the admission is made by a party or not does not arise at all'. It was sufficient that the statement was made by the child's guardian. The statements should, therefore, be admitted and the case returned to the magistrates for decision.[2]

Whatever the logical basis for this ruling, its effect has been to sanction the presentation of a good deal of evidence that would otherwise be inadmissible. As one local authority solicitor remarked:

> What I do if there is a bit of a problem here (on hearsay) is I get the social worker to pump mum or dad or guardian because that added to whatever the mum or dad or guardian says normally we can get it in. {182}

By getting the social worker to put allegations to parents and note their responses, these statements can be introduced within the *Humberside* principles without falling foul of the hearsay rules.

The second major restraint is the common law rule excluding evidence of opinion by persons other than experts. If such evidence were generally admitted, it could lead to an evasion of the hearsay rule, since the opinion might reflect nothing more than hearsay (Cross and Tapper 1979: 452). Should, however, the court accept a witness as an expert, his opinion may be allowed, even if it is on the question to be decided by the court, provided that the factual basis of the opinion has been proven by admissible evidence. There are no *a priori* rules about who is or is not to be considered as an expert. This is a matter for the court's discretion so that, for instance, we observed a number of cases where experienced foster-parents were accorded this status while inexperienced professionals were not.

Much seems to depend on the attitude of the local authority's solicitor. Doctors and health visitors seldom found their credentials challenged but a minority of the solicitors were reluctant to treat social workers as experts. As one put it, 'their judgement doesn't convince us; why should it convince the magistrate?' More typical, however, is the declaration of another solicitor that 'we always treat our social workers as being expert witnesses' or a third asserting, 'I take the view that (social workers) are professional witnesses and this has never been questioned by the clerk'. All of the lawyers agreed that the acceptability of a particular individual might be contingent on his or her standing or experience but, if the advocate presented the person as an expert, in his or her judgement, this was unlikely to be challenged directly. In the hearings we observed, solicitors for the child or parents might question individual social workers about their experience, apparently in an indirect attempt to discredit their standing, but we did not see any categorical attacks on social workers as a class. Once again, the general discretion of the magistrates' courts has recently been reaffirmed by the Divisional Court, in *F* v. *Suffolk County Council* [1981], which held that evidence on mental development from a psychiatrist was not essential given the availability of material from an experienced social worker and an experienced health visitor.

A third common law rule which might seem important, at first sight, is that which states that, in civil proceedings, evidence of the character of the parties is inadmissible (cf. Phipson 1976, para. 527). The justification is that in most civil cases, breach of contract, for instance, the parties' moral disposition is indeed irrelevant. {183} Wigmore (1940: 477), however, notes that:

> . . . it may be maintained that the reasons of policy apply in ordinary civil cases only and that where a moral interest is marked and prominent in the nature of the issue, the defendant's good moral character should be received, as in criminal cases.

As Graham Hall and Mitchell (1978: 74) have observed, in care proceedings 'the disposition or character of a child's parent will always be relevant to the issue of the child's need for care or control. It will sometimes also be relevant to the proof of the primary condition'. Character evidence is always allowable in respect of a witness's credibility, so that a lawyer may make imputations against a parent who gives evidence. Finally, as Wigmore (1940: 513) warns, evidence of character is not the same as evidence of habits and conduct, from which, of course, the court may still draw inferences about a person's moral disposition. As we shall see, however, the acceptability of evidence on parental character never seems to be made into an issue: indeed it is often the central substantive dispute.

It cannot be stressed too strongly that the rules of evidence sit rather lightly on care proceedings. This is not to say that they are ignored or disregarded: rather, as we saw in our discussion of representation, the participants in the hearing are operating within more general notions of fairness or equity which are only partially coincident with the statutory framework, although, of course, when disputes arise, resolutions may be achieved only be resort to legality. Even here, though, the rulings have consistently supported the commonsense organization of care proceedings rather than the strict construction of the statutes. The courts we observed were persistently hostile to attempts to introduce technicalities, a finding which was supported by our interviews with solicitors and court clerks. We shall present an example later in this chapter, but the approach was perhaps best captured by a clerk who remarked that it was only a desperate solicitor who relied on points of law.

THE COURT HEARING

It is, then, with such considerations in mind that we approach the examination of court hearings. We shall begin by discussing the evidence led by the local authorities as applicants and its treatment, before proceeding to consider the nature of parental defences. The {184} local authorities' evidence can be divided into three elements: the child's condition, the competence and character of the parents and the child's future if the application were to succeed.

The condition of the child

Court hearings almost invariably began with medical evidence as to the child's condition at the point of intervention. As we saw previously, this is often presented in an impersonal factual form, although necessarily depending upon normative judgements linking clinical observations of an individual case to probabilistic generalizations about the likelihood of that case occurring by chance. This tends to be most apparent in neglect cases where, for instance, a child's weight gain can be matched against a normal distribution. Patterns of gain and loss, as the child goes in and out of substitute care, and metabolic tests, can be used to assess the relative credibility of parental negligence, illness or heredity as the cause of failure to thrive. Such findings are difficult to challenge and, in fact, we never saw a solicitor seriously question them.

Abuse cases were more contentious because, as we have observed, it is hard to rule out alternative explanations solely on clinical grounds, except in so far as tests are usually carried out to exclude clotting disorders or brittle bones. Even here, however, we saw only three solicitors in two cases, Dickens and Leonard, seriously cross-examine medical witnesses, and all that they could do was to advance the parents' own explanations, which the doctors simply rejected.[3] In both of these, as in other abuse cases, the local authority sought to substantiate its allegations by placing the child's physical condition into the context of the parent's general competence and moral character, just as we have shown throughout the decision-making process. The hearings, in effect, came to depict the children as neglectfully raised *and* abused, a shift which was particularly marked when the Leonard case was appealed, as we show later.

The least reliance on specialist evidence occurred in those cases where the child's emotional or psychological development was the focus for concern. In the Dawson case from our County data (pp. 83-5 {pp. 92-4}), for instance, the evidence of physical neglect was supplemented by descriptions of the two-year-old boy deliberately banging his head against furniture and rocking back and forth. The interpretation of this as evidence of psychological disturbance was given by an (unqualified) family welfare worker and a senior social worker. In two Shire cases, Leonard and Illingworth, social workers and, in one {185} case, a foster-mother drew the inference that excessive friendliness towards strangers, destructive play and failure to cry signified emotional disturbance. In a third Shire case, Canning, a social worker and a health visitor testified about the likely effects on a child's emotional development of a minor act of sexual abuse (a five-year-old boy had allegedly been made to grasp a man's testicles).

Several factors seem to be involved in the apparent consensus about the validity of non-specialist evidence. Firstly, psychiatrists and psychologists characteristically like to observe children over a period of time. For both the local authority and the parents, however, time is a real pressure: both want a quick decision on the child's fate in order to minimize a recognizedly damaging period of uncertainty. Secondly, most local authority social workers in all three study areas were highly critical of the possible contribution from psychology or psychiatry, occupations whose relevant skills were thought merely to duplicate their own.[4] Thirdly, the solicitors distrusted 'expert' opinion on such matters. They tended to feel that any person experienced with children could form a commonsense judgement about the normality or otherwise of any particular child against the background of that experience. The same can be said for the adverse effects of a child's general environment, which again were seen as a matter for common sense rather than specialized knowledge.

The consequence of the definition of child development as a non-specialist matter was, of course, that anybody might properly argue about it. When allied to the inherent ambiguity of evidence for abusive treatment, it reinforced the pressure towards making parental character the central issue and, in effect, replaying the sequence of assessments we have already described: allegations of deviation from conditions or behaviour based on a socially constructed view of normality and the attribution of responsibility to parents. The difference here is that parents now have some opportunity to formulate a specific defence by means of justifications and excuses which seek to deny or mitigate that responsibility.

Parental competence and character

As we have already seen, parental character may be assessed in many ways and it seems redundant merely to reiterate chapters 3 and 4. We have, therefore, chosen to concentrate on one particular case, Jamie Leonard. This case is especially relevant because it illustrates our contention about the essential ambiguity of injuries and {186} because it was strongly contested by a solicitor, giving his services to the child's parents without charge, and subsequently appealed. As a result the case incorporates features which occurred throughout our data and may be treated as paradigmatic.

The central question, it will be recalled, was whether a burn to the ear of a three-year-old boy had been caused by his mother applying a hot iron or by the child himself in play. While the doctors disagreed with the mother's explanation, they could not unequivocally reject it from the nature and extent of the injuries. As we have already stated, this uncertainty had led to one of the rare debates between doctors at the case conference and when the matter came to court both gave evidence. This itself was unusual, especially as the first doctor to see Jamie was an experienced general practitioner with a strong specialist interest in child mistreatment.[5] However, it was known that the parents intended to argue that this interest led him to over-diagnose abuse and neglect, and the admitting house officer from the Victoria Hospital was also called. Two comments are worth making here. Firstly, the rarity of such duplication of evidence indicates the participants' own sense of the immunity of clinical data to serious challenge except in exceptional circumstances where essentially nonclinical attacks could be made. Secondly, the sensitivity to the possible criticism of the GP in the Leonard case is a further sign of the cautious orientation built into the agency system. Its defence requires that the workers involved in the case can, if necessary, show that coercion is a reluctant last step. Here, then, the alleged over-enthusiasm of one doctor might be countered by the independent testimony of another with no known special interest at stake.

Both of these doctors gave evidence which was fairly closely confined to the questions of the extent of the injury and its congruence with various possible causal explanations. They were closely questioned by both the parents' and the child's solicitor, who elicited a discrepancy in their accounts of bruising on the child's body. This could have been explained by the lapse of time between the two examinations but introduced a further element of uncertainty. The medical witnesses, however, gave their evidence after a social worker's characterization of the social context of the child. Again, this was uncommon, although it also occurred in Parry, where a health visitor played a similar role. If we recall our general argument, we can suggest that, whereas the normal procedure was to attempt to present clinical descriptions unambiguously and follow this with social evidence as to how they should be explained, in these {187} cases ambiguous or disputable clinical descriptions were preceded by social evidence to set a frame in which they could be heard as less disputable.

The social worker stated that she felt that the child was overactive in a manner 'not typical of a child of that age'; that the parents were concerned 'to punish rather than to understand' him; that their income was low and their marital relationship strained. She said that 'they would sometimes agree that they needed help, but would not accept the suggestions that I made'. She concluded by saying that they were doing their best, but that 'the parents' interests always came before those of the children'. We can see, in this single piece of testimony, a number of features which, we have argued earlier, characterize the identification of mistreatment. The burn by itself would not be sufficient to allow such an identification, let alone establish it in a court. A picture is built up of a flawed relationship between parents and child. The possible excuse of love in the relationship is undercut by reference to the child's apparent emotional insecurity and the punitive attitudes of the parents. They are responsible for this state of affairs: they may not be able to help their economic plight, but were showing distinct lack of success in managing their marital relationship. Most significant of all, they have not co-operated when help was offered, as (it is implied) any reasonable parent would do. These factors combine to allow the final, overall judgement to be made on their parental incompetence: they place their own interests before those of the children.

The parents' solicitor attempted to deal with this by attacking the social worker's competence as a childless unmarried woman to make judgements about children and families. In leading his own evidence, he called the child's foster-mother and a neighbour. The neighbour gave evidence of the parents' normality by the standards of the neighbourhood and pressed the allegation of undue zeal against the GP by describing his intervention in relation to one of her own children whom she had recovered from a place of safety order. The foster-mother's evidence proved to be a mixed blessing. Although she spoke with immense practical experience, the substance of what she had to say was that Jamie was a rather disturbed child who had responded to her skilled management. Despite the parents' solicitor's attempts to minimize the significance of her contribution, all the participants we spoke to treated this as the critical material in swaying the magistrates towards granting the authority's application for a care order.

This case was one of the two in our study which went to appeal. {188} The route for appeals lies to the Crown Court, which deals with more serious criminal cases, reflecting the delinquency-oriented basis of the 1969 Act. Despite the higher level of legal input – a professional judge and representation by barristers – the effect of this further challenge was to place the social evidence even more firmly at the heart of the case.[6] Here is an early exchange between the local authority barrister, the general practitioner and the judge:[7]

LAB: Have you dealt with the family since (the incident)?

GP: Yes.

LAB: With the other child, Suzy?

GP: Yes.

LAB: Have you seen her on one or more occasions since then?

PB: I must object here. We're only dealing with Jamie in this case; it's not right and proper to discuss other members of the family in this way.

JUDGE: Well, I think we're finding out about the environment to which we're being asked to send Jamie back.

PB: But I think it's only right that the matters of this case should be restricted to the child, Jamie.

JUDGE: Well, if you wish to maintain your objection, I shall have to rule on it, but I must say that I'm bound to take a view, if I were to think you were trying to shut out evidence here. I think that in this case we have to consider the present situation, although it may be adverse to your client's interests.

PB: In the circumstances I must withdraw.

Notice here how the attempt to raise a technical point is cut off by the judge making what appears to be a commonsensical rather than a legal ruling. The parents' barrister is put in a position where he must lose: either the evidence is admitted or his stand on a technicality will be treated as indicating that his client has something to hide. This should recall our earlier discussion of compliance and moral character. A reasonable person will comply with the dictates of common sense since he or she has nothing to conceal. Conversely, {189} attempts at concealment can justify suspicions about the sincerity of the moral claims being made. In the present case, the local authority barrister proceeded to elicit that the general practitioner had been called to see the second child the previous night and had found bruises on her which he thought had been caused by slapping.

As the appeal progressed, the social evidence expanded. The social worker augmented her previous contribution with statements to the effect that Mrs Leonard would often be in her night-clothes late in the morning, that 'the whole house smelt' and that there was 'a lack of capable management'. To this evidence on the material condition of the household was added a detailed moral inquiry. The couple's marital relationship, a minor element at the initial hearing, had deteriorated to the point of a divorce petition being filed but it was now claimed that a reconciliation had taken place. While an examination of this in court could be justified by reference to the 'care or control' test and the child's future prospects, it was clear that the authority's attempts to show that this reconciliation was a sham were also directed at establishing Mrs Leonard's general untrustworthiness as a witness and destroying the credibility of her account of the iron incident. This line of attack surfaced at several points, as in the following extract:

LAB: Were there ever other people staying overnight at Mrs Harper's? (a neighbour of the mother with whom the mother was living in her husband's absence. CSLS)

MRS L: Well, there was me.

LAB: Apart from you?

MRS L: Well, Connie stayed occasionally.

LAB: Anybody else?

MRS L: Mrs Harper's boyfriend.

LAB: And was there anybody else?

MRS L: No.

LAB: Has there been anybody else when Mrs Godfrey (a Family Aide CSLS) has come in the morning?

MRS L: No. {190}

It is difficult to catch the tone of innuendo in this passage, but neither of the observers nor, we presume, the judge was in any doubt that Mrs Leonard was being accused of sleeping with other men in her husband's absence and of lying in her answers. This effect derived partly from a change of pace by the barrister, in that this sequence was run more slowly than other parts of the examination, and partly from the inferences which listeners were projected as drawing through the fact that the barrister felt he could warrantably ask these questions. Any listener could suppose that the barrister must know *something* to Mrs Leonard's disadvantage and her apparently evasive answers could be heard as acknowledging that without admitting it. In so far as she did not admit what she appeared to acknowledge, her credibility could be questioned. Later in his cross-examination, the barrister dealt with this more frontally.

LAB: Have you changed your mind about the reconciliation?

MRS L: No.

LAB: Are you sure you're telling the truth here?

MRS L: Yes.

LAB: It's not always true that you've been honest, though.

MRS L: What do you mean by that?

LAB: Haven't you recently been in court for claiming supplementary benefit for Jamie while he's been in the care of the local authority?

MRS L: Yes.

JUDGE: And you've been claiming benefit for Jamie?

MRS L: Yes.

JUDGE: Did you do it deliberately?

MRS L: Well, I was claiming it before Jamie went into care; I didn't tell them he was taken into care.

LAB: Weren't you also concerned with Mrs Harper and her boyfriend in a case involving a stolen motor car?

MRS L: I was offered a lift in a stolen car. {191}

JUDGE: Who had the car been stolen by?

MRS L: Ron stole the car; that's Mrs Harper's boyfriend, and he offered me a lift in it and I went to see Jamie.

LAB: Mrs Leonard, it seems that you've not been behaving very sensibly of late.

MRS L: No.

We must not be understood as suggesting that the social services have intervened *solely* because they have adversely evaluated the competence or moral character of the parents, or that the court is being asked, directly or by implication, to make the desired order only on the basis of a similar evaluation. As we have shown, evidence of this kind provides a necessary context for the interpretation of clinical evidence, whether in or out of court. These attacks deal with the vital issue of parental incorrigibility, that there is no choice but to intervene coercively because these parents are fundamentally incapable of voluntary compliance. It is this question which accounts for the following passage, again relating to Jamie's sister, whose welfare is not officially before the court.

LAB: Wasn't Suzy in hospital shortly after she was born?

MRS L: Well she was about eight months old.

LAB: And you discharged her?

MRS L: Yes.

LAB: Why was that?

MRS L: Because there was nothing wrong with her.

LAB: Is that what the doctor said?

MRS L: She was losing weight and the social worker had her admitted to find out why. The doctor said there was nothing wrong with her.

JUDGE: You did take her out against the doctor's advice?

MRS L: I asked the doctor if there was anything wrong.

JUDGE: You took her out against advice. {192}

MRS L: He said that they couldn't find anything wrong.

LAB: But you were not prepared to accept their advice that she shouldn't go?

MRS L: I signed Suzy out because there was nothing wrong with her.

Mrs Leonard's barrister was well aware of the centrality of this issue. He specifically asked her whether, despite her past attitudes, she would be prepared to accept help now, and the only question asked of her by the representative for the child was whether she would be willing to 'go to a Centre to learn more about child care'. The mother's counsel subsequently called witnesses to testify to her character, and when the judge asked what their evidence was directed to, the barrister replied: 'To Mrs Leonard's ability to co-operate with the helping services.' This theme recurred throughout the cases we observed. We saw, for example, the paediatrician in the Illingworth case adding to her description of the condition of the child as observed in hospital: 'I must emphasize that her withdrawal (from hospital) was against the hospital advice', and the social worker in the same case telling the court that Mrs Illingworth had told him that 'these were her methods of child care and they weren't going to alter them'; the social worker in the Marryat case stated that the mother always found 'some excuse' for not attending at the clinic and a good deal was made of the aggressive attitude of the parents to social workers in Dickens.

Conversely, we see the parents, either in person or through their (or the 'child's') legal representative, endeavouring to persuade the court that, whatever may have been the case in the past, they are now ready to cooperate with the authorities. This argument was central to the other, successful, appeal in our study, that of the Conrads, whose case has already been outlined (pp. 84-7 {pp. 94-7}). The family and the local authority had reached an agreement prior to the magistrates' hearing that the authority would settle for a supervision order in exchange for a public commitment by Mr Conrad to spend more time with his family, either by working from home or taking them abroad with him. Unfortunately, we were unable to observe the hearing, where a care order was made, but the Conrads' solicitor and the local authority's solicitor both told us that Mr Conrad had made an unfavourable impression by lecturing the court on his importance as an export earner, an analysis which was supported by a second-hand report of some rather indiscreet comments by one of the magistrates {193} at a subsequent social occasion. The outcome of the hearing was the making of a care order.

At the appeal, however, both parents were closely questioned by their own barrister and by the children's barrister, who favoured their return home, to establish that they recognized the legitimacy of the authority's intervention and were capable of future compliance. This example is from the examination of Mrs Conrad by the children's barrister.

CB: The local authority have a duty under law to look after children in their area. Do you see the course of action that the local authority took, especially through Mr Brittan and other social workers, in taking the children into voluntary care at Bidney as reasonable?

MRS CONRAD: Yes. That was reasonable.

CB: After your first overdose was it reasonable that they should take a Place of Safety Order?

MRS C: I was less happy about that.

CB: Do you see their position?

MRS C: Yes.

CB: Was it reasonable?

MRS C: At the time it was reasonable.

CB: Somebody was crying wolf and they had to take notice (. . .)

The same themes could be observed in the Conrads' examination by their own barrister, as he explored the issues of disposal to which we shall turn shortly:

PB: If no order were made, would you still make use of the social services?

MRS C: Probably, yes. Although there would be less need if my husband were at home.

PB: Would you feel the need to see (the psychiatrist)?

MRS C: He says he doesn't want to see me again. {194}

JUDGE: Unless something is wrong?

MRS C: Yes.

PB: Have you felt the need to see him?

MRS C: No.

PB: Because of the trauma of the children being taken away into care, has that affected your determination to cope?

MRS C: Yes, definitely. It has pulled me up and given me a shock.

PB: Is that the support of the care order, as (senior social worker) suggests?

MRS C: It is not the support of the care order. I would rather be without that.

PB: After the experience of the last six months, you will be more sensitive in future; your eyes have been opened?

MR C: I think so; regardless of any external orders, I am determined not to allow this situation to arise again. For personal reasons, I will not separate myself from my family again.

PB: If no order is made in the future, and things began to build up again, what would you do?

MR C: We would look for whatever co-operation we could get from the social services agencies.

(...)

MR C: Any kind of order is a hindrance. But if it was felt that there were grounds a supervision order would be preferable. It would give us more security. A feeling of greater control over our own destinies (. . .) little things make it slightly infuriating – to tell people what you are doing all the time, not being treated as a responsible adult, being treated as though you were a child yourself. Like today, we wouldn't have brought the children to court but the County Council insisted. They are with us but they are not our children.

In effect, Mr Conrad is asserting the implicit values which we saw the social workers using in chapter 4 – independence, responsibility, autonomy. {195} His credibility is built up by references to his social standing ('We are not dealing with a recalcitrant Bermondsey docker here'); the fact that they are an intelligent family ('We are dealing with two highly intelligent children with parents who, when Mrs Conrad is all right, are more than adequate. They are materially well off and the children are happy') in which there are good interpersonal relations ('Do you get the impression of a united and loving family?'). The conflict has arisen from misunderstanding and lack of communication rather than obstreperousness, foolishness rather than bloody-mindedness.

The judge's statement of his reasons for upholding the appeal reveals the persuasiveness of this strategy.

JUDGE: The first thing is that, in our view, it is absolutely plain that the local authority took an entirely proper course in May of this year when they sought a place of safety order after the telephone call and meeting between Mrs Conrad and Mr Brittan. She then told him she was unable to cope and feared she might batter. There was only one possible course he could pursue. He did that. He had the children's interests at heart (. . .) The general effect of (the GP's) evidence was that (the children's) material needs were satisfied and that this was a united and loving family (. . .) It is not fair to conclude without saying that the local authority were correct in taking their actions. We would like to express the hope that Mr and Mrs Conrad will not harbour any resentment and, more important, will feel able to go and seek assistance again because that can only be in the interests of the children and we feel they are sufficiently devoted to appreciate that fact. So that means the appeal will be allowed.

PB: My clients have not been legally aided. We are not criticizing the local authority. We are not aware of any money authorized from central funds.

JUDGE: We would not take the view that this is a case where costs should be allowed. What was done had to be done. The chain of events brought us here. We feel there has been a useful clearing of the air.

PB: My clients agree.

179

The outwardly satisfactory appearance of the children and their home and of their parents' marital relationship is linked with the parents' sense of moral responsibility and their acceptance of the {196} legitimacy of intervention to permit the conclusion that coercive measures are now inappropriate. To the extent, though, that the Conrads have brought the case upon themselves, by negligently disregarding previous warnings about the consequences of Mrs Conrad's behaviour in her husband's absence, it is proper that they should, in effect, be fined their own costs (about £400). Nevertheless, their unimpeachable moral character underwrites the credibility of their assurances about future co-operation so that the care order can now be discharged, in contrast with the Leonards, whose unreliability necessitates the maintenance of control.

The future of the child

The importance of the debate on compliance and its implications for control of parents in the future is reflected in a further distortion of the official structure of the hearing. In principle, care proceedings, again by analogy with criminal cases, fall into two parts. The first concerns whether the authority has established that one or more of the conditions specified in section 1(2) of the 1969 Act is satisfied and that the child needs care or control which he or she will not receive unless *an* order is made. If the authority succeeds here, the court goes on to consider *what kind* of order is appropriate, with the benefit of a social inquiry report from the social services department detailing the home circumstances without the supposed constraints of the 'official' rules of evidence. If this division is taken seriously, discussion about the child's future should not occur during the first stage.

In fact it proves virtually impossible to exclude such debate. Hilgendorf (1981: 103), using restrictive criteria, found that 12 out of 30 observed cases failed to separate the two stages at all, while in none of the hearings we observed was the issue of disposal entirely absent from the first stage. The majority of the local authority solicitors we interviewed would have preferred to keep the two stages quite separate, an account which was consistent with our observations of their practice. Nevertheless, other lawyers or the magistrates themselves commonly raised questions about disposal and the local authority solicitors could not object without falling into the trap illustrated in the Leonard case of the negative implications to be drawn from an insistence on procedural exactitude. For the other advocates and the court, however, an exploration of the respective merits of supervision and care orders is an important element in evaluating parental compliance. The weakness of supervision orders {197} in mistreatment cases is sufficiently widely recognized for courts and lawyers to assume that the local authority will be asking for a care order, whether this has been explicitly stated or not.[8] Indeed, the cases where local authority solicitors did announce their intentions were those where supervision powers were being sought. Discussion of the merits of the different orders can serve to soften the evaluations of local authority witnesses about the past and future compliance of parents with external intervention. If concessions are extracted by forcing authority witnesses into the dilemma of not wishing to say harsh things about parents for fear of compromising future work as against staying with an agreed line that parents have had a sufficiency of 'last chances', the opposing solicitor or the court can find arguments to the effect that the shock of the hearing has been sufficient or that only a weak order is necessary because the local authority has acted precipitately. Again there is some recognition of this in the local authority solicitors' concession that their reason for announcing applications for supervision orders was often to acknowledge the weakness of their case in the hope that the magistrates would be more disposed to find in their favour for a 'soft' disposition.

While there may be good theoretical arguments for separating the two stages of care proceedings, they founder on the central common-sense question: is this child (or family) in need of care or control which it would not receive without compulsion? Is voluntary compliance possible? If the family can be made to display this as a serious prospect, then the need for an order disappears.

PARENTAL DEFENCES

Our discussion of the Leonard and Conrad cases introduced some of the features of successful and unsuccessful parental replies to the local authority's allegations. These defences can, of course, be advanced at any point in the decision-making process, as we indicated in chapter 5. Nevertheless, their most formal and explicit presentation occurs in the course of court hearings when parents get their first opportunity publicly to confront the agency system as a whole. When considering the persuasiveness of these accounts, then, we are not just considering their credibility in court but also their prospects of success in defeating the possibility of a hearing at all.

Unlike agency accounts which, as we saw earlier, are designed to analyze whole categories of cases, parents' accounts are, naturally, {198} tied much more closely to individual circumstances. As such, they fit quite closely to the typology formulated by Scott and Lyman (1968).

Parental justifications

These, as we have seen, concede the facts of the alleged deviance but argue

181

that the act has been misinterpreted either because the observer has incorrectly applied correct standards or has correctly applied incorrect standards. In either case, parents are attempting to show that their treatment of a child is permitted or required by considerations which, once stated, they hope that the audience will recognize and accept. Scott and Lyman describe six sub-types of this account: denial of injury, in which the deviance is admitted but its consequences dismissed as trivial; denial of the victim, in which it is argued that the victim somehow deserved the injury; condemnation of the condemners, in which the deviance is admitted but claimed to be irrelevant because others commit the same acts and are not condemned; appeal to loyalties, where the deviance is admitted but held to be the result of higher allegiances; sad tales, where the deviance is asserted to be the just outcome of an unfortunate past; and self-fulfilment, in which the deviance is said to be the consequence of a desire to expand the actor's sense of his or her own human possibilities. Examples of all these can be found in our data:

1. Denial of injury, and *2. Denial of victim:* These are, perhaps, the most common and acceptable justifications in a society which permits and, indeed, encourages the physical punishment of children. In the instance of abuse, it is argued that the injuries are of an acceptable degree or that they are somehow deserved by the child for its wilful misconduct. The following extracts are typical. They are taken from statements to the police in one of our Shire cases, Parry, which were read in court during the care hearing. Sandra Parry is the mother of three children, two toddlers by her former husband and a baby by Jimmie Black, her present cohabitee. The case followed the discovery of cuts and bruises on the younger toddler by a health visitor. On examination by a paediatrician, the child was found to have twenty bruises on her face, back, shoulders, buttocks and legs and a large swelling on her wrist.

> (Black) I can take only so much arguing and then I give my authority. Sandra disciplines them until I feel that enough is enough and then I shout. If she tells them off or spanks them, well, that is her problem. {199} If I feel that it's gone on long enough then I have my say. If I feel they need their backsides smacked, I smack them. Or I will tell them to go to bed. If they do wrong with their hands then I smack their hands. Otherwise I only smack their backsides or the backs of their legs. I never hurt any other part of their body or head. If I do smack them I use the flat of my hands, never my fists but sometimes I used a leather belt but I have never inflicted any injury by using the buckle of the belt. I will admit that when I do smack I smack hard so that it will sting but never with intent to mark them. I want to make them realize they have done wrong. This doesn't mean that they get a smack for every little thing. I will either send them to sit on the stairs or to the bedroom. (...) But I do remember that Carl had a bruise on his backside. I believe I

caused that by smacking his backside a bit hard with my hand when Sandra was out at bingo and Carl had wet himself. I had been watching TV and the door opened and Carl had come down the stairs and he stood there and wet on the floor so I smacked him and went to get him clean pyjamas. There was none dry so I told Carl to go and put on his underpants but instead of going and getting his own clothes he came back with Susie's so I smacked him again for being a bit stupid. I told him to use his potty by his bed.

(. . .) My personal view towards children is that none of this is intentional and we want to have the children back in a normal home life. I know from experience what child care is like. As far as parentage is I look after all the children as if they were my own and I hope that some good will come of this.

(Parry) I admit that I also probably hit them a bit too hard but never on their backs, their chests or their shoulders. The marks on the children's backs are done by Jimmie. I saw Jimmie hit Susie with a belt which had a buckle and caused bruising. Last week I hit her on her mouth for swearing and it bled but that was the only time I know I hit her on the face.

Mrs Parry and Mr Black were quite surprised to find themselves in court for what they considered to be reasonable and justifiable chastisement. They may, indeed, have been unlucky in the chance of a health visitor calling when some of the injuries were very fresh. As far as they were concerned, the children had been punished only when they had misbehaved and the punishment had been proportionate to the offence. There was no qualitative distinction between their standards and those applied to them, merely a quantitative difference in the amount of punishment that was legitimate. The case of the martinet officer offers a further example of such justifications. As we asked at the beginning of this book: what is the line between firm discipline and physical abuse? {200}

Similar denials occur in neglect cases. Parents, for instance, may seek to justify severe nappy rash by claiming that it is the child's fault for wetting or soiling or that the rash is within acceptable limits. Similarly, parents may argue that an undersized and apathetic child is typical of all children in their experience. The child's development is not so delayed as to be worthy of concern or reflects factors within the child rather than parental failure.

3. Condemning the condemners: Scott and Lyman seem to be thinking of politicized criminals who seek to justify their actions by reference to the greater crimes perpetrated by the existing social order. Who had clean hands with which to judge them? In fact, we did not find any openly political justifications of this kind in the three areas we studied. More broadly, however, this denial works by attacking the moral status of frontline workers. What is their right to define acceptable behaviour? The commonest example, which should be too well-known to require illustration, is the challenge to single, childless women on their right to tell others how to bring up children without any practical experience of their own.

4. *'Sad tales'*: This justification involves references by parents to their own past and its failings, both by way of accounting for their current inadequacies and as an awful warning of the fate which they wished their children to avoid. As such, this account upholds the legitimacy of the front-line worker's standards, by recognizing and conceding past departures. The parent, however, has been deprived of the opportunity to learn what may be properly expected and his or her capacity-responsibility is deficient. Moreover, as someone with a deficient past, they know from experience about the implications of normative failure in a special and unique way. It is, therefore, right that they should be more zealous in dealing with their children than an average parent who cannot possibly know just how bleak the alternatives are.

In the extract just quoted, Jimmie Black hints at his own past as a child in care as a justification for his standards of parental discipline. He elaborated that theme into a 'sad tale' at the court hearing. The first passage is in the course of examination by the child's solicitor, the second is questioning by the local authority solicitor.

> (. . .) If only someone could devise a way of stopping children from being naughty. I don't want them to land up before a court like I did. They are very well-mannered children and I am proud of them for that. {201} Since our children have been taken away and they said it would only be for 28 days we have had nothing but problems. Sandra is in tears every bleeding, sorry, night. I want them back even if someone comes in to see that they are not ill-treated. Not even the court knows what effect this can have on a child to be taken away. I was taken into care at the age of seven and that leaves a scar on you for the rest of your life. I was taken into care, all six of us were and we thought that our parents didn't want us which was quite untrue. This is an exact double going on. We mean those children no harm at all. (. . .)

LAS: So you were taken into care under a fit person order.

BLACK: Oh I don't know what it was called, I was seven at the time.

LAS: Was it for ill-treatment?

BLACK: You might call it that. I don't know, all I know is that I was happy with my father and when I was taken into care I did nothing else except run away from the hostel. (. . .)

LAS: Do you think that use of a belt on a three-year-old girl is right?

BLACK: No, not after this. But I used to have a stick used on me in the children's home.

(The principal adviser sitting next to me winces slightly at this point)

The point is not to do with the truth or falsity of the account but the object it is organized to achieve, in this case to persuade hearers that his disciplinary practices are understandable and acceptable in the light of his own childhood experiences.

5. Appeal to loyalties, and *6. Self-fulfilment*: These are discussed together because they can both be seen as principled deviance. In each case, the acts complained of are admitted but justified by reference to alternative philosophies of life. They are distinguished from (3) above by their positive statement of a different set of moral choices rather than a negative attack on the status of the front-line workers. In effect, they pose the dilemma of liberalism in its sharpest form. Just how free are parents to dispose of children in their power?

For reasons we discuss shortly, these cases are rare in our data. Using other sources, however, we can identify two categories which correspond roughly to the appeal to higher loyalties and to self-fulfilment. {202}

The first of these is exemplified by certain sorts of religious sect where particular child-rearing practices are legitimated by scriptural authority. In Sweden, for instance, a new law to introduce an objective test of abuse by declaring any physical punishment of children to be unlawful, even in the course of 'reasonable chastisement', was opposed by religious groups who claimed a biblical warrant for beating their children.

> A spokesman for the small religious Maranata Sect, which operates its own schools declared: We will go underground if we have to, but we will continue to exercise our natural rights. (. . .) The Maranata Sect considered physical chastisement by parents to be a natural means of correction and an 'ethical, moral and religious right.'
>
> *(Aberdeen) Evening Express* 19.5.1979

There was a much publicized case in Sheffield in 1979 which raised similar issues. It centred on the question of whether a father of seven children had acted neglectfully in attempting to isolate them from any contact with a society which, apparently on religious grounds, he considered to be essentially corrupt.

We did have a small number of cases reported to us, especially in County, which came into the second category. In their original discussion, Scott and Lyman referred to the example of hippies taking drugs where their deviance was acknowledged but justified in terms of consciousness expansion. These were also the sort of households where children might receive particular diets or be managed in a free-wheeling fashion. In 1979, two articles in the *British Medical Journal* (Roberts et al., Tripp et al.) reported 19 cases of malnutrition in London infants fed on macrobiotic or other cult diets. In 1977, *The Guardian* (15 June) reported a case in Winchester where care proceedings had been taken on two small children whose mother believed that children should develop naturally, unaided or unencouraged by anyone. Both children exhibited signs of developmental retardation as a result.

Parental excuses

The other device which may be used to defeat or mitigate a charge of deviance is the offering of 'excuses'. In this case, the actor admits the deviant nature of his or her conduct but denies moral responsibility by virtue of an impairment of his or her capacity. As a result, the actor could do nothing to prevent what is recognizably a deviant act. {203} Scott and Lyman suggest four ways in which excuses may be formulated: appeal to accident, that the deviance is a chance occurrence resulting from generally recognized hazards in the environments or the inefficiency of the body and its control systems; appeal to defeasibility, that the deviance is due to insufficient knowledge of the act's consequences or to an impairment of free will; appeal to biological drives, where the deviance is said to be due to generally recognized but uncontrollable natural impulses; and appeal to scapegoating, where it is alleged that the deviance is a response to the behaviour of another.

As in our discussion of justifications, we could present actual examples of all of these excuses from our data. Rather than prolong the analysis unduly, however, we shall confine ourselves to describing their general character in the context of child abuse and neglect.

In response to allegations of mistreatment, appeals to accident typically take the form of admitting that the child was hit but claiming that the major injuries result from the child falling on to some object as a consequence. They are not proportionate to the severity of the original blow and its intended effect. It is that intention that should be judged rather than the outcome, since the parent is incapable of controlling for a chance event. Appeals to defeasibility are found where the total capacity to control will or knowledge is depressed, temporarily or permanently, by intoxication, psychiatric disorder or mental subnormality. The parent is not able to act as others do but has attempted to regulate his or her own behaviour to the best of limited capacities. Again the intention is sound but the outcome is deviant. Biological drive excuses are frequently produced by sex offenders, who will seek to deny their capacity to act responsibly by virtue of overwhelming urges or impulses (cf. Taylor 1972). Finally, scapegoating appears where the child is seen as so provocative that nobody could contain their reactions. This is different from the justification of denying the victim in its fatalistic quality. It is not a matter of proportionate corrective action but of overwhelming pressure. Such excuses might be found in respect of handicapped, subnormal or disturbed children. Once again, some kind of mysterious force overwhelms the possibility of human agency.

The acceptability of parental accounts

The accounts offered by parents are evaluated within the same framework as that used in formulating allegations. Their acceptability, then, turns on the degree to which this framework can be manipulated {204} by parents. Although, as we have seen with the Conrads, this can be done, the chances of success are slim. Most justifications implicitly attack the quality or legitimacy of the agencies' judgements which, as we saw earlier, is likely to be interpreted as further evidence of parental incorrigibility. As Emerson (1969: 165-71) also found, the courts are reluctant to accept challenges to socially licensed regulatory agents.

> To question their motives or character is to threaten the basic presumption of competence and objectivity that justifies the performance of such intrinsically dirty work . . . [and] the elaborate system of legitimation . . . (Emerson 1969: 170-1)

The parent who repudiates the good faith and social necessity of regulation sets him or herself outside the liberal order as one who does not respect its basic principles. Coercion is, therefore, unavoidable.

Only two kinds of justification seem to make any serious impact on agencies and courts: 'sad tales' and appeals to principle. The former operate mainly to mitigate the disposition of the case. If successful, the teller accepts the propriety of the intervention but reveals a troubled history and begs for a further chance. Appeals to principle fix on the vulnerability of agencies and courts to charges of oppressive intervention to restrict individual liberty. The prospects of success are greater if the parents have any sort of group support which might help to define their thinking as a cultural statement rather than an individual eccentricity. In both cases, however, successful defences require the establishment of what Emerson (1969: 167) describes as their proponent's *absolute rectitude*. As we saw in chapter 8, the agencies attempt to produce a total denunciation of the family to warrant such a drastic step as compulsory intervention. Their right to do this is underwritten by their charters and licences. Any kind of response which is not to be made available merely as further evidence of the parents' spoiled character must be set against a picture of moral impeccability. Thus the Parrys' sad tale fails because the household is so discreditable on other counts, while the Conrads' succeed through a conspicuous demonstration of their loyalty to the liberal moral order. Similarly, one can see, in the reported cases, differential responses to religious zealotry, which is often allied to a fastidiously-kept material environment and an explicitly moralized interpersonal environment, and to free-wheeling hippy groups whose whole way of life is conspicuously deviant. {205}

Excuses rarely seemed to make much impact on their audience, largely, we suggest, because of the potency of the notion of natural love. It was virtually impossible to find ways of accounting for its breakdown without either introducing elements of intention, as with the consumption of drink or drugs or even with minor mental disorder, or portraying oneself as defective in one's essential humanity, as with biological drives or scapegoating. Accidents seemed a limited exception to this, although, again, their success as an excuse was contingent on establishing the absolute rectitude of the parents.[9]

If we look at the court hearing as a whole, far and away the most striking feature is the way in which it recapitulates the decision making process analysed in the preceding chapters. The courts, it would seem, are making much the same sorts of judgements on much the same sorts of issues using broadly commonsensical rather than strictly legal criteria. This observation has two important implications.

The first is that the impact of the law on agency practice is procedural rather than substantive. In the nature of things, it is rarely possible to produce direct evidence of mistreatment in the way that is characteristically done for homicide, burglary or fraud. The events do not take place before witnesses or are subtle processes rather than single incidents. What the court requires local authority witnesses to do is to demonstrate that they have dealt with the case in a procedurally correct fashion, not in the trivial sense of following an agency manual but in the fundamental sense of correct reasoning. The witnesses must show grounds for regarding accidental or adventitious explanations as implausible, primarily by undercutting the moral character of parents, who can be shown to be incredible, in a literal sense. Moreover, the authority must show that it has no choice but to adopt compulsory measures, that voluntary intervention is impossible either because parents are incapable of compliance or because the mistreatment is so grave as to represent an unacceptable risk. Local authority applications succeed by fitting the magistrates' sense of the spirit of the law rather than the letter. That sense, however, is essentially a lay sense which is imposed on all the competing professional assessments and asserts the fundamental primacy of the judgements of ordinary men and women. Its effects may vary from one locality to another but this may not necessarily be a ground for criticism where the central activity is the moral evaluation of parents and the appropriateness of demands that they conform to some minimally defined local standard of acceptable child-rearing. {206}

The second implication is that, if the local authority has done its job properly, relatively few applications will fail. Care proceedings are the end of a very long line of decisions where alternative outcomes are preferred at each and every stage. While critics of the present system have latched on to the high success rate of local authorities as evidence of a rubber-stamping approach by courts, we find it more plausible to analyse the 75 per cent rate in our study and the 92 per cent in Hilgendorf's as reflecting the exhaustive processes of discussion which have taken place within the local agencies prior to an application being lodged.[10] As Parker et al. (1981: 165) conclude, for a slightly older population:

> In short, the goal to *prevent* children and adolescents or parents being taken to the care court is primary, the responsibility through law to take over parental rights, to remove children is only apparent when routine work fails or when a real crisis or emergency arises . . . we should be clear that the 'push-in' is *not* a natural tendency in the professional ideology dominating social welfare as with the police faced with alleged delinquency.

Care proceedings are an extreme remedy for an extreme situation.

10

Social Regulation and the Family in a Liberal State

{207}
The picture of decision-making in child mistreatment that has emerged from this study clearly contradicts one fashionable view: that child protection agencies are rapaciously scouring the homes of the poor for children to seize. We have clearly shown that, at each and every stage, the structures of the organizations involved and the practical reasoning of their members have the effect of creating a preference for the least stigmatizing interpretation of available data and the least overtly coercive possible disposition. Officially-labelled cases of mistreatment are, quite literally, only those for which no excuse or justification can be found. Compulsory measures are employed only in those cases where parental recalcitrance or mental incompetence leave no room for voluntary action. At the same time, we think it would be wrong to interpret our findings as support for the contrary proposition: that agencies are catastrophically ineffectual in enforcing optimum standards of child-rearing. Caution should not be confused with weakness. While our personal conclusion might be that agency staff are over-respectful of parental liberties and that 'justice for children' may require more rather than less state intervention, we recognize that these deficiencies, by our standard, do not represent failings by the individual agencies so much as the inherent limitations of the licences and charters which we, as citizens, have granted to them.

Both of the current critical positions rest, in our view, on misunderstandings of the nature of the task of child protection and the appropriate way of analysing the relationship between families and the state. Our task in this chapter will be to elaborate our passing references to the societal context of agency practice and discuss the normative environment within which child mistreatment is managed. We shall establish that the 'deficiency' position fails to reflect the {208} complex balance which agencies must strike between child protection and adult freedoms. First, however,

191

we propose to deal with the 'rapacity' argument, to consider its origins and empirical substance. Just what is the case for agency imperialism?

CONSERVATIVE ANXIETIES AND AGENCY IMPERIALISM

Parton (1979, 1981) has shown very clearly how child abuse and neglect are formulated as social problems, in Waller's sense, within a conservative analysis of the supposed failings of post-War British society. These failings, it is argued, are the consequence of the declining effectiveness of the family as an agency of moral socialization. This analysis, as we noted in chapter 2, first emerged in the United States as a reaction to the perceived civil disorder of the sixties and was imported through the NSPCC, an organization with a strongly evangelical Christian tradition. It achieved significant state sponsorship during Sir Keith Joseph's tenure of the DHSS (1970-74), linking, as it did, with conservative Jewish social thought. As Parton stresses, however, the formulation of child mistreatment as a social problem should not be identified with any particular political party. It forms part of a more general populist anxiety which generated a number of pressure groups, most notably the NVALA and the Festival of Light, that cut across party lines. Some of the concerns for family integrity and its apparent disintegration were as evident in the speeches of James Callaghan, the Labour Prime Minister, as in those of any member of the present Conservative government.

Echoing arguments put forward by Hall and his colleagues (1978), Parton contends that the state has come increasingly to adopt a 'control' posture as a response to such pressures.

> . . . social workers have been increasingly encouraged and constrained during the 1970s into a more directive and interventive role in their work with families and their approach to child care . . . (the emphasis has shifted) towards increased surveillance and direct control of certain families . . . . There has been an increasing use of intervention that is 'authoritative, intrusive and insistent' . . . (Parton 1981: 392)

The response has been the emergence of counter-groups like the self-styled Family Rights Group and Justice for Children. Morris et al. (1980: 8-9) write, for instance, in a volume under the latter title: {209}

> This manifesto for action includes compromises between ideological beliefs and social realities, but these compromises are peripheral to our main principle: the limitation of compulsory state intervention in the lives of children . . . . Compulsory intervention in the lives of children must be limited in nature, not subject to indiscriminate intervention on the basis of current moral panics.

They go on to argue for a set of institutional and legal changes designed to restrict the powers of social workers and courts and to make it more difficult to take compulsory measures in respect of either delinquent or mistreated children.

The conventional critical wisdom, then, is that there is more political concern about child mistreatment, which has led to social services departments and allied agencies becoming more expansionist in their surveillance of the population and more directive in their treatment of clients. Put in these terms the thesis looks very reminiscent of the fashionable analysis of medicalization and medical imperialism, whose empirical base, as Strong (1979b) has demonstrated, is tenuous, to say the least. On inspection, the same proves to be the case for child mistreatment. The first point, admittedly, is well-established. At a macro-level, there does seem to be more expressed concern than in the early sixties and Parton's characterization seems unexceptionable. The real problems emerge when one looks at the evidence adduced for the implementation of these concerns at an organizational or interpersonal level.

Parton relies on two sources. The first is a table, derived from Hallett and Stevenson (1980), showing an apparent rise in place of safety orders as a result of the Maria Colwell inquiry (1974). What does this actually mean? If, as our data suggest, compulsory intervention is related to both interpersonal and organizational factors, these figures could indicate that parents have become less compliant or reflect the increasing elaboration of inter-agency consultations, which reduces the likelihood of containing marginal cases. Both of these could operate independently of any tendency towards more aggressive agency practice. Parton's other source is a postal survey by Tredinnick and Fairburn (1980 a and b, Fairburn and Tredinnick 1980) of social services departments about children taken into care at birth over a period of eleven-and-a-half years. A 61 per cent response yielded 160 such cases, although only 83 actually ended up with caretakers other than their natural parents and some of these were with close relatives. There appears to have been a sharp increase {210} since the mid-seventies, but the numbers are very small to place much weight on year-to-year fluctuations, and the effects of two reorganizations of social services in 1971 and 1974 must cast doubt on the reliability of the early figures in the series. In the absence of further data on practice, Parton can only assume that the processes which he identifies very convincingly at a macro-level are in fact paralleled at others.

Morris et al. (1980) present no serious evidence to support their polemic against the present state of child care law.[1] Much of their effect is purely rhetorical. Statistics, for instance, are characteristically presented in absolute terms: 'On 31 March 1977, over 100,000 children were in the care of local authorities in England and Wales (p. 85)'. Phrased like that, it appears to be a large number of children, but if we express it as about 0.75

per cent of the eligible population, the figures take on a rather different significance. On other occasions, the authors simply rely on assertions: 'Lawyers experienced in this field can quote numerous cases . . . (p. 97)' or 'It is certainly the experience of many of our social work colleagues . . . (p. 97)'. In the four chapters dealing with this topic, the book cites six anecdotes, seven reported court cases and three public inquiry reports – Colwell (1974), Godfrey (1975) and Brewer (1977). We have no way of knowing how representative the anecdotes are, although they are presented as typical of national practice, and the point about public inquiries and appealed cases is precisely that they are atypical.

The impact of this book and a similar volume from Taylor et al. (1980) cannot be understood in terms of the empirical substantiation presented so much as the resonance of the thesis with chic radicalism. It has nothing to say about the degree to which agency staff themselves participate in the same libertarian culture, about the counter-pressures from attempts to reduce or contain welfare expenditure or about the growing movement from the radical Right to roll back the frontiers of state intervention to an extent which the proponents of this argument would plainly anathematize. As an increasing number of writers have been observing, we need much more sophisticated conceptions of law, medicine and social welfare if we are to understand their complex and sometimes contradictory roles in advanced societies.[2]   Merely dismissing them all as agencies of social control presents a one-dimensional picture of a subtle reality. In so far as the criticism results from extrapolations from an unverified theory, then, our task must be to displace that theory by one which is grounded in systematic empirical inquiry. {211}

THE FAMILY IN LIBERAL SOCIETY

We have already encountered the basic elements of the 'deficiency' position in our earlier discussion of strict liability approaches to mistreatment (pp. 27-33 {pp. 31-7}). The tone of its proponents' morality is well caught by a recent paper from the President of the British Association for the Prevention and Study of Child Abuse and Neglect, Dr A. W. Franklin (1982: 16), a leading paediatrician:

> What is needed is for all countries, including our own, to accept the overriding importance of the growth and development of children to their full potential and of the need to make this a conscious goal. Each country should then accept certain responsibilities – to examine the ways in which this goal can be achieved, to examine those attitudes and practices which hinder the achievement of this goal and to renew, in the context of their own society and culture, the priority to be given to the achievement of this goal . . . . Yet many children will continue to have as

raw a deal in the world of the eighties as children have ever had . . . . As to life in the world to come this receives diminishing attention as the decades pass.

The heavy-handed paternalism and religiosity of these sentiments are characteristic of many of the best-known writers on child mistreatment. It is argued that child welfare should and must be an absolute social priority. Anyone failing to accept this whole-heartedly may then be justly criticized.

While this is a wholly legitimate political position, however, it is by no means clear that it would receive majority endorsement to the extent that its adherents demand. As the French writer Donzelot (1980) has pointed out, questions about the nature of the family cannot be extricated from questions about the nature of the state and of the good society. Child protection agencies develop within a particular set of answers to these questions. If we are dissatisfied with the answers, it is not necessarily appropriate to attack the agencies so much as the reasoning by which they are produced. Such an analysis, however, depicts agencies as balancing several partially conflicting objectives and points to the real disadvantages of an unreflective pursuit of child protection as an overriding goal. Agencies operate within a liberal 'guardian state' rather than the absolutist 'paternal state' advocated by writers like Kempe, Fontana and Franklin. As a fuller discussion shows, the necessary failures which result are not necessarily ignoble. {212}

The entanglement of the family in Utopian debate is, as Donzelot observes, the consequence of the relationship between the family and the pre-industrial social order. The family was a key instrument of social regulation. Economic power was concentrated in household heads, who were backed up by a bevy of legal powers, which reflected their accountability to the state for the conduct of all those under their roof. Donzelot characterizes this as a government of families, which is to say that the authority of the family head over other members of the household was the most local manifestation of the state. With the overthrow of that form of society, the family was necessarily drawn into political debates on the nature of the relationship between citizens and the state. What was to replace the household head as the point of connection? Socialists looked to the family's destruction and replacement by a welfare state dealing directly with each citizen on the basis of need rather than kinship. Liberals, on the other hand, saw the family as an important check on the excess of state power. The authoritarian power of household heads should be replaced by a more democratic internal regime, but this should remain sufficiently insulated from external supervision to allow members to support each other against an over-mighty state. The socialist vision, to them, seemed totalitarian, satisfying needs at the expense of diversity and liberty. For the socialists, the liberal argument was a reactionary one, seeking to revive a discredited paternalist authoritarianism.

In the course of this continuing debate, Donzelot observes, few attempts have been made to analyse the positive part taken by the family in the organization of the liberal state. As he puts it, 'the question is not so much one of knowing what the family is used for in a liberal economy as one of understanding why such a setup works'. (Donzelot 1980: 53). What problems does the family contribute towards resolving in a liberal society? Donzelot identifies two: the economic and social dislocation of industrialization; and the advance of social differentiation:

> the appearance of divisions with respect to living conditions and mores that ran so deep within the social body that they risked generating cataclysmic conflicts, thus posing a challenge to the very principle of a liberal society. (Donzelot 1980: 54)

If we are to understand the modern family and the status of children, we must take the liberal social order as an object of study rather than of criticism. {213}

SOCIAL REGULATION IN THE LIBERAL STATE

The classical theory of liberalism views social order as the product of a series of free contracts between responsible individuals, responsible, that is, both in the sense of being knowing and intentional actors and in the sense of being accountable for their own actions. The state has a limited role as the ultimate and residual guarantor of the conditions under which free contracts can be made.

This is, however, a highly problematic form of social organization, especially with the advance of the division of labour. The differentiation of individuals and their contributions increases the interdependence of society members and the necessity of trust between them at the same time as it enhances the possibilities for deceit in the anonymity and segregation of social relationships and the diminishing ability of citizens to evaluate each other. In some sense people become more free, while finding that the incentives to abuse that freedom are also increased. How can this paradox be resolved? The answer is to be found in the refinement of social control or, as we prefer, social regulation.[3] This is the process whereby members of a society place limits on each other's conduct in such a way as to achieve sufficient order to make joint action possible and to ensure the society's reproduction. In this sense, social regulation is a necessary condition for human society. The means by which this objective is achieved are, of course, historically specific.

Given the residual role of the liberal state, the first preference is for regulation by individual initiative, and any departure from this requires a special justification. Indeed, most problems of social order are solved without recourse to specialized assistance or by its purchase in the market: most illness is treated without doctors; most disputes are settled without lawyers; most personal troubles are resolved without social workers. One of the ways in which this preference is facilitated is by the social and legal distinction between public and private spheres of activity. In the private sphere of small-scale, continuing, face-to-face relationships, epitomized by the family, it is feasible for each participant to check out the moral character of the others, and the incentives for deviance or deceit are limited by the prospect of repeated interaction over a period of time.

> Perhaps one of the most important characteristics that distinguish a free from an unfree society is indeed that, in matters of conduct that do not directly affect the protected (i.e. private CSLS) sphere of others, the rules which are in fact observed by most are of a voluntary character and not enforced by coercion. (Hayek 1960: 145-6) {214}

In the public sphere, however, relationships are segmented and anonymous to a degree which renders it difficult for individuals to carry out regulatory actions on their own behalf, either through lack of specialized knowledge or through the practical obstacles to scrutinizing each and every person and their products that one encounters in a complex modern society.

If large-scale social organization is to survive, with the social and economic gains from the division of labour, some substitute regulation must be developed to control the impact of private deviance on others, as in public health matters, or on confidence in the whole system, as with fraud. It is here that the liberal state becomes involved, through its role as a guarantor of last resort. That state is, itself, founded on market principles, in the competition for votes between parties and for powers, between legislature, judiciary and executive. Such competition, in effect, mimics the accountability of citizens to each other through their market relationships.

Two broad types of regulatory response can be discerned. The first is the development of specialized agencies. These do, however, have serious disadvantages. Some means must be devised for ensuring that they are socially accountable rather than undesirable accretions of state power. As we saw in chapter 5, this is not a simple task. Moreover, such agencies tend to be able to act only in a *post hoc* or retributive fashion after deviance has occurred. The second option, then, is a detailed concern with the morality of the citizenry so that the problems arising from social differentiation and the eschewal of absolute power may be resolved by a focus on socialization. Can people be so thoroughly imbued with the principles of liberalism, or such incentives be constructed, that they will choose to constrain their actions in a way which will permit the liberal order to survive?[4]

Childhood is obviously a critical point in this respect. Indeed, it first becomes an issue in English social policy, under the Elizabethan Poor Law, through the perceived threat to social order from children who are being raised by vagrant, dissident or criminal parents and learning false values. The moral socialization of children remained the central policy issue until the beginning of the twentieth century, when their physical welfare became a matter for concern against the background of a declining birth-rate and the unfitness of the population for military or industrial service. Attention was focused first on protection *from* children and only latterly on protection *of* children. They are threats before they are victims (Eekelaar et al. 1982).[5] For the liberal, however, the unresolved problem is how child-rearing can be made into a matter of public concern and its qualities {215} monitored without destroying the ideal of the family as a counterweight to state power, a domain of voluntary, self-regulating actions.

THE POLICING OF FAMILIES

The dissection of this problem is Donzelot's most important contribution as he describes the successive techniques used by the French to regulate the moral socialization of children while preserving some sense of family autonomy. He characterizes this as 'the policing of families' where 'policing' is used in an eighteenth-century sense.

> The science of policing consists . . . in regulating everything that relates to the present condition of society, in strengthening and improving it, in seeing that all things contribute to the welfare of the members that compose it. (von Justi, *Elements Generaux de Police*, 1768, quoted in Donzelot 1980: 7)[6]

Although Donzelot does not make the distinction clearly, two types of family problem were perceived to require intervention: the abuse of *paternal* power and the abuse of *parental* power. Liberal morality required the internal reorganization of the family, so that, as Anderson (1979) points out, individuals today probably enjoy greater independence, through the differentiation and segmentation of social life, than at any previous time in history. The values of liberalism have gradually penetrated family relations so that these are 'to be evaluated in terms of their contribution to *individual* welfare' (Anderson 1979: 68 original emphasis). The problem, however, is what happens to those individuals or relationships that constitute liabilities rather than assets? In this respect, policies for children may be compared with attempts to develop policies for the elderly, the chronically sick, the mentally ill or the handicapped. The peculiarly intractable difficulty presented by children, though, is their social potential, the way in which their moral and physical welfare represent matters of concern to the future survival and character of the nation but whose maintenance depends upon the invisible actions of a myriad caretakers.

As Smith (1974: 6) has observed, the private/public distinction is reflected in the gender order:

> The public sphere is that sphere in which 'history' is made. But the public sphere is the sphere of male activity. Domestic activity {216} becomes relegated to the private sphere and is mediated to the public sphere by men who move between both. Women have a place only in the private domestic sphere.

The same point can be made even more forcibly in relation to children. Women and children remain subject to a regulatory regime which owes more to the idiosyncrasies of particular men than to the restraints men place upon the agencies which regulate their own, public, conduct. The (male-defined) boundaries of the private sphere constitute social and legal barriers to women and children who might seek to enlist regulatory agencies in their own defence. While, in our view, these barriers are primarily associated with resistance to external incursions, they plainly create a potential for paternal absolutism which is, itself, antithetical to liberal principles.

One possible solution would be to give other family members greater access to those agencies already set up to regulate the use of coercion in the public sphere and to protect the private. J. S. Mill, for instance, argues such a case in relation to the rights of women. The intervention is still consistent with family autonomy because the boundaries are breached only at the request of a family member. While this may be an appropriate remedy for abuse of paternal power, it is, however, inadequate as a response to abuse of parental power. Although some writers (e.g. Hoyles 1979) have put forward arguments for allowing children access to regulatory agencies on their own behalf, these founder on the physical limitations of the youngest and most vulnerable. Parental power can be restrained only by external surveillance.

Donzelot argues that the key institutional development in the accomplishment of this task was the evolution of philanthropy as the product of a 'search for a calculated distance between the functions of the liberal state and the spread of techniques of welfare and administration of the population' (Donzelot 1980: 55). The philanthropic institutions were voluntary associations rather than state agencies. In so far as they applied moral pressure, then, this was not the homogeneous coercion of a totalitarian state so much as the conditions set by one citizen for interacting with another. This is reflected in the two techniques developed by these associations, which Donzelot terms *moralization* and *normalization*. The former was used primarily by institutions offering economic assistance. It involved a linkage between poverty and moral failure such that charitable relief would be available only to those families who could {217} prove that their distress was the result of circumstances entirely beyond their control, that they had otherwise lived in an exemplary fashion. The latter technique related to the spread of specific norms either by education or, less commonly, by legislation. It was particularly associated with medical-hygienism. This involved the development of supportive agencies which used women's complaints about paternal power as a point of entry into the home, an alternative to Mill's proposals to extend their civil rights. In return for their support, however, these agencies obtained a moral leverage. Women might be helped, but not necessarily on their own terms.[7] Where legislation was involved, the activities of these visiting or missionary agencies gave it an indicative rather than a coercive force.[8]

Both of these techniques, in effect, enticed families and individuals towards a liberal morality. By complying with particular notions of respectability, families might avoid intervention or at least mitigate its harshness. A poor family that professed adherence to liberal values might be aided by volunteers rather than humiliated by their state (cf. Fido 1977). They were, however, equally vulnerable to parental obstruction. If parents refused to apply for assistance or to co-operate with inspection visits, the philanthropic institutions were unable to regulate the conditions of children. Since the problems of moral socialization did not disappear, and in some sense became even more acute with the rise of socialist movements, and since new problems of the physical quality of social reproduction emerged, more so in Britain even than in France, new approaches were required.

Donzelot analyses these in terms of an institution variously translated as *tutelage* (Hodges and Hussain 1979) or *wardship* (Donzelot 1980). This involved the absorption of philanthropic activity by the state and the introduction of surveillance. Parents were no longer to decide for themselves whether to apply for financial aid or to give more than public compliance to liberal norms. They were now to be the subject of a preventive intervention, designed to anticipate deviance. Resistance to surveillance, the discovery of unannounced need or private non-compliance were all to be taken as indicators of moral deficiency. This was obviously a development of the greatest importance in relation to the supervision of children's moral and physical welfare, since it provided a means of overriding parental power. 'The family', Donzelot (1980: 168) concludes, 'ceases to exist as an autonomous agency. The tutelary administration of families consists in reducing their horizon to supervised reproduction and in the automatic selecting-out of 'socializable' minors.' {218}

THE LIBERAL COMPROMISE

Donzelot's discussion of the evolution of family policing obviously has important implications for the interpretation of our data. The transformations of assistance and medical-hygienism into what he describes as the tutelary complex are highly pertinent to the activities of doctors, social workers, health visitors and lawyers. On the other hand, like other writers influenced by Foucault, Donzelot tends to understate the resistance to surveillance. We are still well short of the panoptic state of their pessimistic vision. The resistances, as we have seen, lie in both the culture and the structure of the tutelary complex.

The cultural limitation is embodied in the rule of optimism. As Donzelot notes, incursions into the family have frequently been legitimated by exploiting internal conflicts, especially between men and women. By allying themselves with the weaker members, agencies have gained access with a degree of consent rather than by compulsion. What the analysis understates, however, is what the agencies are offering in return. It is not a simple question of assisting women in the redress of grievances: dependence on such assistance can be counter-productive in a liberal moral order by discrediting the recipient's own self-reliance. Moreover, as sociologists of law have frequently observed, an aggressive insistence on rights and enforcement also tends to rebound as indicating an unreasonable or irrational reluctance to negotiate or conciliate.

The process needs a more subtle characterization. The rule of optimism is incorporated in the bureaucratic framing of encounters with tutelary agents, to provide that, where alternative interpretations of observed conduct are available, they will prefer the least discrediting. Such a preference is facilitated by the existence of two standard accounts, holding that any style of child-rearing may be justified as a valid cultural statement which should not be illiberally suppressed and that the parent/child relationship is a natural rather than a social phenomenon, with the implication that a charge of mistreatment is equivalent to an allegation that the parents involved do not share in our common humanity. The two combine to produce an attitude of acceptance towards parental accounts and a sense that an accusation of parental failure is a matter of almost inconceivable gravity.

On top of this need to be laid the structural constraints in agency organization. The incorporation of philanthropy by the state has not produced the integrated and harmonious family police depicted by {219} Donzelot. In the three different principles adopted for the organization of the major agencies, we can see different attempts to reproduce the arm's-length relationship between voluntary associations and the state while maintaining a degree of moral and financial accountability. The medical and legal professions retain many of the features of the market; health visitors are employed by quasi-autonomous nongovernmental organizations (cf. Hague et al. 1975); and, while social workers are public bureaucrats, they are accountable to the decentralized bodies of local government and only loosely subject to central direction. Compulsory actions can, in general, result only from agreement between people who have quite different lines of accountability and styles of relating to clients, differences which institutionalize tension and conflict. Moreover, there seems to be a discernible trade-off between accountability, power and intrusion. The most intrusive surveyors, health visitors and doctors, are the least subject to state direction and have the fewest resources to enforce or entice compliance.

Taken together, these restrictions constitute a powerful acknowledgement of the continuing force of family autonomy. Uninvited surveillance is possible only as the result of a compromise which minimizes the likelihood of identifying malpractice. The result is a system which is fully effective neither in preventing mistreatment nor in respecting family privacy but which lurches unevenly between these two poles. A degree of 'agency failure' is inherent in this compromise.

The circumstances which do lead to intervention reflect the character of this metaphorical agreement. Optimism is justifiable only where nothing is hidden. If there is nothing to hide, there is no reason to resist surveillance by standing on one's rights. The discredit derives from the act of rejecting the surveyor's legitimate charter or licence, together with the degree to which an adult's refusal of access by insisting on the right to privacy compromises a child's rights to protection from parental abuse. Scrutinizing the discharge of power by one citizen over another is one of the proper roles for the state recognized by most liberal theorists. A refusal of co-operation gives reason to question the parents' adherence to the normative framework within which surveyors are legitimated, and their respect for the rights of those in their power. The second circumstance reflects those occasions where private conduct breaks out into the public domain and surveillance agencies fail to contain it. They may then be faced with demands that they fulfil their moral charter by taking coercive action. Public knowledge brings public pressure on publicly accountable bodies.
{220}

THE DILEMMA OF LIBERALISM

This theoretical account allows us to respond to the criticisms we identified at the beginning of the chapter. It should be clear why agencies will always fail to recognize more than a selected proportion of child mistreatment. They cannot be given the legal power to underwrite an investigative form of surveillance without destroying the liberal family. At the same time, the state cannot opt out. There is a collective interest in the moral and physical well-being of future citizens, in the quality of social reproduction, as a necessary condition for the survival of this particular type of society. Liberal theorists from Mill to Hayek have repeatedly insisted that parents cannot have unrestricted liberty in child-rearing. The parent/child relationship is an unequal contract, which children do not enter freely. At the same time, both children and the society as a whole have a vital interest in the success of that relationship, in cultivating the capacity for responsible moral action. The only body with the legitimacy to survey the whole population is that which, in liberal principle, is accountable to the whole population – the state. Whatever machinery is devised, however, it will always remain vulnerable to criticism from Utopian libertarians whose ideals break on the brute physical reality of children's dependence on adults.

Our argument, then, is that the practice which we have described in this book is consistent with attempts to resolve the liberal dilemma presented by the twin roles of the family as a bastion of liberty, Lasch's (1977) 'haven from a heartless world', and as a nurturant of future citizens. While there may have been a moral panic about child mistreatment since the late sixties, this is better seen as a rather narrowly based concern about social disorder and the search for a specific aetiology. Its objects are not children as victims of mistreatment but mistreated children as threats to civil order, the dominant image in English social policy since the Tudors. Within the organizations, comparing our observations with those of Satyamurti (1981), Smith (1980) and Dingwall (1977a), all reporting field-work from the early seventies, libertarian principles appear to hold greater sway, both as a reflection of the resurgence of radical and neo-conservative individualism and as justifications for rationing increasingly scarce resources.

These conflicting pressures have heightened rather than resolved the inherent difficulties of child protection work and placed increasing strains on the legal and institutional fabric. In our final chapter, {221} we shall turn to review the objectives of any child protection and consider in detail the elements which might properly constitute it, as a basis for possible repairs to the English structure or as a possible model for the assessment of other nations' practice.

11

Children's Rights, Adults' Liberties: Towards a Proper Balance?

{222}
For a greater part of this book, we have concentrated on an ethnographic description of *how* the system of child protection agencies operates in one modern liberal society. In the last chapter, we attempted to show *why* the system is so organized. Our remaining task is to ask *whether* it should continue to operate in this fashion. At this point, of course, our own values and preferences must come to the fore as we move from explication to evaluation. It is here that we encounter the intrinsic dilemma of all social studies: that we make our judgements in the role of citizens as much as in the role of scientists. We noted in the last chapter that debates about the family were necessarily also debates about the nature of the good society. Experts and specialists cannot usurp the right to decide such issues, although they may hope to clarify them. Our response, then, is to attempt to indicate why we have formed the policy conclusions that we have in terms of a series of decisions on underlying principles. We hope, thereby, to furnish a set of criteria for the assessment of other institutional arrangements and to stimulate discussion at the level of moral rather than technical choices.

Our first decision is to avoid transcendental criticism of the nature of Anglo-American society. This is not to deny the legitimacy of such contributions but rather to recognize the prevailing, more or less liberal, social order as a given fact for the purposes of this study. We are bringing back a report on a small corner of the world which may illuminate other arguments and may serve as a case study but which is designed to appraise the present order in its own terms. Thus, while it may be possible to conceive of forms of social organization which would, as it were, design out mistreatment, these do not seem to represent realizable alternatives at this point in history, although {223} their very existence represents a stimulus and challenge to accepted arrangements.

In beginning with a discussion of what we perceive to be the basic rights of children, then, we are not trying to use this as a strong form of assertions about the priorities of social policy or opinions about how children should be treated. Rather, our objective is to see how far the language of 'rights' can help us to understand the relationships between parents, children and the state presently ascribed by law as they are interpreted and implemented in the way this study was documented. From this base, we then propose to review the existing English social and legal institutions and their practice.

THE RIGHTS OF CHILDREN AND PARENTS

The meaning of the statement 'X has a right' has been much debated in jurisprudence. Our analysis here follows Hohfeld's (1919) classic formulation that a right, in the strict sense of the word (often called a 'claim-right'), could be said to be held by X if and only if Y is under a duty to perform the act to which X has the right.[1] While a right can exist only if someone owes a correlative duty to the right-holder, it does not follow that a right always exists where a person is under a duty. This brings in a social dimension: to use the language of rights we must be able to identify with reasonable clarity who is the beneficiary of the duty (cf. Finnis 1980: 202). Only by stretching the imagination can our duty to complete our tax returns be said to constitute the confirmatory element in a 'right' of (the Revenue? the Crown? the community-at-large?) to receive correct ones. Similarly, it is difficult to consider duties not to be cruel to animals as elements of some right of animals to be free from mistreatment, not for analytic reasons concerning the nature of rights, but because it is unclear whether the interests to be protected are those of the animals, of people who may be distressed by their condition or of the perpetrators who may be corrupted by their own conduct. In the case of children, though, it does seem to be meaningful to talk in terms of rights which justify placing appropriate duties on their caretakers.

Thus, apart from the general duties normally enforced by the criminal law which each of us owes to children, as to all persons, to respect their physical integrity, additional duties may be placed on those who are in a peculiarly strong position to affect a child's life. These duties, however, exist within the context of a social and legal system which also attributes certain rights to parents, rights which {224} have a much longer history of recognition than those ascribed to children. Such rights are expressed in the legal rule that a child's parents are his or her natural guardians and, as we have seen, are embedded in the culture and structure of family regulation. These are, however, claim-rights only in so far as third parties, whether individuals or agencies, may not exercise them except in legally defined situations. Parental rights are different from, say, a property-owner's rights to enjoy his or her own property, in that they must be exercised for the child's benefit. In this respect, the rights of parents also have some of the characteristics of duties. As Eekelaar (1973) argued, they are 'duty-rights' which parents are not free to abandon, extinguish or waive so long as the child is in their care.

Perhaps, then, the best legal model for analysing the relationship between parents and children is that of a trust (Beck et al. 1978). Trustees have rights over the relevant property which they can defend against third parties but which they must use in the interests of the beneficiaries. If they fail to do this, whether out of misconduct or incompetence, the beneficiaries may call them to account before a court with a view to their appointment being terminated. In the case of parents, the object of the trust is the promotion of children's welfare. Where they prove deficient, for whatever reason, the beneficiaries have a ground for legal action in respect of the negligent discharge of their trustees' duties.

If we recognize such rights for children, we must accept corresponding restrictions on parents' rights and on family autonomy.[2] We must also acknowledge, however, that, if children's rights are to be taken seriously, their interpretation and enforcement must find some institutional expression. Many mistreated children are physically unable to initiate their own remedies: others must be licensed to do it for them. This poses, as we have seen, difficult problems about the degree of social policing that is necessarily involved in such an exercise. Our first objective, however, must be to consider the terms of the parental trust as these are defined in law, since these establish the parameters for the whole system.

THE STATUTORY FRAMEWORK

When looking at child protection statutes, then, we keep three issues in mind: the way in which they define the overriding goals of child-rearing; the duties which they place upon caretakers; and the means which they provide for their own enforcement. {225}

Attempts to define the goals of child-rearing must steer a narrow course between the Scylla of being so vaguely drafted as to be ineffective controls on state intervention and the Charybdis of being so tightly restricted as to exclude numbers of mistreated children. The trend of American legal opinion (e.g. Wald 1975, Buckholz 1979) has been towards reducing the scope of permissible grounds for intervention by limiting the recognized objectives of child protection statutes. Goldstein et al. (1980), for instance, would eliminate all references to the promotion of emotional well-being and concentrate purely on the physical protection of children. This movement has not had a great impact in the UK and we consider that the scope for controlling agency and court assessments solely by legal definitions is rather limited. As we observed repeatedly, where statutes and regulations did not fit the commonsense perceptions of social workers, doctors, health visitors, solicitors, magistrates or judges, they were either ignored or adapted, either to exclude or to include particular children and their troubles.

We suspect, then, that the exclusion of, say, 'emotional' harm by statute would simply result in the re-definition of cases rather than their actual exclusion. For instance, it is argued that emotional deprivation can retard physical development. If the former ground were no longer available, then the latter would become more prominent. The courts would be presented with children suffering avoidable developmental delay who happened to be emotionally mistreated rather than emotionally mistreated children who happen to be exhibiting physical signs. Similarly, qualifying terms like 'substantial' risk or 'imminent' danger remain matters for individual or institutional interpretation. We would argue that the real impact of statutes and legal review is in the prospect of public accounting which obliges agency staff to develop defensible lines of reasoning in their case management. The juvenile court and its input of lay opinion, whether through lay justices in England or politically appointed judges in the USA, is only one part of a complex of checks and balances.

Given this, we consider that the drafting of section 1(2) of the Children and Young Persons Act 1969 provides a satisfactory statement of the overall objectives of child protection in attempting to underwrite a child's rights to minimum standards of physical, psychological, emotional and moral care. The principal ground for intervention, that the child's 'proper development is being avoidably prevented or neglected', clearly encapsulates the conjuncture of clinical and social evidence which permeates the decision-making process. {226}

There is only one feature of the wording which it seems necessary to review, namely that, apart from the same household grounds, the conditions are all phrased in the present tense. This might be unduly restrictive in two ways: by excluding children who have not suffered demonstrable mistreatment but are in clear danger; or, if literally interpreted, by excluding children who *have been* mistreated but have already been removed from danger, by consent or otherwise. The ellipsis in the statutes has not been filled by superior court decisions, with the partial exception of children already voluntarily placed in care under section 1 of the Children Act 1948.[3] The same reasoning, however, could be used to exclude children who were in a place of safety, like a hospital, at the time of the application for an order in care proceedings.

In practice, the question is resolved on the basis of interpreting the statute to cover the state of affairs to which the application relates and from which the child has been removed, provided, of course, that the child is not in voluntary care.⁴ To do otherwise would plainly make a nonsense of the provisions. It is arguable that the statute should be re-drafted to incorporate this explicitly. This might facilitate moves towards a unified approach to child protection in English law. At present, children in voluntary care may be detained through a procedure which concentrates on the fitness of parents to care for them rather than on the children's interests in being returned home. By encouraging an administrative integration of the two categories, '1948 Act children' and '1969 Act children', it might be possible to develop a more child-centred approach which would resolve some of the acknowledged deficiencies of the parental rights procedure under the 1948 (now 1980) Act.⁵

The question of whether it should be possible to bring care proceedings *solely* on the basis of the probability of future mistreatment, apart from the circumstances already covered by the same household grounds, is more controversial. Participants in our study were divided as to whether the local authorities wanted or should have such a power or whether it was not rather absurd to have to wait for an expected injury before intervention. As we saw with the Conrad case, it was sometimes possible to stretch the present drafting to cover the difficulty, on that occasion by arguing that the threat of mistreatment in the future was emotionally damaging in the present. More commonly, however, the gap is filled by wardship proceedings so that the question is less one of *whether* probabilistic intervention should occur than of *how* it should be done.

Wardship proceedings are heard before a judge of the Family Division {227} of the High Court. They are based on the old Chancery jurisdiction and the only statutory restriction is that the judge's estimate of the welfare of the child must be his 'first and paramount consideration' (Guardianship of Minors Act 1971, s. 1). Once a child is made a ward, all parental power is vested in the court and no important decision may be taken without its consent. Under section 7(2) of the Family Law Reform Act 1969 the court acquired the power to commit a child into the care of a local authority 'in exceptional circumstances making it impracticable or undesirable for a ward of court to be, or to continue to be, under the care of either of his parents or any other individual'.

As Lowe and White (1979: 89) suggest, such restrictive wording would seem intended to indicate a sparing use of committals. The courts, however, do not appear to have felt in the least inhibited from making such orders and have encouraged local authorities to apply for them. Reviewing a magistrates' court decision in *Re D (a minor)*, for instance, it was stated that

> Far from local authorities being discouraged from applying to the court in wardship, in my judgement they should be encouraged to do so, because in very many of these cases it is the only way in which orders can

be made in the interests of the child, untrammelled by the statutory provisions of the Children and Young Persons Act 1969.[6]

Those of our local authority solicitors who had experienced wardship proceedings generally regarded them with favour. They allowed more discretion in the grounds for intervention, the procedure was less formal with a looser interpretation of the rules of evidence,[7] and the range of dispositions was greater. Our solicitors had more confidence in the judges' decision-making, welcomed the readier availability of legal aid and appreciated the contribution of independent assessors like the Official Solicitor or the court welfare officer.

These alleged advantages, however, largely reflected recognizable deficiencies in care proceedings, in the present case with the available grounds and, as we show later, with the procedural rules. Wardship actions are expensive and time-consuming for local authorities and the uncontrolled judicial discretion threatens to subvert the libertarian compromise on state intervention as it is embodied in the various Acts of Parliament creating the governing charters for the child protection system. Remarks like Ormrod, L. J.'s in *Re CB (a minor)* [1981] are profoundly disturbing: {228}

> It has always seemed to me that when a serious dispute arises about the welfare of a child it is asking too much for the social workers to be made to be judges as well as social workers in these cases, and that it is to the advantage of all parties, including the local authority, to resort to the court in order that a judge may take responsibility for the decision.

The point, surely, is that the court's role in care proceedings is to review the applicants' case by reference to the defensibility of the agencies' actions in the context of the definitions established by Parliament. It should not be the function of the courts to second-guess the legislature and substitute their own predilections for those enshrined in statute. This is, incidentally, a further reason for preferring a jurisdiction with a substantial lay element which can draw on local moral sentiment as an indicator of the justifiable operational interpretations of the statutory provisions.

Rather than encouraging the growth of wardship, then, we would prefer to see its use restricted by reforms to care proceedings within a unified child care statute. We think that it would be appropriate to introduce a ground allowing intervention on the basis of apprehended mistreatment. This should not be seen in isolation from our other suggestions for procedural reform, but it is already established in Scotland, under section 32(2) of the Social Work (Scotland) Act 1968, within the much less restrictive legal setting of the children's panels, and no serious problems have been reported.

The duties of caretakers

If we are analysing child protection statutes in terms of the rights of children, then, following our earlier argument, we must also see them as statements about the duties of those acting as their trustees. The American legislation that we discussed in chapter 1 almost invariably recognizes this in explicit mention of parents. They are, however, quite absent from the British legislation. Indeed, in so far as children are made the respondent parties in care proceedings, it could be argued that they are the only people with duties – not to have their development impaired, not to fall into moral danger, not to commit offences or whatever,

Such references did exist in the previous legislation. Under section 2 of the Children and Young Persons Act 1963 a child was considered to be in need of protection if conditions broadly similar to those presently in effect were established and the child was not 'receiving {229} such care, protection and guidance as a good parent may reasonably be expected to give.' The substitution of this test by the present vague 'he is in need of care or control which he is unlikely to receive . . .' was justified by the Home Office (1970) on the grounds that the previous version 'directed attention solely at the quality of parental care; and it meant that proceedings inevitably appeared to cast blame for the child's situation or behaviour directly on to his parents or those looking after him'.[8] We have repeatedly identified the difficulties which the confusion of troublesome and troubled children has caused for agencies and courts. The quality of parental care is *the* central issue throughout decision-making in child protection. If the child's condition does not result from their acts of commission or omission, the case fails.

We think that there are good grounds for reintroducing such a provision, which is still in effect in Northern Ireland.[9] It imposes, in legal terms, an objective test of parental behaviour so that impairments of parental responsibility such as alcohol addiction or mental deficiency would not constitute defences. In this respect it modifies the sense of 'avoidably' in the present drafting of the proper development ground: the disadvantages of a child born to constitutionally inadequate parents could be said to be unavoidable. On the other hand, it leaves some room for the operation of relative judgements: a good parent can only be expected to take his or her economic, social and cultural environment as given, within marginal limits. The provision would also circumscribe the operation of the new probabilistic ground since *both* lack of parental responsibility *and* apprehended harm would have to be established.

This change would, of course, raise problems if the statute continued to cover both mistreated and delinquent children. We have already hinted at the desirability of a unified child care statute, covering both voluntary and compulsory care. It seems to us that the 1969 Act has failed in its laudable objective of decriminalizing and, to some degree, destigmatizing juvenile delinquency. In part, it must be said, the apparent failure is because the Act has never been implemented as its designers intended. The result can be seen as almost a re-stigmatization of local authority care and the erosion of the attempt to overturn Poor Law attitudes to 'children of the state' since 1948. We suspect that, even if the 1969 Act had been brought into full effect, the same problems would have arisen because of the fundamental difference in the central issue for protective and corrective types of care proceedings. Nevertheless, it is now abundantly clear that the constituency of support for the spirit of that Act has {230} effectively disintegrated. We are witnessing a return to a much more legalistic approach in England (although not in Scotland) and in North America, with a greater emphasis on due process, on proportionate sanctions and on criminal responsibility (cf. Freeman 1981, Tutt 1981). We have some sympathy with these arguments but we do not necessarily consider them applicable to child protection. By separating the two issues, we would be able to design different systems and procedures for dealing with their (rather different) features.

This raises one minor question for our earlier argument about the existing grounds: namely, whether commission of an offence should remain a ground for protective care proceedings. We would like to see this continue to be covered since prosecution will not always be appropriate where, for instance, a child commits an offence at the instigation of an adult. However, it may be that this could adequately be achieved by restoring the broad Victorian sense of 'moral danger', which, in recent years, has become restricted to sexual misconduct. The deletion of the offence provision would emphasize the difference between child care and child delinquency statutes. A similar case might be made in relation to truancy.

More importantly, however, a separate statute would allow the recognition of the central adversarial contest: between state and parents. The issue is the parents' adequacy as trustees, where the state is acting as a guardian of last resort for those unable to protect themselves. We have already amply documented the strains placed on care proceedings by the unnatural opposition of children and the state as the contesting parties and the exclusion of parents from an inquiry where their character and competence is under grave attack. We shall work through the procedural implications of this shortly.

Enforcement

As we have repeatedly insisted, statutes are not self-interpreting and self-enforcing. A detailed discussion of the operation of the relevant agencies is better postponed. For the present, however, we simply want to consider what the implications of recognizing particular types of applicant might be. In England, proceedings may be initiated by the police, the NSPCC or the local authority. If our arguments about the desirability of a separate child care statute are accepted, it seems hard to justify the continuing status of the police as possible applicants. While they obviously have an important part to play in preliminary decision-making, in assembling evidence and {231} in initiating criminal prosecution of parents, if thought appropriate, these do not require that they have an independent right to initiate protective care proceedings. This is a power which reflects the delinquency concerns of the 1969 Act and is inappropriate for mistreatment cases. Indeed, it is so rarely used that we cannot imagine serious objections to its discontinuation. The NSPCC also makes little use of its privilege, despite its attempts to retain applicant status during the passage of the 1969 Act. Our reservations here derive from the intrinsic lack of public accountability in any voluntary body. If we accept the reasoning set out in the previous chapter, then, although there may be valuable work to be done by voluntary associations, the state must properly retain a monopoly on compulsory powers in such an area. We think, then, that only local authorities should have the right to initiate protective care proceedings, although, as we argue later, there might be a case for requiring health authority participation in certain instances.

It should be stressed, however, that these arguments do not necessarily apply equally to countries with less developed state welfare provisions. England has a uniform system of local government which enables more or less equal access to social services throughout the country.[10] Where state facilities are less evenly distributed, there may be stronger arguments for allowing other agencies standing in protection cases. Here, however, we may need to revise our conceptions of what a police force is in a sparsely-settled rural area or how a church-run welfare agency is accountable in a strongly clerical community.

THE AGENCY SYSTEM

In devising an agency system to operate child protection legislation liberal states must, as we have seen, reconcile two conflicting objectives: respect for family autonomy and effective surveillance of child-rearing. American states have generally attempted to do this by means of mandatory reporting laws. Any member of a number of recognized occupations in health, education, welfare or law enforcement, or sometimes any citizen, who has adventitious contact with a child whom he or she has reason to suspect of having been mistreated is required, usually under threat of prosecution, to report these suspicions to a specified state agency. This is, however, a haphazard means of surveying the child population and, in particular, gives very limited access to the smallest and least socially visible children, who {232} may well be those most in need of outside protection. While there may be certain justifications for this in some of the remoter parts of the United States, it is hard to regard this as a very satisfactory basis for an effective and equitable system of child protection. The complex agency system which has evolved in England can, however, be seen to incorporate a number of ingenious attempts to resolve this problem, which we have collectively discussed as the division of regulatory labour. This, in effect, splits the processes of identifying, managing and, if necessary, compulsorily intervening in child mistreatment between a variety of autonomous but accountable state agencies.

At the heart of the English system lies the remarkable innovation of health visiting. Its crucial legitimations have been well identified by the American paediatrician, Kempe.

> To be successful in providing access to the child and to assure acceptance of this concept, it is necessary that it be provided in an equalitarian and universal manner. It must not only be for the poor or members of minority groups but must be for all children starting with newborn infants. (Kempe 1975: 693)

What is important about health visiting is that all children are surveyed with the implication that they may all be equally in need of protection from adult irresponsibility. Kempe (1976: 944) draws an analogy with compulsory education and the recognition that children must be adequately prepared to act as responsible citizens. Public scrutiny of child-rearing before school is the logical extension of that well-established obligation. It is not intended to impose a particular model of family life so much as to draw a bottom line in the quality of care provided, above which parents would be free to act as they chose.

Kempe's (1976: 943) enthusiasm leads him to propose that participation in a health visiting programme should be compulsory and to criticize the relatively passive attitude of health visitors in the face of certain client problems or resistance. We are less persuaded of the virtues of compulsion. The voluntary nature of the health visitor's access is a significant restraint on her intrusions into the privacy of the family and her lack of coercive powers emphasizes the importance of gaining the consent and cooperation of parents. As we saw in the previous chapter, it institutionalizes a preference for persuasion which is intrinsic to the liberal order. While it may well be that health visitors ought to be more suspicious than they sometimes {233} are, it does not seem appropriate to give them the investigative powers of a regulatory inspectorate.[11]

The main problem with health visiting is its lack of public accountability. In part, this is obviously achieved in the voluntary quasi-market relationship with clients; a health visitor who steps out of line finds doors closed to her. On the other hand, health visitors are public servants with collectively-defined objectives to promote. Their conduct and judgements cannot be purely a matter of individual fieldworkers' consciences or local client pressures. In this respect, we think that the supervisory powers of first-line managers need to be strengthened and a more bureaucratic relationship established. We consider that the current attempts to mimic general medical practice, by basing quality control on self-regulating work groups with little management contact, are fundamentally misguided in a nationalized health service.

Medical services, as we saw, are the other main points for identifications. We have, however, underlined their considerable deficiencies in making use of the information available within the various settings for doctor/patient contacts. There is no one simple solution to these problems, since many of the deficiencies reflect local rather than general organizational features. It would not, for instance, necessarily be appropriate for major teaching hospital accident departments to shift power towards nurses in the way that a district general might. A more relevant innovation might be a section on the patient record to allow receptionists or ambulance staff to enter comments indicating possible suspicions to prompt a more, investigative approach by the examining doctor. Similarly, the problems of doctor/community relations are rather different for a general practitioner working single-handed in a rural area and for a partner in group practice in an urban setting. In the former, we were impressed by the value of an enlarged clinical role for community physicians in deflecting the immediate problems of primary care doctors whose patients had no alternative source of medical attention.

The most important need on the medical side is for somebody whose job it is to fit the various elements of the service together and ensure that, whatever division of labour is locally adopted, it has some rationale and coherence. In theory this should be the duty of a community physician, but it is by no means clear that this is generally acknowledged or acted upon. We would take the view that every health authority should have a formally agreed policy statement on the responsibilities of hospital, community and primary care doctors, which should be regularly reviewed and monitored by a committee {234} representing all three groups under the chairmanship of a community physician. It might well be useful to consider the virtues of the Dutch system, where a designated Confidential Doctor (*vertrouwenarts*) acts as a central referral point and co-ordinator of services (Christopherson 1980, 1981). The system operating in the County authority in our study had many similarities. Again the logical person to fill this role is probably a community physician, using established referral networks. If mandatory reporting were ever thought desirable in England, then it could be implemented in parallel with infectious disease notifications, where the law requires similar technical breaches of confidentiality and confers immunity from civil actions.

We were generally impressed by the social services departments which we observed, although it must be recognized that we were studying a high-priority area which was, to some extent, insulated from the increasing pressures on resources and where skilled and experienced staff were concentrated. Through the operation of various assortative processes, it seems that local authorities end up, by and large, with the staff they deserve. Thus, although by the standards of the professional leadership some of the practice we saw might have been considered inadequate, it would be hard to argue that it was unacceptable to the local social services committee to whom, of course, the social workers are actually accountable. Although some authorities, of which Shire was an occasional example, appear to have difficulties in enforcing that accountability through the bureaucratic line of management and supervision, this often reflected divisions within the authority itself. In general, then, social workers seemed to be carrying out their assigned tasks to the best of their ability.

There were, however, three specific problems which we identified. First, the intake system could operate to screen out an unjustifiably high proportion of referrals, particularly from health visitors. In part, this was because health visitors were not very skilled at making referrals in a form which would oblige the recipients to accept them. In part, it was a matter of occupational rivalry. In part, it was due to the increasingly stringent approach to all referrals which the departments appeared to be adopting as their budgets were reduced. Second, some departments, including one of those studied, have a rather complaisant attitude to the risks of violence against their staff. In at least one case among those studied, a proper investigation was not carried out because the young woman social worker was afraid of a male cohabitee with a record of serious assaults. A colleague {235} had recently been stabbed by a client on another case and the department had refused to provide her with either administrative or legal support in a private prosecution and application for criminal injuries compensation. Violence is an intrinsic hazard for social workers but the risks do seem to be increasing with the growth of investigative work and the reduction in resources available to meet client needs. A more explicit recognition of this fact by employers seems overdue.

Finally, we were concerned about the distorting effects on the balance of social services work that appeared to be deriving from the pressure to conduct child protection work in a defensible fashion. It is arguable that some work is now being over-supervised and over-reviewed. More to the point are the implications of a static or growing share of a decreasing pool of resources going into child protection, as opposed to the support of the increasing population of dependent old people or the discharge of mentally ill or handicapped persons from large institutions to smaller, locally-based social service facilities. We are not convinced that any highly specialized or intensive mode of preventive social work intervention has demonstrated its success so overwhelmingly as to justify its cost at the expense of basic service provision for other groups. This is not, of course, an argument against funding such experimental or demonstration projects from other sources, but it is intended to strike a note of caution about further investment, as opposed to a more efficient or effective use of present resources.

If we were to point to a single problem with the present agency system, however, it would have to do with the lack of pressures for effective coordination. As we saw, the areas which had developed workable models had done so largely as a result of historical accident, and there were inherent problems with the stability of these solutions. On the other hand, too closely integrated a system would jeopardize the division of regulatory labour which, we have argued, is an important restraint on the oppressive potential of family regulation. Thus, we would not favour setting up unified health and social service authorities on the Northern Irish model. Two possible remedies have occurred to us. One would be the partial absorption of ARCs into a broader framework of joint planning, through which central funds might be channelled for demonstration projects involving health and social service collaboration. The other is the notion that where protective care proceedings are being considered on physical, psychological or emotional grounds, these should be on the joint application of health and local authorities. As we have seen, {236} evidence from both sources is essential in such proceedings anyway, so that prior agreement is already, *de facto,* essential. Our proposal, then, would merely formalize this. Its real impact, however, is intended to be organizational in that it would require the development of explicit procedures for identifying the distinct responsibilities and judgements of the key participants in the proceedings. If representatives of either party wished to block the other's desire to proceed, this would have to be clearly documented, in order to defend the decision at subsequent review. Similarly, in cases of disagreement, an arbitration procedure would be required, involving senior staff in much the same way as at present in County and Borough. The proposal is not intended to favour one occupation or agency at the expense of another but rather to recognize an existing situation and to underwrite what we regard as good practice in its resolution.

THE PROCESS OF ADJUDICATION

If the statutory framework provides for the goals of child-rearing and the agency system the means for their enforcement on parental trustees, the trinity is completed by the institutions created to determine the appropriateness of the agencies' complaints about the apparently inadequate discharge of the trust. In most Anglo-American jurisdictions, this means the juvenile court.

The quality of justice in juvenile courts has come under increasing criticism in recent years. Freeman (1981: 210) asserts, for instance, that

> Juvenile courts were once hailed as the best plan 'for the conservation of human life and happiness ever conceived by civilised man' (Hoffman 1927). We know better today . . . One of the most unsatisfactory features of juvenile justice is that in reality there is very little justice.

He goes on to criticize the use of social inquiry reports, the lack of legal representation, the co-option of magistrates by probation and police, the indeterminacy of dispositions and the lack of proportionality between dispositions and offences, concluding that

> Children have the right to claim that they should be treated like adult offenders. Concessions made to protect them have been revealed for what they are: measures which undermine their rights. (1981: 225)[12] {237}

The irony is, of course, that the implicit standard for evaluating juvenile justice is based on a model of practice in adult courts which have themselves been subject to exactly the same attacks (e.g. Carlen 1976). Silbey (1981: 14), summarizing the American literature, concludes:

> The most basic criticism is that within these courts there is very limited adversarial process, the result of which is an attenuation of the due process rights of defendants . . . The lower courts emphasize rapid case processing and volume control, outcome rather than process . . . Observers report that judicial arbitrariness is common, that noncompliance with rules, haphazard administration, racial discrimination, corruption and nonfeasance are pervasive.

As Atkinson and Drew (1979: 17) comment, in relation to the work of Carlen and Emerson, the difficulty with such analyses is that, having noticed specific features of court proceedings by reference to extrinsic theories or metaphors like 'capitalism', these are then used to warrant descriptions of those features as 'inefficient' or 'oppressive' without asking what specific problems within the setting such features might be resolving. Although these remarks are principally directed at the study of formal exchanges in courtrooms, they are more broadly applicable. This is reflected in the emergence of what one might call a 'revisionist' school of court ethnography which is still comparatively little known outside North America. Basically this asserts that courts are best analysed as examples of organizations rather than as a special category of social institution. As such they exhibit many of the features of all organizations which result from attempts to make them work in a way which will be reasonably satisfactory for members, clients and sponsors or regulators over time. Feeley (1979: 25) remarks:

> To the casual observer, the dizzying array of rationales for decisions may appear arbitrary and chaotic but to one familiar with the court there is a logic – even if it is unwritten and unarticulated – to the process. The importance and intensity of these various visions of justice have often been ignored by observers of the criminal courts. After looking at the courts and failing to find full-fledged adversarial proceedings they too quickly conclude that all concern for justice has given way to the pressures of heavy caseloads, organizational security and bureaucratic self-interest. The abandonment of a concern with one form of justice is too often incorrectly seen as an abandonment of *all* concern for justice. {238}

Silbey (1981: 21) refers to Weber's (1954: 230) description of English magistrates' courts as a kind of Khadi justice.[13] As she stresses, however, Weber attached no stigma to the lack of formal rationality in this empirical and particularistic style of court. It might not be part of an ordered scheme but could still flow from a due exercise of reason and judgement. The researcher's task is to reconstruct that deliberation and elucidate its principles.

This work does not, so far, seem to have impinged on studies of juvenile justice, although both Silbey and Feeley point to possible cross-overs. Silbey (1981: 23) comments:

> There is a social interest in seeing that, when a hurt is translated into a legal issue, the hurt gets taken care of too. There is the public interest in preventing the damages that flow from the accumulated personal hurts such as alcoholism, drug abuse, child neglect, etc. Yet the modern ethic of responsive justice with solutions tailored to fit individual problems creates a paradox for the system . . . Within such a framework of individualized justice, emphasis is placed upon information and perspectives which are inconsistent with formal legal rationality and adversarial due process . . . psychological 'evidence', therapeutic diagnoses and social history of the family are relevant to a just and equitable consideration of the case. However, these factors are uncomfortably out of place when they are tailored to the requirement of legal evidence, proof of guilt and considerations of legal responsibility. Yet they are the stuff of decision-making and adjudication in the lower courts.

In his study of the New Haven Court of Common Pleas, Feeley (1979: 284-6) goes even further:

In many respects the decision-making process in the Court of Common Pleas is strongly related to the practices and theory of juvenile courts. The modern theory of juvenile justice argues for individualized justice tailored to treat a wide range of factors as relevant and to respond to the 'whole' person. It de-emphasizes the strictly 'legal' proceedings, and purposefully expands its inquiry beyond and away from the provoking incident in order to determine the root of the child's trouble and consider appropriate alternative responses . . . . The same tensions long recognized as a serious problem within the system of juvenile justice seem to exist in much the same form in the lower criminal courts as well. If I am correct, the central problem of the court is rooted in neither the poor quality of the personnel nor the {239} tendency to avoid responsibility; it is entrenched in the officials' aspirations to do good, in the impulse for flexibility and substantive justice which gives rise to competing conceptions of justice. The freedom to pick and choose among these conceptions undercuts the morality of all of them, and ironically the impulse to provide justice seems to foster a sense of injustice.

Most of this discussion has, of course, related to criminal justice. Nevertheless, these arguments would be equally applicable to care proceedings, which are, officially, civil in nature. Quite apart from the fact that they are heard before a court whose major work is with criminal juveniles and dealt with under a statutory framework designed for delinquents, the procedural rules governing civil matters are drafted to leave more discretion to the courts. The burden of proof is, formally, weaker and magistrates have been encouraged by the then Lord Chief Justice, in *Humberside County Council v. DPR* [1977], to regard such cases as 'essentially non-adversary . . . an objective examination of the position of the child.'

It is the essence of magistrates' justice that it is a commonsense justice which seeks to resolve the tension between formal legal rationality and individual human troubles. Such discretion may produce results unpalatable to those who make a fetish of formalism, but this is not necessarily a ground for discrediting it unless the practice of the courts can be shown to be seriously flawed, whether by reference to the actualities of case processing or outcomes. We have stressed this point because it is easy to produce superficial criticisms of courts, as with all organizations, by making ironic contrasts between practice and abstract ideals. All ideals have to be operationalized, however, and without a proper appreciation of that process, changes in formal rules or procedures may have remarkably little impact, unless they are seen to coincide with the practical reasoning of those who must operate them.

The various attempts to reconstitute child welfare legislation to produce a degree of perceived justice are, in many ways, a tribute to the flexibility and ingenuity of the juvenile courts. At the same time it is obvious that there is likely to be a great deal of local variation and that much depends upon the relationships of the participants. Local variation is not necessarily an undesirable feature if we accept the essentially subjective nature of the standards which are being applied. If the children coming before a court are those whose circumstances offend local sensibilities, as mediated through the {240} locally-controlled social services departments, then it is arguable that applications should be locally evaluated.

The success of the system, however, depends upon the mutual trust of solicitors, courts and public authorities. Each must have confidence that a departure from legality will not adversely affect their interests. In the provinces, this is sustained by the continuing relationships into which the participants are bound. They are all 'repeat players', people who are dealing regularly with each other and who anticipate doing so again in the future. Sharp practice in any particular case may bring success but so compromise future dealings as to negate its own value to the perpetrator. This is a particular constraint on private practice solicitors who might have most to gain from a technical assault on the local authority, but it also acts as a restraint on the local authority in ensuring that it is seen to have put up a reasonable case and justified the court's attention. The latter is of particular importance in county areas, where the cases tend to be dealt with at a specially convened court rather than being mixed with the regular juvenile business.

Such an arrangement is, of course, rather fragile. We suspect that many of the problems in London are associated with the density of juvenile courts and the overcrowded market for young barristers which means that many of the advocates appearing against the local authority are 'one-shot' players who do not have the same continuing interests at stake.

The danger is, of course, that this system built on mutual confidence could degenerate into mutual back-slapping. We saw no evidence of this in any of the areas we studied but the danger was well-recognized. It may be noteworthy that the authorities with more integrated health and welfare systems tended to have more distant relationships with local courts but this could have been coincidental. In our view, however, the main deterrent to a rubber-stamping approach was the division between local authority legal and social services. The former's defence of their own position and, indeed their conscience, led them to stress the uncertainty and rigour of court proceedings which deterred the presentation of all but the most evidentially sound cases. In our opinion, and it can be no more than that, none of the successful cases in our study could be said to be legally inadequate.

Nevertheless, these *ad hoc* arrangements cannot be said to represent a sound basis for regulation, do leave scope for procedural abuse and may give rise to concern over issues of substantive or territorial justice. In our view, though, it may be better to build any {241} reform on an attempt to codify existing practice as representing a workable organization of events and procedures which already command a sense of fairness and justice in the settings where they operate. Changes which do not respect that are likely to be similarly evaded and fail in their objectives.

We have already argued for an overt recognition of the *de facto* adversarial character of the conflict between the authority and the parents. In our view, protective care proceedings ought properly to be conceptualized as a dispute between parents and state agencies over the appropriate care of a child. The logic of this is that parents should be respondent parties with full participation in the hearing and access to legal aid. If this is conceded, however, should children retain separate representation? The case for this has been espoused by a growing number of commentators, mostly lawyers, on both sides of the Atlantic and the present British government has edged towards it in the Criminal Justice Bill before Parliament as this book went to press. In our view, however, the arguments in favour are so weak that such provision ought to be regarded as an extravagance in the present economic climate.[14] Given the complexity of the identification of mistreatment, there is an element of unreality, especially where young children are concerned, in the concept of an 'independent' person representing the child's interests as if they were an objectively discoverable entity which only awaited a mouthpiece. At best, such a person can merely offer an opinion to the court on matters which it is for the court to decide within a clearly adversarial contest between parental and local authority versions of a child's interests. At each stage the court has only two options: to find the mistreatment established or not; and, if proven, to order supervised parental care or removal into state care. We have a great deal of sympathy for the local authority solicitor who remarked that if he was not in court in the child's interest, what was he doing there? This study has clearly disproved the proposition that local authorities are bringing unjustifiable cases. If they were, the greater resources available to parents as parties would permit a more effective operation of the normal adversarial restraints. In exceptional cases, especially if it is likely that a child will be removed from his or her home, there may be an argument for a discretionary power for the court to commission a report from an officer of its own appointment, on the wisdom or propriety of the local authority's action, but there seems no justification for the presence of three lawyers and teams of witnesses, all at the public expense, when two will do the job quite adequately. The suppression of separate representation of children {242} would, of course, effectively make this a nil-cost reform, since they are almost invariably represented by a publicly reimbursed lawyer at present.

If these cases were more vigorously contested, as a result of recognizing parents as parties, some elements of the present commonsense fabric might be threatened, with associated risks of a further drift from care to wardship. As we have already indicated, we think such a development should be discouraged and it seems appropriate to introduce safeguards against legalistic mischief-making. In fact most of these could be provided by extending the provision of the Civil Evidence Act 1968 with its more liberal attitude to the treatment of hearsay and agency records, principles which have already been broadly endorsed by appellate decisions. It might also be worth clarifying, by regulations, the status of opinion evidence from field-workers, especially social workers and health visitors, again on the basis of regularizing current practice. A Regulation could, for example, provide that opinion evidence as to (i) the child's physical and emotional condition; (ii) the standard of care afforded to him and its effects on his condition; (iii) the competence and willingness of the parents to provide or seek proper care for the child, and any other matter relevant to these questions, may be given and afforded such weight as is appropriate having regard to the qualifications and experience of the witness and his or her opportunities for forming the relevant judgements. We would hope that such a provision would prevent the exclusion of important evidence by appeals to technicalities and encourage the more experienced social workers to bring to court cases which they believe fall within the terms of the 1969 Act but which they at present feel reluctant to bring due to uncertainty as to their status as witnesses. Of course such witnesses may be asked the grounds upon which they base their opinions, and increased co-operation between legal and social services departments should encourage social workers to pay more attention to crystallizing and recording such grounds.

Suggestions have been made that courts should have the power to order the compulsory production ('discovery') of local authority records.[15] We do not feel that this is appropriate. If proceedings become more adversarial, the risk of irresponsible disclosures could inhibit authorities from bringing legitimate cases. Our own observations tend to the conclusion that there is little in the records which is unavailable elsewhere that would help parents' solicitors. There would be a clear danger that the power would be used to enable the parents' lawyers to rummage for evidence of bias or prejudice which {243} would then mislead the court from paying proper attention to the evidence actually presented by the authority, on which alone the issue should be decided.

There are two further points on which we should like to offer comments, although they are rather on the margins of our study. The first of these relates to the range of dispositions available to the court. We want, particularly, to note the deficiencies of supervision orders in mistreatment cases. These are designed for dealing with young delinquents as a weaker version of probation. Consequently, they confer only powers relating to a juvenile's conduct, whereas the need in protection work is a power to direct parents. This might be done in two ways: first, the parents might retain their rights to the child but the authority be given express power to direct their discharge; or, second, *all* parental rights might be transferred to the authority, except that of removing the child, and delegated back to the parents on such terms as the authority thought fit. In either case, the authority should acquire a right of entry to the home or, at least, refusal of entry should be a ground for obtaining a warrant under section 40 of the Children and Young Persons Act 1933, as it is already in the case of privately fostered children or children protected under adoption legislation.[16] We also think that, in either case, the authority should acquire an emergency power to remove the child for a period not exceeding eight days without recourse to a place of safety order. This period could be extended on application to the court if a case was being prepared for a 'full' care order. We do not believe it would be right to give the court powers to direct local authorities in their supervision of parents but, as a safeguard against abuse, it might be appropriate to restrict the duration of the order to one year. We are sceptical about the efficacy of such intervention for a longer period and consider that the authority should be compelled to justify extensions of its supervision. It should, of course, be possible for parents to apply for an earlier discharge, on the grounds that the order's existence or operation are not in the best interests of the child.

The court should retain power to order a child's removal under a care order. With these extra safeguards, however, we think that a supervision order could become a more satisfactory alternative. Our view is that, in several cases in our study, the authority would have been willing to leave a child at home, if such powers had been available to enforce parental co-operation. We also suspect that it would be a more satisfactory disposition for preventive intervention, if a probabilistic ground were introduced. {244}

Our other point relates to appeals. If our arguments about the changes in party status were accepted, then parents would acquire a clearly established right of appeal. Were it thought fit to separate delinquency and mistreatment cases, however, there might also be good arguments for giving local authorities that right. The present restriction reflects the influence of criminal models where the prosecution characteristically has few grounds for appealing from an acquittal. This is not the case in civil actions and we see no reason to exclude protective care proceedings. More importantly, we would argue for the transfer of appeals from the present criminal line via the Crown Court to the Queen's Bench Division into a civil line via County Courts to the Family Division. This would not impose any increase in cost or other barriers to access but would begin to consolidate family jurisdiction in the courts which already have extensive experience in such work. It might also provide a more satisfactory basis for rationalizing the relationship between care and wardship proceedings.

All of these institutional reforms, however, can at best have a limited impact without the cultivation of more critical child protection practice. Legal or organizational changes can facilitate this but much ultimately rests on the way all sorts of people actually carry out their daily work. As we have shown, child protection raises complex moral and political issues which have no one right technical solution. Practitioners are asked to solve problems every day that philosophers have argued about for the last two thousand years and will probably debate for the next two thousand. Inevitably, arbitrary lines have to be drawn and hard cases decided. These difficulties, however, are not a justification for avoiding judgements. Moral evaluations can and must be made if children's lives and well-being are to be secured. What matters is that we should not disguise this and pretend it is all a matter of finding better checklists or new models of psychopathology – technical fixes when the proper decision is a decision about what constitutes a good society. How many children should be allowed to perish in order to defend the autonomy of families and the basis of the liberal state? How much freedom is a child's life worth?

Postscript • 1995

The Protection of Children was first published in 1983. In the intervening years, there have been many changes in the institutions we described. The legal framework has been radically amended by the Children Act 1989. The health services have been reorganized twice, on the basis of the 1983 Griffiths Review and the 1989 White Paper, *Working for Patients*. Social services departments have seen more incremental changes, but the cumulative impact has been to create at least as much turbulence in their organization. *The Protection of Children,* then, no longer stands as a description of a particular set of institutional arrangements. Why should there be a case for republishing what is, by now, an historical study? There are two ways of answering this question. One is to note that the rationale of parts of the Children Act and the current structure may be more apparent if we understand the context from which they emerged. The second, and much stronger, justification is that, although the institutions may have changed, the practical problems and moral dilemmas of child protection work have not. As an analysis of those dilemmas, *The Protection of Children* has a continuing relevance to everyday practice, to organizational design and to legal drafting or adjudication.

THE CRITICAL RESPONSE

The first edition of this book was generally well-received by its reviewers, both in the UK and in North America, and had an identifiable impact on both an academic and a policy audience. Three points have been made, however, which merit a particular reply.

A number of reviewers commented on the lack of methodological {246} justification and suggested that there should have been an additional chapter or an appendix which explained and defended the use of an ethnographic method. It has been suggested that this omission might be explained by the economics of publishing. In fact, it was a deliberate decision on our part. We saw no reason why we should feel obliged to write a specific justification simply because we had chosen to use a qualitative approach. The same challenge is rarely made to quantitative studies which are simply asserted as the right way to address some problem. The same is true here. The questions posed, partly by the team and partly by the Department of Health when they became involved, addressed issues of process which were most appropriately handled with some sort of qualitative method. The justification lies in the persuasiveness of the analysis produced by this method rather than in a philosophical or theoretical defence (cf. Silverman 1989). There are plenty of other texts designed for that purpose. What we actually did is described on pages 17-26 {pp. 20-30} and associated footnotes.

Some reviewers, particularly King (1983), were critical of the decision not to give more attention to the perspectives of the families on the receiving end of the child protection system. As we pointed out in our reply (Dingwall et al. 1984), *The Protection of Children* is a study of *organizational* decision-making. What are important are the representations of families constructed by the investigative and definitional work of child protection services. Suppose we had interviewed the families and formed a different view from that of the agents involved? Why should the results of our investigative procedures be any more valid than theirs? We were not interested in producing an ironical analysis and are profoundly sceptical of the idea that anybody can produce a "true rate" of child abuse (see also Graham et al. 1985; Dingwall 1989a). This study is about the way in which child abuse is socially constructed by those groups who are licensed to define the condition. An account could, of course, be written of the alternative constructions that might be possible, as a problem in the sociology of knowledge. This, in some measure, is what Nigel Parton (1985; 1991) has attempted. However, it was not what we were trying to do.

Finally, there has been recurrent confusion about one of the theoretical ideas which has gained most currency from the book, namely the idea that one of the elements in the framing of any organizational decision was an institutionalized preference for positive evaluations of clients; what we called the *rule of optimism*. (As Stimson 1985 has pointed out, organizations may also operate under a rule of pessimism, where all clients {247} are evaluated negatively until proven otherwise.) This has been read by, for example, Louis Blom-Cooper in the *Report of the Inquiry into the Death of Jasmine Beckford* (1985) as if it were describing a psychological property of individuals. This leads to a picture of child protection agents as naïve and easily deceived, which has many echoes of the tabloid press images of social workers. Our usage, as Dingwall (1986) stressed in a review of the Jasmine Beckford report, was quite different. The rule of optimism is a dimension of the organizational culture of child protection services which is founded on the deep ambivalence that we feel in a liberal society about state intervention in families. Although the rule is, of course, operated by individuals, they do so as members of organizations whose structures, incentives and sanctions are designed to sustain the preference which it embodies.

RESEARCH AND WRITING SINCE 1983

As might be expected, six years' work yielding two million words of data was difficult to compress into a single volume. Various parts of *The Protection of Children* have, then, been supplemented by other analyses of the data published elsewhere. A number of these were in print at the time of original publication and appear in the main bibliography, including Dingwall (1980) on the organizational problems of teamwork in primary care, Murray et al. (1983) on local government lawyers and Dingwall and Murray (1983) on the management of children in accident departments. Two subsequent papers also address empirical issues.

Dingwall and Eekelaar (1984) extended the argument about trends in state intervention through an analysis of child care statistics between 1951 and 1981. This demonstrated that many of the arguments about the growth of intervention were based on misinterpretations of the data, particularly the elementary mistake of failing to correct raw numbers for the changing size of the population at risk over the period. The likelihood of a child being taken into care appeared to have remained more or less unchanged over that period and the increase in numbers during the 1970s was almost entirely accounted for by the rapid growth in the child population during that decade. This paper also contains the results of a follow-up inquiry in 1980 into the care careers of the 34 children considered for removal into care in Shire during 1977-78. Of the 15 children who became subject to care orders, 7 were still away from home, all but two being either physically damaged by the original abuse {248} or lacking kin who might be available to act as alternative caretakers.

Dingwall (1989b), which is essentially a summary of Chapters 2-4 commissioned for an Open University text, adds some brief comments on the definition of sexual abuse. We had systematically sought to collect data on this topic throughout the original fieldwork but found so little that it did not justify a discussion in the original report. Although most informants recognized that this formed part of the agenda for child protection work, and some acknowledged its prevalence in their own locality, there was no organizational framework within which these perceptions could be articulated and made into dimensions of practice. Where these cases did arise, however, they were fitted into the same sorts of framing as we described for physical abuse and neglect.

We have also continued our explorations on the historical background to child care law and the debates around the nature of social control in liberal states (Dingwall 1992; 1994a; Dingwall and Eekelaar 1986; 1988; Dingwall and Robinson 1990) and on the theoretical basis of trusteeship and children's rights (Eekelaar 1991; 1993; 1994a; 1994b).

Although there has been considerable criticism of the general argument in *The Protection of Children* from people who adopt a different value position (Fox Harding 1991 has a good review of this debate), the findings of fact have proved remarkably resilient. Corby (1987) reported on a comparable study in two metropolitan areas in the North West of England, which seem to fill the sampling gap acknowledged by the present authors. He also found the preference for non-intervention (pp. 58-9), although he explained this in a slightly different way, and supported the analysis of the difficulties of case conferences and their *de facto* role in organizing cases for intervention (pp. 74-5). He endorsed our view that care proceedings were a 'last resort' form of intervention (p. 75). More recently, Thorpe (1994) has presented data from a career study through agency records of child protection cases in Australia (655 cases) and the UK (100 cases). These provide additional support for the analysis in Chapters 3 and 4 of the moral filtering of the population of physically damaged children and, in particular, of the role of noncompliance with voluntary interventions in precipitating coercive actions. Thorpe notes some differences in the treatment of Aboriginal children in Australia, compared with our discussion of minority ethnic groups: however, he also indicates that these seem to have their roots in an older, assimilationist tradition which was giving way to an ethnically sensitive (or culturally relativist) approach. The official policies had, in any case, been undercut by the exigencies of everyday work in the way {249} we describe on pages 74-78 {pp. 82-86}. Thorpe (1994: 168) quotes a service manager in a remote area: 'If they asked me to strictly apply these definitions [of child abuse] and act on them in this region, then we would be taking nearly all the Aboriginal children into care'.

WHAT HAS CHANGED?

These studies all pre-date the Children Act 1989 and the intensive educational campaigns launched around this and addressed to all the professionals involved in child protection work. Although the Department of Health has commissioned a number of studies of the operation of this legislation, they have not replicated the study described here and there is, as yet, little indication of the extent to which practice has changed at street level, if at all. There are, however, signs from other sources that the Act and associated procedural changes have had a limited impact.

In a way, this should not be too surprising: to the extent that a number of the changes reflected a desire to align the law with practice, then we might not expect to see major differences in the way cases are actually handled. Examples of this might include the articulation of the 'last resort' nature of care orders in the 'no order' presumption; the redrafting of the grounds for intervention, including the incorporation of apprehended risk as a ground; and the introduction of civil evidence rules. Others, such as the restraint on local authorities' use of wardship, would have an impact restricted to particular areas which had local reasons for working outside the previous statutory provisions. However, these 'tidying up' elements of the Act did sit uneasily with others that were intended to produce more fundamental changes in child protection practice (Dingwall and Eekelaar 1990; Bainham 1990; Cretney 1990; Parton 1991; Eekelaar 1991). These sections leaned more in the direction of parents' rights by emphasising the primary nature of parental responsibility, enhancing their status in legal proceedings and their right to be consulted over any planned intervention. The result seems to be a more open forensic contest before the court, between local authority, parents and guardians *ad litem*. The hearing has become the point at which it is most apparent how the Act has privileged parental responsibility and the procedural rights associated with it, a message reinforced by the report of the Butler-Sloss inquiry in Cleveland and the training packages sponsored by the Department of Health. The 'rule of optimism' remains intact: only it is now explicitly underwritten by the {250} Act and policed by the courts.

The obsession with proceduralism has been noted by others (e.g. Harris 1990; Thorpe 1994). Having undercut the legitimacy of the local state and its child protection services, central government has sought to shore up the structure by elaborating the framework within which action occurs and the procedural rights of the people who are affected by it. This is well-illustrated in the Report (1988) of the Butler-Sloss inquiry into the Cleveland affair. Between February and July 1987, two consultant paediatricians had diagnosed 121 children as having been victims of sexual abuse, the majority then having been removed into care by the social services department under Place of Safety Orders. In context, this can clearly be seen in evidence submitted to the inquiry as an attempt by the social services to operate under a 'rule of pessimism' following Louis Blom-Cooper's strictures in his report on the death of Jasmine Beckford (1985) (Dingwall 1989b). In effect, the evidence of the paediatricians was taken on the kind of 'strict liability' basis that we sketched at the beginning of Chapter Two. The result was politically unacceptable, with a wave of complaint from parents that found a ready audience in a traditionalist local Labour MP and sections of the tabloid press. The subsequent inquiry made no attempt to evaluate the correctness or otherwise of the diagnoses or whether the children's return home had actually favoured their welfare. It simply dealt with the affair as a matter of procedural correctness. The processual failures compromised the legitimacy of the intervention, whether justified or not.

The Cleveland Affair overtook the lengthy process of consensus-building which civil servants had been carrying out jointly with the Law Commission during the 1980s in what came to be known as the Review of Child Care Law. It gave a great boost to the parental rights critics of the system as we described it, who had already received significant support from mid-1980s research findings that parents who had been on the receiving end of care interventions had poor relationships with social workers (e.g. Packman et al. 1986; Milham et al. 1986). This work was picked up and endorsed by the Department of Health (e.g. 1991a: 39-40) and linked to the reconceptualization of voluntary care and to the elaborated procedural role of parents as a form of partnership which made the local authority 'accountable to the parents'.

We have always been rather sceptical of the way in which these studies interpreted their data. Our research had suggested that poor relationships between parents and their social worker might well be a precipitant rather than a consequence of care interventions. As we also pointed out {251} (Dingwall et al. 1984), Voysey's (1975) analysis of the possible accounts available to parents with children in trouble, in her case with severely handicapped children, makes it difficult to suppose that a care intervention could be presented positively to an inquirer. The moral nature of parenthood in our society is such that it is almost impossible to conceive of a way in which someone could simultaneously claim to be a good parent who loved their child and that they were on friendly terms with the social workers who had removed the child because of some alleged mistreatment. My status as a parent depends upon my contestation of the right to be the primary caretaker with those who have declared me unfit or incompetent. However, these methodological problems have not been allowed to get in the way of politically convenient conclusions. It is the classic role of research as 'window-dressing', providing a legitimation for a predetermined policy (Cohen and Taylor 1972: 205-7).

The effect is the preoccupation with proceduralism and legalism that has dismayed an increasing number of observers. The issue is no longer one of taking the *right* decision in a child protection case but of taking a *defensible* decision. This may confer a false sense of security at considerable resource cost. As Dingwall (1986) remarked, increasing the complexity of a system increases the number of points at which errors can occur. It is not clear that care hearings with a minimum of three lawyers, all paid for from public funds, calling evidence and examining witnesses, are the most cost-effective way of taking a quality decision. The elaboration of inter-agency procedural codes can simply slow decision-making and tie up resources in monitoring compliance. Dealing with the complexity of the code itself becomes a disincentive to action. At the same time, the codes' elaboration increases the risk to individuals: with increased complexity, an inquiry into any specific failure is more likely to be able to find some breach that can be used with hindsight against those involved. It is much safer to find a reason not to identify a case as a candidate example of abuse or neglect in the first place. While these changes may appear to deal with the problem of legitimacy, they do so at the cost of reinforcing the bias against intervention.

These structural changes are complemented by changes in the culture of child protection services. The new buzzword is 'empowerment', particularly in social work but, to a lesser extent, also in health visiting and other psychosocial agencies. Ward and Mullender (1991: 21) point to the way in which the term has been adopted to cover a wide range of philosophies from New Right consumerism to radical anti-professional {252} user movements. They argue that it needs to be associated with a more specific notion of oppression, both as a state of affairs and as a process that institutionalizes and reproduces the interests and values of particular groups, not as overt repression but 'moderating and containing conflict and defining what is to be seen as 'normal' and 'acceptable' through, for example, the workings of the law, the media and the educational system (p.23)'. Empowerment is a systematic form of resistance to this. It cannot be based on individual action as consumerists claim but requires some form of collective mobilization where people are helped to see their private troubles as expressions of public issues (see Wright Mills 1970: 17-20). This collective mobilization can be facilitated by the self-denial of professionals, who can assemble groups of people with common troubles without presuming to direct their analysis or action.

In this respect, Ward and Mullender are declaring themselves heir to the radical social work ideas of the 1970s which we discuss on pages 74-75 {pp. 82-83}. However, as Page (1992) observes, the result is no more coherent. What constitutes 'anti-oppressive mobilization' is still decided by professionals. A group of white working class youths mobilizing around their private trouble of unemployment might conclude that an appropriate response would be to join the British National Party and campaign for discrimination in their favour. This could be experienced as empowering, as the result of a user analysis and user-determined action but Page thinks it unlikely that Ward and Mullender would want to facilitate it. They have no answer to results of user action which do not lead to their preferred strategy of general collective mobilization against all forms of oppression. Page also note their lack of realism about the pragmatic obligations of practitioners working in organizations with public resources and a structure of accountability to politicians and taxpayers who expect them to deliver practical responses to practical problems. Do Ward and Mullender really want to see abused women refused referral to refuges which aim solely to provide a safe haven rather than a transformative experience, if the former are the only resource available in a crisis? This approach, Page concludes, enables practitioners to 'cling to the vestiges of a personally rewarding form of 'radical' practice' while offering little to the disadvantaged themselves.

The fundamental problem, which Page does not address directly, is the radicals' misunderstanding of the nature of society (see Strong and Dingwall 1989). Society is the means by which human passions are ordered and limited. Power in itself is neither good nor bad: it is simply *there*. It upholds a framework of relationships which limit human choices {253} in ways which make joint, co-operative action possible. There can, of course, be a variety of forms of social organization but all of them involve some element of oppression in Mullender and Ward's sense. Indeed, as Page implies, their own paper only envisages the substitution of one form of regulation for another, the decision of the psychosocial practitioner as to whether to facilitate the emerging user analysis and actions or to destabilize them until the preferred outcome is achieved.

In the process, however, the ideology of empowerment undercuts the legitimacy of such power as child protection agents are expected to employ, in much the same way as the idea of cultural relativism did in our original analysis. The use of power by child protection agents in the interests of children is in contradiction to the empowerment of their parents to resist the oppression which is thought to be responsible for their abusive behaviour. We still see a device which operates to push candidate cases of abuse out of the system. More perniciously, however, it may also lead to the co-option of parents in ways which nullify the legal protections which the Children Act is supposed to have introduced.

This is a more speculative conclusion in the absence of good ethnographic data on the new-style case conferences. In passing, we may note the resilience of the traditional case conference, restyled the 'strategy discussion' (Department of Health 1991b; cf. Parton 1991: 127-31), where the agencies come together to review evidence and plan investigations, much as they did when we were studying them. Case conferences are now supposed to be the embodiment of the spirit of partnership under the Act, where parents and professionals seek to reach an agreement about a plan for a child's protection. However, it seems arguable that, in practice, they may simply reproduce many of the procedural defects of the old-style care proceedings, with parents being confronted with the professionals' case against them and asked to accept this without serious forensic test. The parent who does not 'volunteer' to cooperate and to share in making a plan whose parameters are predefined by the professionals, is likely to find this treated as further evidence of their incorrigibility, legitimating compulsory action. We have never thought that parental participation in case conferences would be the panacea that parents' rights groups claimed and have yet to see any evidence to challenge this proposition. Even Stevenson (in press), an author sympathetic to the policy, accepts that there have been and continue to be serious problems with its implementation.

The greater emphasis on proceduralism and legalism has been interpreted by some commentators (e.g. King and Piper 1991; {254} King and

Trowell 1992) as indicative of a kind of legal colonization of the child protection system. This critique, which is mainly theoretical and owes much to Teubner's (e.g. 1988) writings on the sociology of law, asserts that law reconstructs social reality in terms of its own discourse which is irreconcilable with the discourse of the helping professions. This is not the place to explore the problems with this analysis, but like so much German Idealism, it has difficulty in responding to some fairly obvious empirical objections. Law as an academic discipline and in its formal texts may well take on the appearance of an autonomous and self-reproducing system. In the world of practice, it forms a part of the governance structure of modern states and depends for its own legitimacy on the extent to it can engage in successful transactions with other parts of this structure. Law does not determine its own legitimacy; legitimacy for law, as for any other social institution, is an environmental response to the organization (cf. Meyer and Rowan 1977; March and Olsen 1989). As Cotterell (1992: 65-70) stresses in the course of a more general critique, law is *people's* work not an abstract communicative system. Those people create symbols which others may use to legitimize their own activities but legal symbols, in turn, acquire their legitimacy from their use and from the extent to which others regard them as encapsulating value-statements which accord with their own expectations (see also the discussion of the limited impact of the US Supreme Court on social policy by Rosenberg 1993). The fact that, in market societies, law may have become a preferred source of legitimation does not mean that the legal system is immune or indifferent to the responses of its own environment. The child protection system has not been colonized by law: rather the present mode of governmentality, the interlocking system of ideas and institutions that constitutes the cultural ordering of a society (Foucault 1979; Burchell et al. 1991), treats law as its most powerful instrument of legitimation (cf. Dingwall 1994b).

CHILD PROTECTION IN THE 1990s

The Children Act 1989 was a remarkable piece of legislation. It tried to create a uniform and coherent framework which brought together developments in public and private child care law that had remained separate for centuries (Eekelaar and Dingwall 1990: 1-18). However, the law cannot be isolated from the political context within which it was written. The result is a preoccupation with procedural matters and an {255} elision of child protection and the promotion of child welfare. The political abandonment of the idea that there might be a collective interest in facilitating the physical, educational and social development of children through a search for need and public investment to support private efforts has simply left a more refined system of social policing, in its twentieth rather than its eighteenth century meaning. Although the Children Act was meant to stand for a generation, much as the Children Act 1948 did, a better parallel may be the Children and Young Persons Act 1969, whose aspirations were overturned by political change before the ink was dry from the printer. The Children Act signals the limits of legal routes to change. It could not prescribe organizational coherence much as it might aspire to intellectual coherence. Its full potential may only be realised in a context where it is matched a positive political commitment to the welfare of the nation's children, that seeks to use the permissive sections of the Act to promote their well-being and to offer resources to parents in support of this rather than to wait to react to the failures of overburdened families.

Nottingham, Oxford, Devon
January 1995

We are grateful to Olive Stevenson, Jim Christopherson and Robert Page for their comments and suggestions on this postscript.

References • 1995

Bainham, A (1990) 'The privatisation of the public interest in children', *Modern Law Review* 53, 206-21.

Burchell, G., Gordon, C. and Miller, P. (1991) *The Foucault Effect: Studies in Governmentality,* London, Harvester Wheatsheaf.

Cohen, S. and Taylor, L. (1972) *Psychological Survival: The Experience of Long-Term Imprisonment,* Harmondsworth, Penguin.

Corby, B. (1987) *Working with Child Abuse,* Milton Keynes, Open University Press.

Cotterell, R. (1992) *The Sociology of Law: An Introduction* (second edition), London, Butterworths.

Cretney, S. (1990) 'Defining the limits of state intervention: the child and the courts' in Freestone, D., ed., *Children and the Law: Essays in Honour of Professor H.K. Bevan,* Hull, Hull University Press.

Department of Health (1991a) *Patterns and Outcomes in Child Placement,* London, Her Majesty's Stationery Office.

Department of Health (1991b) *Working Together,* London, Her Majesty's Stationery Office.

Dingwall, R. (1986) 'The Jasmine Beckford Affair', *Modern Law Review* 49, 489-507.

Dingwall, R. (1989a) 'Some problems about predicting child abuse and neglect', in Stevenson, O., ed., *Child Abuse: Public Policy and Professional Practice,* Brighton, Wheatsheaf.

Dingwall, R. (1989b) 'Labelling children as abused or neglected', in Stainton Rogers, W., Hevey, D. and Ash, E., eds., *Child Abuse and Neglect: Facing the Challenge,* London, Batsford.

Dingwall, R. (1992) 'Family policy and the liberal state' in Otto, H-U and Flösser, G., eds., *How to Organize Prevention,* Berlin, de Gruyter.

Dingwall, R. (1994a) 'Dilemmas of family policy in liberal states' in Maclean, M. and Kurczewski, J., eds., *Families, Politics and the Law,* Oxford, Clarendon Press.

Dingwall, R. (1994b) 'Litigation and the threat to medicine' in Gabe, J., Kelleher, D. and Williams, G., eds., *Challenging Medicine,* London, Routledge.

Dingwall, R. and Eekelaar, J.M. (1984) 'Rethinking child protection', in Freeman, M.D.A., ed., *State, Law and the Family,* London, Tavistock.

Dingwall, R. and Eekelaar, J.M. (1986) 'Judgements of Solomon: psychology and family law' in Richards, M.P.M. and Light, P., eds., *Children of Social Worlds*, Cambridge, Polity Press.

Dingwall, R. and Eekelaar, J.M. (1988) 'Families and the state: an historical perspective on the public regulation of private conduct', *Law and Policy* 10, 341-61.

Dingwall, R. and Robinson, K. (1990) 'Policing the family? Health visiting and the public surveillance of private behavior' in Gubrium, J.F. and Sankar, A. *The Home Care Experience: Ethnography and Policy*, Newbury Park, Sage.

Dingwall, R., Eekelaar, J.M. and Murray, T. (1984) 'The new child savers – a reply', *Legal Action*, January.

Eekelaar, J.M. (1991) 'Parental responsibility – state of nature or the nature of the state?', *Journal of Social Welfare and Family Law*, 37-50.

Eekelaar, J.M. (1993) 'From welfarism to rights: family law in the late twentieth century' in McCrudden, C. and Chambers, G., ed., *Individual Rights and the Law in Britain*, Oxford, Oxford University Press.

Eekelaar, J.M. (1994a) 'The interests of the child and the child's wishes: the role of dynamic self-determinism', *International Journal of Law and the Family*, 8, 42-61.

Eekelaar, J.M. (1994b) 'Parenthood, social engineering and rights' in Morgan, D. and Douglas, G., eds., *Constituting Families: Archiv fur Rechts und Soziale Philosophie (Association of Legal and Social Philosophy)* 57: 80-97.

Eekelaar, J.M. and Dingwall, R. (1990) *The Reform of Child Care Law*, London, Routledge.

Foucault, M. (1979) *The History of Sexuality: Vol 1*, London, Allen Lane.

Fox Harding, L. (1991) *Perspectives in Child Care Policy*, London, Longman.

Graham, P., Dingwall, R. and Wolkind, S. (1985) 'Research issues in child abuse', *Social Science and Medicine* 21, 1217-28.

King, M. (1983) 'The new child savers', *LAG Bulletin*, October, 10-11.

King, M. and Piper, C. (1991) *How the Law thinks about Children*, Aldershot, Gower.

King, M. and Trowell, J. (1992) *Children's Welfare and the Law: The Limits of Legal Intervention*, London, Sage.

March, J.G. and Olsen, J.P. (1989) *Rediscovering Institutions: The Organizational Basis of Politics*, New York, Free Press.

Meyer, J.W. and Rowan, B. (1977) 'Institutionalized organizations: formal structure as myth and ceremony', *American Journal of Sociology* 83, 340-63.

Milham, S., Bullock, R., Hosie, K. and Haak, M. (1986) *Lost in Care: The Problems of Maintaining Links between Children in Care and their Families*, Aldershot, Gower.

Packman, J., Randall, J. and Jacques, N. (1986) *Who Needs Care? Social Work Decisions about Children,* Oxford, Basil Blackwell.

Page, R. (1992) 'Empowerment, oppression and beyond: a coherent strategy? A reply to Ward and Mullender', *Critical Social Policy* 35, 89-92.

Parton, N. (1985) *The Politics of Child Abuse,* London, Macmillan.

Parton, N. (1991) *Governing the Family: Child Care, Child Protection and the State,* London, Macmillan.

Rosenberg, G. (1993) *The Hollow Hope: Can Courts Bring About Social Change?,* Chicago, University of Chicago Press.

Report (1988) *Report of the Inquiry into Child Abuse in Cleveland 1987* (Chaiman: The Hon. Mrs. Justice Butler-Sloss), London, Her Majesty's Stationery Office.

Silverman, D. (1989) 'Telling convincing stories: a plea for cautious positivism in case studies', in Glassner, B. and Moreno, J., eds., *The Qualitative-Quantitative Distinction in the Social Science,* Dordrecht, Kluwer.

Stevenson, O. (1995) 'Case conferences in child protection' in Wilson, K. and James, A., eds., *The Child Protection Handbook,* London, Baillière Tindall.

Stimson, G.V. (1985) 'Recent developments in professional control: the impaired physician movement in the USA', *Sociology of Health and Illness* 7:141-66.

Strong, P. and Dingwall, R. (1989) 'Romantics and Stoics', in Gubrium, J.F. and Silverman, D., eds., *The Politics of Field Research: Sociology beyond Enlightenment,* London, Sage.

Teubner, G., ed., (1988) *Autopoietic Law: A New approach to Law and Society,* Berlin, de Gruyter.

Thorpe, D. (1994) *Evaluating Child Protection,* Buckingham, Open University Press.

Voysey, M. (1975) *A Constant Burden,* London, Routledge and Kegan Paul.

Ward, D. and Mullender, A. (1991) 'Empowerment and oppression: an indissoluble pairing for contemporary social work', *Critical Social Policy* 32, 21-30.

Wright Mills, C. (1970) *The Sociological Imagination,* Harmondsworth, Penguin.

Notes

Introduction

1 One of the best examples is the debate around the draft *Standards Relat-ing to Abuse and Neglect* issued by a Joint Commission from the Juvenile Justice Standards Project of the Institute of Judicial Administration and the American Bar Association in 1977. See, for example, Wald's (1975) background paper for the Commission and Bourne and Newberger's (1977) subsequent critique. The comparable UK defences of family auton-omy and limited intervention, like Morris et al. (1980) and Taylor et al. (1980), have not yet attracted a full-scale response, although we shall deal with their position later in this book.

2 We should stress that 'England' is not being used as a loose synonym for 'Britain' or the 'United Kingdom'. Scotland and Northern Ireland have quite different legal and agency arrangements. Those in Wales are the same as England but no Welsh areas were included in the study. Never-theless, we would argue that such differences are likely to be no more sig-nificant than those between England and, say, Massachusetts, given the societal constraints within which child protection is conducted.

Chapter 1 • The Institutional Framework and Research Design

1 The term 'charter' is taken from Dingwall and Strong (1985), upon which this discussion of the interpenetration of formal and informal aspects of organizational life is based. They define a charter as:

> the concept to which organization members orient in their dealings, with each other and with non-members, to establish the limits of legit-imisable action. It refers to the organization's notional contract with other institutions for the co-ordination of a certain area of human ac-tion. (Dingwall and Strong 1985: 217)

Charters need not have a written form but commonly do in formal organi-zations.

2 The relevant parts of the Children Act 1948 and the Children and Young Persons Act 1963 have now been consolidated into the Child Care Act 1980. The Acts are cited as they were in effect at the time of the research.

For a cross-tabulation of the 1948 and 1963 Acts with the 1980 Act, see Jackson et al. (1981: B194-8). There are, of course, numerous other enactments which bear upon the protection of children in a more general sense. Since we are not attempting to write a general history of child welfare legislation, our focus here is necessarily selective, concentrating on those Acts which are most referred to in the management of abuse and neglect. Probably the best review of the whole pattern of current legislation is to be found in Hoggett (1981). We have, ourselves, discussed the 1969 and 1980 Acts in more detail elsewhere (Dingwall and Eekelaar 1982).

3 'Care under the Act of 1948 is often spoken of as "voluntary care", to distinguish it from care under an order made under the Children and Young Persons Act 1969, but it is an inaccurate expression. Care under the Act of 1948 is usually voluntary placement by the parents, but not necessarily. Section 1 of the Act of 1948 covers various situations which are not in any sense "voluntary" as far as parents are concerned'. (Ormrod, L. J., *W* v. *Notts CC,* 3 WLR 964).

4 The sections of the Children and Young Persons Act 1933 which are still in force relate mainly to criminal offences against children. Schedule 1 lists a number of offences to which special provisions apply. It includes the murder or manslaughter of a child or young person, infanticide, abandonment, common or aggravated assault, abduction, procuring, unlawful sexual intercourse, incest, indecent assault and buggery, attempts to commit any of the foregoing or assisting others in committing those offences, or any other offence involving bodily injury to a child or young person.

5 This is not to say that social workers do not have a rhetoric of commitment to prevention as an objective (cf. Handler 1973). There is, however, great uncertainty about how this might be achieved. In practice, what 'prevention' seems to mean is early referral at a stage when, for instance, 1963 Act powers may be used rather than bringing care proceedings.

6 This is a very crude outline of a system whose complexity was positively Byzantine. For a fuller account of the then structure see Levitt (1980). The reorganization mentioned here took place on 1 April 1982 and no good summary description is yet available. The oriental complexity remains undiminished.

7 Health visitors are a uniquely British institution, which has never taken root in the United States. Attempts to establish comparable programmes foundered in the past largely on opposition from the medical profession (cf. Rothman 1981). Kempe's (1975, 1976, 1978) recent attempts to reawaken interest have been bitterly attacked by fellow-physicians, partly on libertarian grounds and partly out of economic self-interest. See, for instance, the letters from Klein, Rubenstein and Reiss and the editorial comment in *Pediatrics* 57, 577-9, following Kempe's 1975 article. The debate is discussed further by Dingwall (1982b).

8 This figure is based on published DHSS statistics. There are, however, certain difficulties in interpretation as the local work returns are based on first visits during the relevant year. As a result of migration, children may be counted more than once. The English figures for 1979, for instance, show 111.6 per cent of new births being visited. If we assume that this

overstates a true rate approaching 100 per cent, the proportion of children under five being visited falls to 80 per cent. Further, if visits to children aged between one and five are overstated by a similar proportion, the true visiting rate will be of the order of 73 per cent. This does not, however, materially affect the point at issue.

9 These figures are taken from *Fit for the Future: Report of the Committee on Child Health Services* (Court Report) 1976, paras. 4.8, 4.23, 4.38 and the annual *Health and Personal Social Services Statistics*, published by the Department of Health and Social Security. The figures for child health clinics are susceptible to the same double counting as discussed in note 8.

10 This figure is derived from the summaries of state provisions collected by Costa and Nelson (1978).

11 The term 'ethnography' is used here to refer to a body of research drawing on a variety of theoretical perspectives within sociology, most importantly symbolic interactionism and ethnomethodology, which give primacy to the observation of naturally-occurring events as their source of data. The methodological literature has grown considerably in recent years and has recently been the subject of a useful review by Emerson (1981). Probably the most accessible introductory text is the collection edited by Filstead (1970) and the most influential statement of the philosophy of method is still Glaser and Strauss (1967).

12 It is difficult to find a neutral term for some of the implications of parent/child relations. 'Rights', 'duties' and 'obligations' should, therefore, be interpreted in a very loose sense rather than carrying specific connotations.

13 The County Social Services data includes material on the Director, three Assistant Directors, a Principal Adviser, the Administrative Assistant responsible for the Area Review Committee, two Area Directors, two Senior Social Workers, five Social Workers, and a Medical Social Worker. From County Health Services, we have interview data from one consultant in each of Community Medicine, Paediatrics and Accident Services, a Clinical Medical Officer, a GP Casualty Officer, the Area Nurse (Child Health), Divisional Nursing Officer (Community), three Senior Nursing Officers, eight Health Visitors, ward sisters in the District General Hospital Accident Department and in a Peripheral Casualty Department, the Administrative Assistant for the NAI Register and the Secretary of the local Community Health Council. On the legal side, we interviewed two local authority and two private practice solicitors, a court clerk, the Chief Probation Officer and a Chief Superintendent and an Inspector from the local police. Our County file also includes field notes on one care proceedings hearing, one meeting of the Area Review Committee's standing panel on individual cases and several single days' observation with social workers and health visitors.

14 In Borough, we saw the Director of Social Services, an Assistant Director and a Principal Adviser for Fieldwork, two Area Directors, two Senior Social Workers, six Social Workers and a Medical Social Worker. Within the Area Health Authority, we spoke to the Area Nursing Officer, the Area Nurse (Child Health), the Divisional Nursing Officer (Community), the Senior Nursing Officer and the two Nursing Officers for health visiting, six

Health Visitors, the Specialists in Community Medicine for Child Health and for Local Authority Liaison, one Consultant each in Paediatrics and in Child Psychiatry and a General Practitioner. The legal data includes interviews with one local authority and one private practice solicitor, two court clerks and the Chief Probation Officer. Others we interviewed were the Chief Education Welfare Officer and a local representative of the NSPCC. Our field notes also cover two hearings, one meeting of the Area Review Committee's standing panel on individual cases and several single days' observation with social workers and health visitors.

15 In so far as there is any association between child abuse or neglect and household poverty, it may be worth recalling that Townsend's (1979: 545-64) major study found the latter to be widely dispersed rather than a problem exclusively, or even largely, of the inner cities. Further material on the roles of the police and of the education services might have been desirable, but their role seems peripheral and we consider our present data enable us to account adequately for their marginality. A greater omission might appear to be the limited attention given to the NSPCC. This does in fact reflect the local experience in the three areas we examined. The NSPCC Inspectorate was a negligible feature, although in two cases long-serving inspectors has been of some significance in the past. However, neither of those vacancies had been filled and it is clear from other sources that the NSPCC's field staff are now stretched extremely thinly. We consider then, that this omission is much less important for current practice than a historical account might suggest. The NSPCC's practical influence may be more strongly felt through its Special Units' publications and its political connections than through the activities of its inspectors.

Chapter 2 • The Child as a Clinical Object

1 Although we did not encounter it in the course of this study, there is, in fact, another version of this model exemplified, for instance, by the work of Gil (e.g. 1975, 1978). This argues for the self-sufficiency of social evidence. In a capitalist society all children in the specified circumstances are victims of abuse or neglect resulting from social inequality. Parental responsibility is equally irrelevant, since these failures result from inevitable historical processes rather than individual actions.

2 Strong actually refers to 'role formats' in the text cited. In recent communication, he has indicated that he regards that notion as essentially synonymous with 'frame' and now prefers the latter word in the interests of restricting the unnecessary proliferation of terminology.

3 In a personal communication, Strong suggests that we have slightly shifted the emphasis from his original formulation, which concentrated on the *overt* treatment of parents and left open the assessment of their essential moral character. We tend to argue here that this overt treatment frames the subsequent official response, as opposed to department gossip, in a way which makes it difficult to discredit the ascribed moral character. To all intents and purposes, then, this ascription can be seen to curtail possible alternative inferences and to constitute a statement about the parents'

inherent moral nature. Our grounds for this stronger line will become evident as our data are presented.

4 The enforcement of a clinical perspective in American medical training is discussed at length by Carlton (1978) who shows how it emerges as a rational response to the indefinite boundaries of professional practice, 'the selection of a small segment of all possible considerations as the basis of physician insight' (p. 82). As she comments, however, this focus also involves a selective inattention to the social and moral dimensions of medical work, an inattention which, we would argue, inevitably compromises the possibility of identifying mistreatment. Holter and Friedman (1968: 137), in studying the emergency department at the University of Rochester Medical Center, report further data consistent with this analysis, underlining the parallels between English and American practice in this setting.

> . . . children with medical problems are seen by the pediatric house staff, but children with traumatic injuries, such as burns, fractures and lacerations, often are seen only by the surgical house staff. The obvious problem receives prompt medical attention; but, in general, no continuing medical care is planned for the children and their families.

5 The crucial role of demeanour in agency assessments will be familiar to sociologists. Two celebrated examples are Piliavin and Briar's (1964) analysis of its impact on police arrest decisions and Emerson's (1969) discussion of its contribution to juvenile court dispositions. Sudnow (1967: 103) underlines the importance of social and moral considerations in American emergency rooms:

> . . . there seems to be a rather strong relationship between the age, social backgrounds and the perceived moral character of patients and the amount of effort that is made to attempt revival when 'clinical death signs' are detected (and, for that matter, the amount of effort given to forestalling their appearance in the first place).

6 This is, of course, a tricky issue for parents in a bureaucratic frame: documenting that one is caring may involve presenting minor injuries which *might* be more serious. In some respects, though, it is merely a special case of the general problem, which all patients face, of deciding, in advance, what doctors will define as trivial, without actually having access to the medical knowledge on which that categorization will be based (Bloor and Horobin 1975).

7 This is not a universal practice: one Area where one of the present authors had done research previously seemed to operate quite successfully with a checklist of examination items which had to be scored for each child. Particular scoring levels led automatically to specialist referral or reassessment one month later. We found nothing like this in the present study.

8 Davis (1982: 40-60) provides a much more extensive analysis of local authority medical work (Child health clinic services were provided by local authority health departments until the latter's absorption by AHAs in 1974). Although he does not specifically discuss the issue of mistreatment,

Davis's account substantially confirms our own discussion of the emphasis on normalizing children and discounting possibly inconsistent findings. Davis also notes the pressures on staff which arise from the voluntary nature of the clinic/parent relationship and the way in which these constrain attempts to moralize at clients. This book incorporates a valuable exploration of paediatric out-patients which shows similar constraints on investigative treatment of parents and reliance on the evidence of demeanour as a basis for inferences about moral character.

9 Bittner and Newberger (1981: 205) make a similar point for the US:

> The opportunity to observe parent-child interaction and the child's physical and psychological milestones (which might yield insight into the familial causes of a child's injury) may not be available to a physician in his office or in the emergency room. Nurses in clinical and public health settings can and do, however, make such observations, which are fundamental in case-finding and evaluation. The input of these nurses contributes uniquely to diagnosis . . . .

10 Rather than having doctors doing nothing other than be in attendance for legal cover, we might also question what their presence could actually contribute. Health visitors already screen children for pertussis vaccinations to identify those obviously at risk of complications. The main hazard which the doctors are covering is anaphylactic shock, an allergic reaction to the injected material which can be fatal. What needs to be asked, and this is not a question we are competent to answer, is whether this is not so rare that a trained health visitor could not recognize it as readily as an average doctor and whether, if it does occur, a child's best hope of survival does not lie with a 999 call rather than anything within the resources of the typical clinic. There are suggestions that a child who dies too quickly for an emergency transfer to hospital would be unlikely to survive anyway. We must stress again, however, that this is a matter for research in social epidemiology rather than one which this study and its staff were intended to consider.

Chapter 3 • The Child as a Social Object

1 The term 'licence' is used here in the sense developed by Hughes.

> An occupation consists in part in the implied or explicit *license* that some people claim and are given to carry out certain activities rather different from those of other people and to do so in exchange for money, goods and services. (Hughes 1971: 287 original emphasis)

As with the term 'charter', which Dingwall and Strong (1985) develop by deliberate analogy with 'license', the referent is a notional or literal contract between a certain group and the remainder of its host society which legitimates the execution of a particular set of activities in a particular way.

246

2 The position summarized here is based on the work of Schutz (1962, 1964, Schutz and Luckman 1974) as developed by Garfinkel (1967) and Sacks, in his unpublished lectures. Our ideas about 'normal' family life are, to some extent, modelled on Sudnow's (1965) discussion of 'normal' crimes. Dingwall (1977a: 47-85) has previously analysed the centrality of lay social theories in health visitor training.

3 Lawson (1980) produces a very similar list of features involved in case assessment by social workers but organizes them into rather different categories. In doing so, she tends to run together features which we discuss separately, most importantly parental compliance and legal admissibility. The difference is probably attributable to differences in the research design: Lawson's is a cross-sectional study of cases at or close to a decision on whether or not to refer to court, whereas our investigation has a more processual character, so that the features oriented to can be placed in a time sequence.

4 Health visiting has significant antecedents in sanitary inspection, and its curriculum was heavily influenced by these until the early 1960s. Since then, however, it has increasingly moved towards social work in emphasizing the interpersonal aspects of its practice. For further discussion, see Dingwall (1977b, 1980) and recent publications from the Council for the Education and Training of Health Visitors, especially (CETHV 1977, 1980). On the other hand, Farquhar and Bacon (n.d.) report that health visitors in their study tended 'to place greater emphasis on the morality, particularly of mothers in single-parent families, and material standards and cleanliness of the home', than did social workers, a finding which they explain by reference to the lower socio-economic background of the health visitors. It is not clear how far this can be generalized without national data, since, in our observation, marriage and migration seemed to have important assortative effects on the nature of the health visitors available for recruitment in any particular locality.

5 It should be stressed that this is a somewhat tendentious presentation of the history of the Page case. Our purpose in quoting it is to illustrate the line which media comment may take. Since the official report did not publish the names of the workers involved, we have followed our practice throughout this book of editing out their identity: the case itself is too well-known for there to be much point in doing the same and preventing the reader from contrasting the press story with our own analysis.

6 Macintyre (1977) discusses this issue in an analysis of decision-making in the careers of single, pregnant women. She points, in particular, to the search for a moral evaluation of the fact of pregnancy as a key issue in referral decisions about termination by general practitioners. While pregnancy seemed to be an unmotivated act for most of her respondents, this did not constitute an acceptable version of events for the workers who might subsequently become involved.

7 The imputation of responsibility to drug-users and drunkards, respectively, is discussed at length by Duster (1970) and by Macandrew and Edgerton (1970).

8 In addition to the circumstances discussed in chapter 1, children may be committed to the care of local authorities, at the court's discretion, under

a variety of powers related to divorce, adoption and guardianship. A more detailed description of these powers can be found in Dingwall and Eekelaar (1982).

9 As Macintyre (1977) shows, though, this acceptance is conditional on the negotiation of a mutually acceptable motivational account between the woman and the workers involved.

10 The formidable pressures to naturalize the most apparently unloveable of children are well brought out in Voysey's (1975) study of families with severely mentally handicapped children. This has recently been extended, in a rather more rigorous fashion, by Baruch (1981) in an examination of transcripts from interviews with parents of children with congenital heart defects or cleft palate/hare lip.

Chapter 4 • The Rule of Optimism

1 The logic of this operation in ethnographic research is set out by Goodenough (1957). Although arrived at by different means, it is useful to compare our argument with Gelles's (1978) finding, as a result of a nationally representative survey, that up to two million American children in any year were the victims of acts capable of being construed as abusive. According to Gelles, the highest estimate based on identified populations was of the order of half a million.

2 The notion of prospective-retrospective interpretation is developed by Garfinkel (1967) and McHugh (1968). Other examples of its employment can be found in Kitsuse (1962) and Duster (1970), which show how any situational performance, by a homosexual or a drug addict respectively, may be used as further evidence of their damaged nature. Satyamurti (1981: 139-42) makes rather similar points about how comparable behaviour by social workers and clients can be read, by the former, as evidence of their own competence and the latter's incompetence.

3 It should be recognized that although this paper has had a great influence on a number of sociologists, including those discussed here, Hart himself no longer subscribes to its original form. He declined to reprint it in his collected essays, *Punishment and Responsibility* (1968), in view of the criticisms by Geach (1960) and Pitcher (1960). On the other hand, it is by no means clear that these attacks fundamentally discredit the parts of the paper which have most influenced sociological thought.

4 Pearson (1975a) has an interesting if excitable discussion of the impact of labelling or what he calls 'misfit sociology'. Dingwall (1977a: 196-7) documents the enforcement of relativist approaches to counselling in health visitor training in the early seventies, a point which is also mentioned by Heraud (1981: 44-50) in his review of the literature on social work education.

5 Such analyses are bolstered by relativist intellectuals. Sutton (1981: 80), citing Loventhal's (1972) description of West Indian societies, ridicules:

... such anomalous cases as a black ten-year-old's being taken to court, and thence into residential care, because his mother was found to be chastising him with a belt, a characteristic means of punishment in the culture in which she herself had grown up.

It must be said that the most reliable study we have on ethnic variations in definitions of mistreatment, Giovannoni and Becerra's (1979: 190-9) work in Los Angeles, found that black and Hispanic groups tended to rate most types of mistreatment more seriously than did white groups. While there were variations within and between ethnic groups, there was no evidence of the greater tolerance for certain kinds of parental misconduct which is often alleged. The application of this finding to UK minorities remains, of course, an open question in the absence of any replication.

6 There were some differences. In both Borough and County a strong sense of geographical identity was apparent, so that remarks on specific districts were located within general characterizations of the area. In Shire, however, there was less of an attempt to describe the area as a whole but lower-level references to particular streets, villages or estates were in evidence. It is possible that these differences are an artefact of our design. County and Borough staff may have felt it necessary to produce area-wide characterizations to justify their practice to us as outsiders on a relatively brief visit. We spent longer with Shire staff and, coming as we did from a base in a comparable county, could be assumed to know what Shire was like. Nevertheless, as it is a rather middle-class area, it is plausible to suppose that Shire staff do not have the same problem of reconciling their own standards with those that they assume to be the norm in that county. In consequence, they may simply not have such well-worked-out justifications at that level.

7 The category of 'nature' is, of course, itself a social product. For instance, 'accidents' as excuses could not exist among the Azande described by Evans-Pritchard (1937) because their theorizing has no notion of chance. All events have a witting or unwitting causal agent.

8 In some respects, of course, this discussion echoes the well-recognized, if unfashionable, concept of the 'blood-tie'. With the decline of cruder theories of genetic transmission, that particular formulation has fallen into disuse. In so far as it responds to real and continuing issues in social work and other occupational practice, however, we must recognize that the basic theme is likely to persist as we have shown here.

9 Emerson (1969: 42-3) reports the arrest decisions of juvenile police officers in identical terms.

This (arrest) can occur in what would otherwise be an inconsequential encounter except that the policeman feels that his authority has been assaulted . . . . In (other) cases the police want the youth 'off the streets' i.e. out of the community where his misconduct is producing a constant stream of complaints . . . .

10 Bacon and Farquhar (1982) explain this predominantly in psycho-dynamic terms, pointing to the sado-masochistic nature of agency staff's relation-

ships with the family. As will become clear in this chapter, we consider that the behaviour can be adequately explained in social organizational terms without needing to impute unconscious motives to the actors involved.

11 Crain and Millor (1978) describe a similar case and echo the difficult issues which arise in protecting children of mentally incompetent parents while respecting the recently-enlarged rights of retarded persons. They underline the dearth of research evidence on parenting which might assist the development of a more coherent policy in such cases.

12 'The word "manipulation" was used very frequently by (social workers) to describe clients and it referred to the attempt on the client's part to influence a social worker's behaviour in a way that was seen by the social worker as illegitimate.' (Satyamurti 1981: 130)

13 Emerson (1969: 126) points to the role of documented legal sophistication in moral denunciation in the juvenile court which he studied. Defendants who 'knew their rights' and stood on them were likely to be regarded as more damaged, criminal-like delinquents and to attract more severe labels.

14 Of the remaining nine cases, three dissolved on evidential grounds before any serious question of compulsory action arose, three were more like delinquency cases in relation to the control of violent or sexually precocious children, in one case the abusive parent was imprisoned on another charge and the need for intervention was seen to lapse, one case involved a teenage girl whose mother had an organic brain disorder and the last case came through matrimonial jurisdiction with a very confused history.

15 This case has some interesting echoes of the childhood of Daniel Paul Schreber, who formed the subject of one of the classic case studies of psychoanalysis published by Freud in 1911. Schreber's life is discussed by Niederland (1974). We are grateful to Alvin Rosenfeld for this observation. One should not necessarily make too much of the military background in this case: Miller (1976), in a useful discussion of American experience and the limited research literature, suggests that there are probably no great differences between military and civilian families in terms of mistreatment. From our observations, what may be more important are the assortative effects of service recruitment and posting in concentrating certain types of family in military housing schemes. There are also suggestions that the mobility of service personnel and their dependants may sometimes precipitate compulsory action in order to detain a family in a locality while a therapeutic programme, which might otherwise have been manageable on a voluntary basis, is completed.

16 This runs counter to American suggestions (e.g. Newberger and McAnulty 1976: 1160) that black children may be preferentially diagnosed as mistreated. However, as Pelton (1978) argues, the dearth of reliable prevalence data means that such suggestions are difficult to evaluate. There may, indeed, actually be more mistreatment among black groups. It might, though, be possible to show that agency reasoning consistently tends to understate a higher true prevalence, if, of course, we could agree on what to count in the prevalence rate to start with.

17 While purely speculative, it is tempting to wonder what contribution such changes might be making to the long-term increase in child-care interventions since the mid-sixties. The decline of working-class deference is, of course, a long-established debate in political sociology.

Chapter 5 • The Division of Regulatory Labour

1 The perspective on the division of labour which underpins this chapter is derived primarily from Durkheim (1964) and Simmel (Wolff 1950). We have not sought to discuss the vast theoretical literature on this topic but simply selected those parts which facilitate our analysis of the data in this study. Our own position is elaborated somewhat further in chapter 10.

2. Strong's choice of term may look odd in this context, but it is possible to see it as a matter of some subtlety in the light of our subsequent comments on the historical relationship between professions and bureaucracies.

3 As Prest (1981: 13) remarks, in introducing a volume of essays reviewing the history of the legal profession, 'There is certainly no lack of material to be worked over or of questions to be posed. The most serious deficiency is our general ignorance about the interaction between lawyers and their clients.'

4 This is reflected in, for instance, Freidson's (1976) research on a prepaid group practice in New York and Thomas and Mungham's (1983) description of the duty solicitor scheme in Cardiff. Both studies highlight the empirical difficulty of challenging less than competent practice. It is equally apparent in corporate settings. Several recent American writers (Arluke 1977, Bosk 1979, Light 1980) have remarked on the role of post-error review conferences in neutralizing professional failures in hospital medicine, and we have shown that the same was true of solicitors in the Shire Administrative Services Department (Murray et al. 1983). Although McGlew and Robertson (1981) suggest that the general practitioner/specialist referral system enhances the possibility for peer review in Britain, a contention we might also extend to the solicitor/barrister relationship, they present no empirical data to support this argument.

5 This apparently elementary point seems to have escaped critics of many persuasions from the radical Right (e.g. Brewer and Lait 1980) to the radical Left (e.g. Whittington and Bellaby 1979) to say nothing of the professionalist segment within social work who see bureaucracy merely as an impediment to autonomous practice (e.g. Butrym 1976, Glastonbury et al. 1980). In fairness, the same neglect is also evident among students of local government in general.

... not one of the major contributions ... has considered the existence of elected representatives, to whom an organization is subordinated and who are themselves accountable to a wide electorate, as a significant contingency operating upon government bureaucracies. Despite the wide variety of studies carried out into *public* organizations (Blau 1968; Meyer 1972; Hage and Aitken 1967, 1969; Hall 1962, 1963) contingencies such as organizational size and the nature of production technologies are treated as the salient variables. The impact of public accountability is either ignored or treated as insignificant. (Greenwood et al. 1980: 109-10 original emphasis)

Two useful accounts of the impact of public funding on intendedly flexible and discretionary organizations are provided by Johnson (1981), discussing an Arizonan shelter for battered women, and Bradshaw (1981), looking at the UK Family Fund for the support of households with severely congenitally handicapped children.

6 The Salmon Committee (1966) was chaired by a leading industrialist and took the organization of private business enterprises as its model for a management structure in nursing. Its most important innovation was the introduction of middle-management grades designed to tighten the line of authority from the director of the service (the matron) to the ward, a line which had become overstretched by increases in the size and complexity of hospitals since the Nightingale pattern was established. The Mayston Working Party (1969) simply extended these principles into community nursing without separately considering their applicability.

7 This may be explained in two ways. First, there are some reasons for thinking that health visiting attracts independent-minded and assertive people who find it difficult to work within the stricter bureaucratic discipline of hospital nursing (Dingwall 1977a). Second, it seems possible that local authority work represents the 'hospital' pole for social workers. Those who cannot accommodate to its organizational pressures drift into other areas of practice. Certainly the local authority social workers in our study tended to regard those of their colleagues who had opted for medical social work or work in voluntary agencies as somehow lacking the stomach for the intrinsically unpleasant parts of the job, particularly its coercive elements, like place of safety orders or mental health detentions, and its rationing of financial and other resources. Both Butrym (1976) and Satyamurti (1981: 100-3) tend to depict the prestige of medical social work in terms of its scope for autonomous action, precisely because these publicly accountable elements of the work are absent. It can approximate more closely to a professional model. More research seems necessary on the balance between our respondents' 'push' motivational account and the alternative 'pull' explanation in terms of the attractions of these other settings.

8 We understand that in some authorities it may even be necessary to refer such decisions for the personal sanction of the Director of Social Services.

9 These systems originated in two sensitive areas which involved contracting out the local authority's responsibility for children while being unable constantly to monitor the discharge of substitute parenting. Indeed, much of the scandal around the death of Denis O'Neill in 1945 and the subsequent debates in the Curtis Committee which led to the Children Act 1948 were over precisely this point. The Boarding Out of Children Regulations (1956) specifically require regular reviews of foster placements by someone not involved in the day-to-day handling of the case. In respect of adoption, this is compounded by the shortage of children, so that authori-

ties are under pressure to formalize their procedures to demonstrate their equitable treatment of would-be adopters. Indeed, in one of the authorities we looked at, the social services committee seemed to have used this argument as a way of clinging on to a Poor Law tradition of approving adoption placements itself rather than relinquishing them to its staff. Bacon and Farquhar (n.d.) also comment on the way in which child abuse procedures have been designed to produce a politically defensible system of case management rather than a basis for therapeutic activity.

10 There are striking similarities with the erosion of the supervisor/foreman's role in industry. See, for instance, Child's (1975) discussion of the literature.

11 These systems are also very time-consuming. Critics of social work (e.g. Brewer and Lait 1980: 86-92) have seized upon the comparatively small amount of time devoted to client contact. If, however, a social worker has a generic caseload, reviews, supervision and the preparation of the associated reports and records must necessarily encroach on the time available for actually seeing clients. The requirements of public accountability oblige social workers to deliver a smaller quantity of services than they could do as professional or bureau-professional workers.

12 There are suggestions that this might also apply to the legal sphere. Flood's (1978) work on barrister's clerks, for instance, has observations about their relations with junior members of their chambers which are very reminiscent of the literature on interaction between sisters and junior doctors. An essential part of the skill of a successful young practitioner is learning how to read indirect messages. Our single observation in this study of solicitor/barrister interaction is also consistent with this thesis, but we should not wish to rely on it.

13 The same is true of medical and nursing records in hospitals. Health visitors may have access to GP records, by agreement within the practice, but these are not used systematically, i.e. if a health visitor has reason to suspect mistreatment, she may pull the relevant record as a preliminary to informal discussion with a general practitioner but she would not expect to enter information on it or to read children's records on a regular basis.

14 There are local variations in health visitors' access to clinical information. In the present study, County had a highly developed system for passing hospital and community medical data to health visitors, partly as a response to acknowledged inadequacies in practice attachment and the limited access of health visitors to GP records. Borough recognized similar inadequacies in attachment but had no comparable system. Shire thought its attachments were generally satisfactory, although our observations would not altogether support this. As we have remarked, the quality of that data, particularly from routine developmental testing, may also leave a lot to be desired. With all these reservations, it nevertheless remains that health visitors are better placed to obtain, and make intelligent use of, clinical data, which gives them an extra ground for scrutinizing parental conduct.

15 Skinner and Castle (1969) and Castle and Kerr (1972) report referral rates from GPs of 3.9 per cent and 2.9 per cent respectively in cases of child abuse, as agency-defined.

16 In the imagery of figure 2, one might wish to move GPs' cut-off for referrals to the left of that for health visitors', which would reduce the number of 'inappropriate' referrals.

17 It was suggested to us by some social workers that, in practice, economic pressures were leading to a more elastic use of at-risk registers since funding for certain kinds of preventive work, like a free day nursery or playgroup place, was effectively restricted to those on the register. Senior management staff maintained that this was a misinterpretation of the more critical attitude now being taken to departmental expenditures. Our data do not permit us to choose between these two accounts, although we may recall W. I. Thomas's oft-quoted dictum, 'If men define situations as real, they are real in their consequences.' Even if area staff are acting under a 'misapprehension', the consequences are the same as if they are acting 'correctly'. The force of this point, however, is the question mark which it places against the allegation that a simultaneous increase in the number of children on at-risk registers and the number of unemployed people implies a causal connection between unemployment and child mistreatment. It seems equally possible that both are the product of the general economic situation as an intervening variable.

18 This is not to say that differences do not exist. Our reliance on hand notes in observing such interaction limits the level of detail we can analyse. In order to resolve this question, it would be necessary to collect and transcribe tape-recordings of health visitors and social workers dealing with comparable groups of clients.

19 The report prepared by a DHSS team on the effects of the 1978-79 social workers' strike in Tower Hamlets draws a very similar conclusion across a broader range of work.

> It was perhaps the health visitors who bore the brunt of the additional work. They are the only other statutory agency with a 'visiting' remit similar to social workers and they are very much in the vanguard in identifying social problems . . . As the strike wore on it became clear that they were having to neglect their own duties in order to take up the responsibility of emergency cases especially those concerned with non-accidental injury to children (DHSS 1979: paras 11.1 and 11.2)

20 Although there have been several attempts to conduct time-budget studies in health visiting, reviewed by Clark (1980), none of these deals with longitudinal distributions of contact time. Very little research of this kind has been carried out in social work. Brewer and Lait (1980) cite two studies, by Harris and Palmer (1976) and Hassall and Stilwell (1976), but Rees and Wallace's (1982) comprehensive review of the evaluation literature does not identify any others or even propose this as a useful line for future investigations. Bruce (1980: 92) reports health visitors' perceptions of the infrequency of social work visits, but these may be functioning as 'atrocity stories' (Dingwall 1977c) and one should be cautious about taking them at face value.

21 This helps to account for the differential commitment of health visitors and social workers to local liaison meetings. Five such meetings occurred

during the course of our fieldwork, but we attended only two since the social workers we were 'shadowing' on the other occasions found reasons to be elsewhere. Members of both occupations volunteered comments to us on the consistent differences in the relative turnout. Health visitors are keen attenders because they hope to bring informal pressures to bear on social workers, the very embarrassment which the social workers hope to avoid.

22 This statement may seem at odds with the fashionable critique of professional imperialism which sees both medicine and law as having wide ambitions to regulate everyday life. As Strong (1979b) has shown, however, the empirical evidence for this is weak, at least as far as medicine is concerned, and reflects the aspirations of specific professional segments rather than the general body of practitioners.

Chapter 6 • Sovereignty and Association: Co-ordinating Intervention

1 The circular suggests that these senior officers would include representatives of the local authority's Chief Executive and Directors of Education, Housing and Social Services; the health authority's Area Medical Officer, Specialist in Community Medicine (Child Health), District Community Physician, Consultants in Paediatrics, Surgery, Obstetrics, Orthopaedics, Accident and Emergency and Psychiatry, General Practitioners, Dental Surgeons, Area Nursing Officer, Area Nurse (Child Health), District Nursing Officers; and a Senior Police Officer, a Senior NSPCC Inspector and a senior representative of the Chief Probation Officer. (Some of the health authority posts mentioned would not exist in the single-district Areas covered by this study.)

2 The Colwell, Auckland, Brewer, Spencer, Peacock, Chapman, Taylor, Mehmedagi, Page and Brown reports are summarized in a recent DHSS (1982) review of inquiries conducted between 1973 and 1981. That also covers several reports not listed here, *viz.* Graham Bagnall (1973), Max Piazzani (1974), Stephen Meurs (1975), Lisa Godfrey (1975), Neil Howlett (1976), all local, Richard Clark (1975), ordered by the Secretary of State for Scotland, Darryn Clarke (1979), ordered by the Secretary of State for Social Services, and Stephen Menheniott (1978), by an internal DHSS team. The Darryn Clarke inquiry also followed parliamentary pressure of the same kind as the Brown inquiry and the Menheniott investigation seems, at least partly, to have been prompted by the difficulties arising from the peculiar constitutional status of the Isles of Scilly. As we completed this text, another local inquiry was published, into the death of Lucy Gates (1982).

3 In this and subsequent extracts, titles are abbreviated as follows:

DIVNO Divisional Nursing Officer (Community)

AD: Area Director, Social Services

SCM: Specialist in Community Medicine (Child Health)

CPO: Chief Probation Officer

PC: Senior Police Officer
LAS: Local authority solicitor
DD: Deputy Director, Social Services
ASD: Assistant Director, Social Services
PAE: Consultant Paediatrician
PSY: Consultant Psychiatrist
PAS: Principal Adviser, Social Services

4 It may be interesting to note that, in a passage not reproduced, the nearest to such a commitment came from the police superintendent, although the Principal Adviser tried very hard to undercut this, an attempt which is visible in the quoted material.

5 Something of the character of this reaction is captured in a useful series of articles by Ann Shearer in *Social Work Today* (9, 16 and 23 January 1979), where she revisited East Sussex, Barnsley, Somerset and Derbyshire, involved in the Colwell (1974), Auckland (1975), Brewer (1977) and Spencer (1978) inquiries respectively. She points out that Barnsley and Somerset have both developed highly centralized systems of at-risk case management, comparable to those described here, and East Sussex had tightened the detailed accountability of social workers to divisional management. Changes in a similar direction in Derbyshire were awaiting the appointment of a new senior specialist.

Chapter 7 • Case Conferences and the Legalization of Mistreatment

1 It may be necessary to qualify this opposition. Analysts of the police (e.g. Banton 1964, Wilson 1968) tend to distinguish two aspects of their work: enforcement and peace-keeping. In the latter, police seem to behave more like health and social welfare workers, using law as an ultimate resource where voluntary measures to deal with problems of public order fail. Conversely, Frank (1981: 172), writing about a specialized Canadian child abuse intervention agency, found staff 'constantly work[ing] with attentiveness to the impending or potential development of court cases'. This orientation may well reflect a difference between the multi-purpose agencies in this study and more narrowly focused organizations.

2 It is this formal quality which, as we saw in the previous chapter, agency staff themselves use to distinguish conferences from other sorts of inter-agency discussions. We observed 32 meetings defined by the participants as case conferences.

3 Frank's account does not make it clear whether the Canadian jurisdiction involved required the identification of an agent in legal proceedings for compulsory powers. In England, a strict reading of the Children and Young Persons Act 1969 does not require such identification. On the other hand, it is a practical necessity in choosing between dispositions. Compulsory action may be redundant if the agent can be removed from the child, or otherwise constrained, by negotiation.

4 Lawson (1980: 152) was similarly impressed by her analysis of case conference records in Hertfordshire, a county rather like Shire.

> On the first reading of each case, I was struck by the way in which attention was paid during case conferences to whether or not sufficient *evidence* was available for care proceedings to succeed. (Original emphasis)

5 But not, interestingly, in Scotland, where section 32(2) of the Social Work (Scotland) Act 1968 permits proceedings where 'lack of parental care . . . *is likely to* cause [the child] unnecessary suffering or seriously to impair his health or development' (Our emphasis).

6 A committal hearing is held in serious criminal cases. It involves the prosecution presenting its case before a panel of magistrates who are required to determine whether there is sufficient evidence to justify a full jury trial. There are similarities to the role of the grand jury in some American states.

7 Several of the others had exceptional features. One was led off by an area director because the child's general practitioner was known to have come to the conference in order to dispute the identification of the child as mistreated and allegations had been received that his motives in so acting were corrupt. Another, on Jayne Wallace, was started by a head teacher but this was essentially a 'subsequent' case conference. These tended to begin rather differently with a solicitor or a social work manager recapitulating the actions agreed at the previous meeting and inviting participants to report back. Bacon and Farquhar (1982) give an example of a conference opened by a child-minder who then leaves so that 'serious' discussion can take place among the professional staff involved. That phase opened with the child's general practitioner. We had one similar case, where a playgroup supervisor reported her observations of the child's injuries and left. No doctor was present on that occasion, however, although the next phase was dominated by two Health Visitors and a Senior Nursing Officer interpreting the clinical significance of the observations for the social workers. (Part of the issue was the difficulty of getting emergency medical examinations for children of service personnel when competent base doctors were hard to reach or involve in case management.)

8 The major exception, a three-year-old child, Jamie Leonard, with a severely burnt ear will be discussed in the next chapter. Briefly, that case involved competing organizations of the presenting signs as resulting from the deliberate application of a hot iron by Jamie's mother or from Jamie injuring himself while pretending that the iron was a telephone receiver. The consequence for the case was an opening debate on the consistency of the signs with each characterization between the general practitioner and a paediatric house officer.

9 Frank analyses a case, also involving a less serious burn to a child's face which is not, in itself, sufficient to exclude an 'accidental' interpretation. The conference, then, examines the child's weight measures and development scores to see if these will yield admissible evidence to corroborate a non-accidental explanation. Can the child be characterized as one who is

neglected and happens to have sustained a suspicious injury rather than one who has been abused? As we show, Jamie Leonard's case goes through a similar transformation.

10 Eighteen times out of 24 in our study with one application for a care order dismissed, three where supervision was granted instead of care and two where care was ordered rather than supervision, and 49 cases out of 53 in Hilgendorf's (1981: 137) study with one case dismissed, two supervision orders on application for care orders and one application for discharge of a care order dismissed.

Chapter 8 • Representing 'The Facts'

1 These procedures are covered by the Magistrates' Court (Children and Young Persons) Rules 1970. The definition of parties and eligibility for legal aid is set out in the cases of *R* v. *Worthing Justices* ex p. *Stevenson* [1976] and *R* v. *Welwyn Justices* ex p. *S* [1978]. The participation of parents is discussed in *R* v. *Milton Keynes Justices* ex. p. *R* [1979],

2 Hilgendorf (1981: 35) identifies three roles for solicitors: as a legal consultant, as a social work advocate and as a legal member of the team. The first two of these represent variants of our Model A and the third corresponds to our Model B. We think the discrepancy arises from Hilgendorf's reliance on the solicitors' perceptions of their role in her five authorities, whereas we looked more to descriptions of their organization and practice. As her data indicate (pp. 35-40), the middle position is difficult to operate and solicitors tend to work towards Model B or to develop something closer to that of an active consultant as described in our Model A.

3 Although Mungham and Thomas (1979: 174-5) do point out that advocacy is generally regarded as a 'young men's game' in a literal sense, partly because of its physical and mental pressures. General fitness is more important than a detailed knowledge of the law, a point whose implications we shall develop in the next chapter.

4 The exception was in the case of a teenage girl whose widowed mother had become mentally incompetent, the central issue of the hearing. In that case a solicitor was appointed by the court at the local authority's suggestion.

5 In the light of some of the conventional wisdom about solicitors' avarice, we should perhaps stress that in none of our three research sites was it uncommon for some private practices to represent parents without fee. Some of these did seem to be 'loss leaders' to build a firm's reputation with neighbourhoods which might be a fertile source of work on criminal legal aid, but others were clearly acts of genuine altruism. Solicitors obviously perceived the limited representation afforded to parents as commonsensically unjust, a view, of course, which reinforces our analysis of the essential nature of the adversarial contest in care proceedings for mistreatment as being between the local authority and the parents. In London and one or two other metropolitan areas, parents may also succeed in obtaining free representation from neighbourhood law centres.

6 The solicitor is also, to some extent, making a pitch for the parents. We shall discuss parents' attempts to defend their moral character in the next chapter.

7 The legality of this practice is somewhat obscure. Once an authority has obtained an interim care order, it acquires parental rights temporarily and would seem to be able to make such an appointment. The court presumably relies on its 'inherent jurisdiction', the discretionary power to regulate its own conduct in areas not covered by explicit procedural rules or superior court decisions. In either case, of course, the appointment of a solicitor precludes parents from representing their child and, as such, could be taken to be an oppressive act. The intention, however, ultimately rests on the other participants' sense of justice, that this is offended by an absence of professional representation.

8 The limited range of appropriate disposals, which we discuss later, precludes the solution to this problem which is available in adult courts, namely plea-bargaining. If Silbey's (1981: 23-4) arguments are equally applicable in the UK, defence solicitors may, at least sometimes, press clients to plead guilty on an evidentially weak case as a device for getting assistance with other problems through the probation service. A negotiated guilty plea spares the lawyer the dilemma he faces in care proceedings, where bargaining attempts are seldom accepted by the authority's solicitors. The incentives for the latter to settle out of court are much weaker, partly because of the perceived strength of the evidence and partly because their caseload pressures are less than those on a prosecuting solicitor or police officer. As Parker et al. (1981: 49-55) found, however, such incentives certainly operate in criminal cases before juvenile courts and are tacitly encouraged by a liberal granting of legal aid to ensure that defendants are represented by professionals who know how to participate in plea negotiations.

Chapter 9 • Charges and Defences

1 Care proceedings would still seem to be covered by the full rigour of the House of Lords judgement in *Myers* v. *DPP* 1965. This is, however, decidedly anomalous since those restrictions were eased for criminal proceedings in the Criminal Evidence Act 1965 and virtually abolished for civil proceedings by the Civil Evidence Act 1968. Care proceedings seem to fall between these two stools.

2 This ruling has caused a great deal of confusion because, of course, the Children and Young Persons Act 1969 quite clearly casts these as adversarial proceedings. It might have been more reasonable and consistent to arrive at the same conclusion by ruling that parents were *de facto* parties and that the common law rule could simply be applied by analogy.

3 Two of these solicitors were representing children, the third parents. One of these was the solicitor who had tried to get independent medical advice, referred to on pages 159-60 {p. 174}.

4 There may be an element of self-selection here. Clearly social workers in psychiatric or child guidance services are likely to have a somewhat different attitude (cf. Goldie 1977).

5 Only in one other hearing, Parry, did two doctors give evidence about the same medical issue, as opposed to, say, a paediatrician and a child psychiatrist describing a child's physical and mental condition. In that case, the admitting doctor was on his first shift as a house officer in paediatrics and the senior registrar was called to anticipate possible challenges to his experience.

6 At the time of this study appeals were comparatively rare, which, of course, meant that Crown Courts faced the problems of inexperience even more acutely than did magistrates' courts. The only person with a clearly established right of appeal was the child, yet another reflection of the 1969 Act's design for coping with delinquency. In the absence of standing, parents had to rely on the court's discretion, although we never heard of this being refused, consistent with our arguments about the commonsense administration of the statute to reflect the perceived reality of a just contest. Since the completion of the study, three superior court decisions, by the Divisional Court in *B* v. *Gloucestershire County Council* [1980], *Southwark London Borough Council* v. *C (A Minor) and Another* [1982] and *C (R., S. and K.) (Minors)* v. *M and Others* [1982], have reconstructed the relevant provisions of the 1969 Act and the associated rules of court to admit appeals by parents. In effect, one can argue that the judges of the Family Division have applied exactly the same commonsense reading to stipulate how ambiguous passages in the statutes and rules are to be interpreted and how lower courts are to deal with matters on which the formal instructions are silent. These decisions provide further support for our finding that where the framework of care proceedings is at odds with permitting parents to be treated as if they were full parties to the contest, the framework will be stretched or disregarded, although, of course, no court has yet ruled that parents should be eligible for representation at public expense (which is not, as we have shown, to say that the legal aid rules are never manipulated in their favour at present). In the absence of financial assistance, though, it is difficult to envisage a massive upsurge of appeals consequent on this clearer definition of parental rights.

7 In this and following extracts LAB is the local authority barrister. PB is the parents' barrister and CB is the child's barrister.

8 The deficiencies of the present supervision order are discussed in detail in chapter 11.

9 As this book was being prepared for press, for instance, the Oxfordshire newspapers were reporting a case where a small child had died from a skull fracture. The child's parents said that this had been caused in the course of a game. After several months' investigation of this otherwise respectable family, the agencies involved accepted the explanation as a freak of nature and the coroner recorded a verdict of accidental death. This can be compared with one of the cases in Shire, where a child sustained serious brain damage from a subdural haematoma. Similar explanations were given but her parents were readily discreditable and she was the subject of

care proceedings. (It should be said that her siblings also came into care after our study finished as a result of apparent abuse).

10 Hilgendorf (1981: 104, 138-9) declares herself less satisfied with the courts' independence by reference to two criteria: compliance with the laid down procedure and length of hearing. These are, however, both somewhat artificial standards. As we have seen, departures from procedure may, in fact, reflect and facilitate the courts' independence. Since Hilgendorf presents only the crudest of quantitative evidence, it is impossible to evaluate her contentions about the qualitative effects of procedural flexibility. The length of a hearing is also a poor guide. Hilgendorf's study does not cross-tabulate this by the grounds of the application but, in our observation, truancy and same household cases are often evidentially straightforward and can be dealt with quickly without detriment to the quality of court decisions.

Chapter 10 • Social Regulation and the Family in a Liberal State

1 Morris et al.'s critique cites and has many similarities with Wald's (1975) arguments for the restriction of compulsory intervention in the United States. Bourne and Newberger (1977) develop comparable criticisms of this paper for its lack of empirical data and its inattention to the genuine ambiguities of agency practice. Wald's concern for deducing a child protection system from first principles obscures the inevitable complexities of everyday work which require a degree of flexibility and discretion that is inconsistent with his legalistic approach.

2 Examples of this work might include Cain's (1979) analysis of solicitors as 'conceptive ideologists', Feeley (1979) and Silbey (1981) on the neglected virtues of departures from strict legality in lower courts, Strong's (1980) discussion of doctors' reluctance to expand their domain of responsibility and Smart's (1982) reproach to feminist assumptions about the uniformly patriarchal nature of family law.

3 Our preference for this term reflects a view that 'social control' has probably become irremediably contaminated by its recently-acquired pejorative connotations. What we are discussing is the minimal level of self-containment which is essential for the formation of human collectivities. This may, of course, become over-determined in particular contexts but it is Utopian naiveté to assume that it could ever be eliminated.

4 This is an important difference between classical liberals like J. S. Mill and a modern theorist like Hayek (1960: 133-47) who argues that, although the state should restrict its use of compulsory measures to those necessary to prevent individual citizens coercing each other, it should not necessarily seek to restrict moral pressures through the force of public approval or disapproval.

If a hostess will invite me to her parties only if I conform to certain standards of conduct and dress, or my neighbour converse with me only if I observe conventional manners, this is certainly not coercion . . . So long as the services of a particular person are not crucial to my existence or the preservation of what I most value, the conditions he exacts from rendering these services cannot properly be called 'coercion'. (Hayek 1960: 136)

5 Pfohl (1977) develops a comparable analysis of US reform movements where, he concludes, 'the primary objective was not to save children from cruel or abusive parents but to save society from future delinquents.'

6 British theorists argued along similar lines. Donajgrodski (1977: 52), discussing the work of Colquhoun, Tremenheere and Chadwick, defines social policing by two features:

> . . . first, that social order was the product of a common morality, which was sustained and expressed by its general diffusion throughout the institutions of society. Thus a social policy which aimed at the preservation of order must include not only consideration of legal systems, police forces and prisons but of religion and morality and of those factors which supported or propagated them – education, socially constructive leisure, even housing and public health . . . second . . . a strong tutelary grasp should be maintained over the poor, whom, it was assumed, were normless, or at least insufficient if left to themselves; liable to be led astray by agitators or to form 'perverted' social systems.

7 We can add to Donzelot's analysis Celia Davies's unpublished observation that these agencies often relied on women, under the direction of men, to police other women. This respect for the gender order might render the intrusion more acceptable, since it could be presented as an extension of traditional forms of woman-to-woman regulation rather than as thoroughly novel. It may be arguable that the reliance on male inspectors by the NSPCC, for instance, provoked some of the early hostility to its work.

8 The distinction is based on Hayek's (1960: 142) discussion.

> This threat of coercion has a very different effect from that of actual and unavoidable coercion, if it refers only to known circumstances which can be avoided by the potential object of coercion . . . The sanctions of the law are designed only to prevent a person from doing certain things or to make him perform obligations that he has voluntarily incurred. Provided that I know beforehand that if I place myself in a particular position, I shall be coerced and provided that I can avoid putting myself in such a position, I need never be coerced . . . In that they tell me what will happen *if I* do this or that, the laws of the state have the same significance for me as the laws of nature; and I can use my knowledge of the laws of the state to achieve my own aims as I use my knowledge of the laws of nature.

Chapter 11 • Children's Rights, Adults' Liberties: Towards a Proper Balance?

1 We do not follow the refinement proposed by Hart (1954, 1973) that the right-holder should be in a position to waive, extinguish, enforce or leave

unenforced the other's obligation. As MacCormick (1976) has shown, this creates insuperable difficulties in formulating coherent concepts of children's and parents' rights.

2 Goldstein et al. (1980: 9) seek to avoid this by attempting to define children's rights in terms of family autonomy, claiming that the right to optimum development encompasses 'the privacy of family life under the guardianship of parents who are autonomous'. When they concede, however, that parents may fail and family privacy become a threat to a child, the authors desert this argument of principle in favour of one of contingency, founded on an empirical claim that the state lacks the means to respond adequately to children's needs, and a political commitment in favour of limiting state action.

3 Lord Scarman, in *Lewisham London Borough* v. *Lewisham Juvenile Court* [1980] thought it 'inconceivable' that 'where a child is in the care of a local authority, there can be proved to exist a condition entitling a juvenile court to make a care order under the Act of 1969'. This had been directly held by the Divisional Court, in *Essex County Council* v. *TLR and KBR* [1979], observing that 'however advisable it may be for a juvenile court to have a wider discretion, it was the duty of the court to give effect to the words of the statute'.

4 This is comparable to the interpretation of the words 'who are living with each other in the same household' in section 1(2) of the Domestic Violence and Matrimonial Proceedings Act 1976 by Lord Denning in *Davis* v. *Johnson* [1979 AC 214, 275]. Jackson et al. take a similar line in their discussion of Essex CC v. *TLR and KBR* in *Clarke Hall and Morrison on Children* Second Supplement to the Ninth Edition, 1981, p. B28 (comments on p. 413 of Ninth Edition).

5. This was left completely unchanged by the consolidation of the Child Care Act 1980. One might, of course, still wish to retain the resolution procedure for some categories of children, particularly orphans, where it may be less damaging than a court appearance.

6 In *A* v. *Liverpool CC* [1981] the House of Lords lent its support to this view. The wardship jurisdiction, according to Lord Roskill, was available to local authorities whenever their own powers were 'inadequate to make the welfare of the child paramount'. See also *Re CB (a minor)* [1981].

7 Lord Devlin, for instance, asserted in *Re K (Infants)* [1965]: 'A judge in chambers is quite capable of giving hearsay no more than its proper weight. An inflexible rule against hearsay is quite unsuited to the exercise of a parental and administrative jurisdiction.' See also Lowe and White 1979: 59-65.

8 The phrasing of the 1969 Act can be traced back to the proposals in the Report of the Committee on Children and Young Persons (Ingleby Report 1960). This had, however, defined its task almost exclusively in terms of responses to actual or potential delinquency in juveniles (cf. Eekelaar et al. 1982: 76-7). Its reasons for dispensing with a reference to parental competence reflect this preoccupation.

... in many cases evidence existed that a child was falling into bad as-sociations or in moral danger but it was impossible to provide satisfactory proof of the shortcomings of the parent . . . it is unreasonable to expect a parent to be aware of everything that his child does.

9 Under the Children and Young Persons Act (Northern Ireland) 1968, s. 93.

10 Such a statement is obviously relative. There are well-documented variations in the availability of social service resources between and within local authorities. On the other hand, by comparison with the limited financial support in certain American states or the simple logistical problems of service delivery in an area like the Northern Territory of Australia, it seems reasonable to emphasize the homogeneity of the English system.

11 This is an important error in Mount's (1982) book, *The Subversive Family*, which was attracting a good deal of political attention as this book went to press. While it performs a valuable service in disseminating the results of recent research in historical demography to a popular audience, it is remarkably unsophisticated in its analysis of the position of children and the consequent necessity for state regulation. Mount's arguments are more reminiscent of certain American commentators who attempt to define marriage solely in terms of a free contract between consenting adults which they may enter and terminate at will and which should not be subject to state intervention. What this ultra-liberal, adult-centred view misses, however, is that children born to that marriage are not free entrants into the contract. In so far as it vitally affects their life-chances, then, the contract must properly be the subject of third-party supervision. As Hayek (1960: 377) acknowledges,

> With regard to children the important fact is, of course, that they are not responsible individuals to whom the argument for freedom fully applies. Though it is generally in the best interests of children that their bodily and mental welfare be left in the care of their parents or guardians, this does not mean that parents should have unrestricted liberty to treat children as they like. The other members of the community have a genuine stake in the welfare of the children.

The virtue of health visiting is precisely that it does not have ready access to what Mount (1982: 174) describes as a 'Stalinist array of powers'. Those powers can be mobilized only by a consensus between independent agencies under legal review within limits set by Parliament. Of course the element of intrusion into family privacy is regrettable: one cannot, however, will the end, of a responsible citizenry, without willing the means, surveillance of child-rearing. The challenge is to develop non-totalitarian institutions for so doing, a point on which Mount remains silent.

12 Similar arguments have been advanced by Morris et al. (1980) and Taylor et al. (1980), while Grant (in Martin and Murray 1976) presents a comparable case against the Scottish system of Children's Hearings. All of these authors make copious reference to American critiques of juvenile courts, especially in the wake of the *Gault* decision by the Supreme Court.

13 A *Khadi* is a judge sitting in an Islamic religious court administering justice by reference to a set of general ethical principles rather than a body of formal law.

14 At 1979 prices, a DHSS working party estimated that the introduction of separate representation would cost about £2 million per annum from public funds. Those interested in the cost-effectiveness of social science research may care to note that this study has cost less than £200,000 in total, at 1982 prices, over six years.

15 See, for instance, Lord Widgery's remarks in *R* v. *Greenwich Juvenile Court* ex p. *Greenwich London Borough Council* [1977].

16 Adoption Act 1958, s. 45, Foster Children Act 1980, s. 13.

References

Anderson, M. (1979) The relevance of family history', in Harris, C., ed., *The Sociology of the Family: New Directions for Britain*, Keele, Sociological Review Monograph 28.

Ariès, P. (1973) *Centuries of Childhood*, Harmondsworth, Penguin.

Arluke, A. (1977) 'Social control rituals in medicine: the case of death rounds', in Dingwall, R., Heath, C. C., Reid, M. E. and Stacey, M., eds., *Health Care and Health Knowledge*, London, Croom Helm and New York, Prodist.

Atkinson, J. M. and Drew, P. (1979) *Order in Court*, London, Macmillan.

Bacon, R. and Farquhar, I. (1982) 'Resistance and rejection in work with abusing families and their children', Cambridge, Child Care and Development Group, mimeo.

Bacon, R. and Farquhar, I. (n.d.) 'Problems in the social work management of child abuse cases', Cambridge, Child Care and Development Group, mimeo.

Bailey, R. and Brake, M., eds. (1975) *Radical Social Work*, London, Edward Arnold.

Bains Working Group (1972) *The New Local Authorities: Management and Structure*, London, HMSO.

Bamford, F. (1976) 'Medical diagnosis in non-accidental injury of children', in Borland, M., ed., *Violence in the Family*, Manchester, Manchester University Press and Atlantic Highlands, N.J., Humanities Press.

Banton, M. (1964) *The Policeman in the Community*, London, Tavistock.

Baruch, G. (1981) 'Moral tales: parents' stories of encounters with the health professions', *Sociology of Health and Illness*, 3, 275-95.

Beck, C., Glavis, G., Glover, S., Jenkins, M. and Nardi, R. (1978) 'The rights of children: A trust model', *Fordham Law Review*, 46, 669-780.

Benson, J. K. (1973) 'The analysis of bureaucratic-professional conflict: functional versus dialectical approaches', *Sociological Quarterly*, 14, 378-99.

Bittner, S. and Newberger, E. H. (1981) 'Pediatric understanding of child abuse and neglect', *Pediatrics in Review*, 2, 197-207.

Blackburn, S. (1980), 'Review of L. Jonathan Cohen, *The Probable and the Provable*', *Synthese*, 44, 149.

Blau, P. M. (1968) 'The hierarchy of authority in organizations', *American Journal of Sociology*, 73, 453-67.

Blaxter, M. and Paterson, E. (1982) *Mothers and Daughters: A Three-Generational Study of Health Attitudes and Behaviour*, London, Heinemann.

Bloor, M. J. and Horobin, G. W. (1975) 'Conflict and conflict resolution in doctor/patient interaction', in Cox, C. and Mead, A., eds., *A Sociology of Medical Practice*, London, Collier-Macmillan.

Blum, A. F. and McHugh, P. (1971) 'The social ascription of motives', *American Sociological Review*, 36, 98-109.

Bosk, C. (1979) *Forgive and Remember*, Chicago, University of Chicago Press.

Bourne, R. and Newberger, E. H. (1977) '"Family autonomy" or "coercive intervention"? Ambiguity and conflict in the proposed standards for child abuse and neglect', *Boston University Law Review*,57, 670-706.

Bradshaw, J. (1981) 'From discretion to rules: The experience of the family fund', in Adler, M. and Asquith, S., eds., *Discretion and Welfare*, London, Heinemann.

Brewer, C. and Lait, J. (1980) *Can Social Work Survive?*, London, Temple Smith.

Bruce, N. (1980) *Teamwork for Preventive Care*, Chichester, Research Studies Press.

Buckholz, Robert E. (1979) 'Constitutional limitations on the scope of state child neglect statutes', *Columbia Law Review*, 79, 719-34.

Butrym, Z. (1976) *The Nature of Social Work*, London, Macmillan.

Byrne, P. S. and Long, B. E. L. (1976) *Doctors Talking to Patients*, London, HMSO.

Cain, M. (1979) 'The general practice lawyer and the client', *International Journal of the Sociology of Law*, 7, 331-54.

Carlen, P. (1976) *Magistrates' Justice*, London, Martin Robertson.

Carlton, W. (1978) *'In our Professional Opinion . . .': The Primacy of Clinical Judgment over Moral Choice*, Notre Dame, University of Notre Dame Press.

Carpenter, M. (1977) 'The new managerialism and professionalism in nursing', in Stacey, M., Reid, M. E., Heath, C. C. and Dingwall, R., eds., *Health and the Division of Labour*, London, Croom Helm and New York, Prodist.

Carpenter, M. (1978) 'Managerialism and the division of labour in nursing', in Dingwall, R. and Mcintosh, J., eds., *Readings in the Sociology of Nursing*, Edinburgh, Churchill Livingstone.

Castle, R. L. and Kerr, A. M. (1972) *A Study of Suspected Child Abuse*, London, NSPCC.

CETHV (1977) *An Investigation into the Principles of Health Visiting*, London, Council for the Education and Training of Health Visitors.

CETHV (1980) *The Investigation Debate,* London, Council for the Education and Training of Health Visitors.

Child, J. (1975) The industrial supervisor', in Esland, G., Salaman, G. and Speakman, M-A., eds., *People and Work,* Edinburgh, Holmes MacDougall.

Christopherson, J. (1980) 'Child Abuse in Holland', *Social Work Today,* 10 July.

Christopherson, J. (1981) 'Two approaches to the handling of child abuse: A comparison of the English and Dutch systems', *Child Abuse and Neglect,* 5, 367-74.

Clark, J. (1980) *What do Health Visitors do?,* London, Royal College of Nursing.

Court Report (1976) *Fit for the Future: Report of the Committee on Child Health Services* (2 vols.), Cmnd. 6684 and 6684-1, London, HMSO.

Costa, J. J. and Nelson, G. K. (1978) *Child Abuse and Neglect: Legislation, Reporting and Prevention,* Lexington, Mass., Lexington Books.

Crain, L. S. and Millor, G. K. (1978) 'Forgotten children: maltreated children of mentally retarded parents', *Pediatrics,* 61, 130-2.

Cross, R. and Tapper, C. (1979) *Cross on Evidence,* London, Butterworth, Fifth Edition.

Davies, C. (1983) 'Professionals in bureaucracies: The conflict thesis revisited', in Dingwall, R. and Lewis, P. S. C., eds., *The Sociology of the Professions: Lawyers, Doctors and Others,* London, Macmillan.

Davis, A. G. (1982) *Children in Clinics: A Sociological Analysis of Medical Work with Children,* London, Tavistock.

Davis, A. G. and Strong, P. M. (1976) 'Aren't children wonderful? A study of the allocation of identity in developmental assessment', in Stacey, M., ed., *The Sociology of the National Health Service,* Keele, Sociological Review Monograph, No. 22.

de Francis, V. (1972) The status of child protective services: a national dilemma', in Kempe, C. H. and Heifer, R. E., eds., *Helping the Battered Child and His Family,* Philadelphia, J. B. Lippincott.

Dennis, N., Henriques, F. and Slaughter, C. (1956) *Coal is Our Life,* London, Eyre and Spottiswoode.

DHSS (1975) *Non-accidental Injury to Children,* London, HMSO.

DHSS (1979) *An Investigation into the Effect on Clients of Industrial Action by Social Workers in the London Borough of Tower Hamlets,* London, DHSS.

DHSS (1982) *Child Abuse: A Study of Inquiry Reports 1973-1981,* London, HMSO.

Dingwall, R. (1977a) *The Social Organisation of Health Visitor Training,* London, Croom Helm.

Dingwall, R. (1977b) 'Collectivism, regionalism and feminism: health visiting and British social policy 1850-1975', *Journal of Social Policy,* 6, 291-315.

Dingwall, R. (1977c) '"Atrocity stories" and professional relationships', *Sociology of Work and Occupations*, 4, 371-96.

Dingwall, R. (1980) 'Problems of teamwork in primary care', in Lonsdale, S., Webb, A. and Briggs, T., eds., *Teamwork in Personal Social Services and Health Care*, London, Croom Helm and Syracuse, NY, Syracuse University Press.

Dingwall, R. (1982a) 'Bureaucratic and bureau-professional organizations: management, supervision and accountability in social work and health visiting', Oxford, SSRC Centre for Socio-Legal Studies, mimeo.

Dingwall, R. (1982b) 'Community nursing and civil liberty', *Journal of Advanced Nursing*, 7, 337-46.

Dingwall, R. (1984) 'Child protection in its social and legal context', in Lloyd-Bostock, S., ed., *Legal Decisions concerning Children*, Oxford, SSRC Centre for Socio-Legal Studies.

Dingwall, R. and Eekelaar, J. M. (1982) *Care Proceedings: A Practical Guide for Social Workers, Health Visitors and Others*, Oxford, Basil Blackwell.

Dingwall, R. and Murray, T. (1980) 'Categorization in accident departments: "good" patients, "bad" patients and "children"', *Sociology of Health and Illness*, 5, 127-48.

Dingwall, R. and Strong, P.M. (1985) 'The interactional study of organizations: a critique and reformulation', *Urban Life*, 14, 205-31. Dingwall, R., Eekelaar, J. M. and Murray, T. (1982) 'Childhood as a social problem: A survey of the history of legal regulation', Oxford, SSRC Centre for Socio-Legal Studies, mimeo.

Donajgrodski, A. P. (1977) '"Social police" and the bureaucratic elite: A vision of order in the age of reform', in Donajgrodski, A. P., ed., *Social Control in Nineteenth Century Britain*, London, Croom Helm and Totowa, NJ, Rowman and Littlefield.

Donzelot, J. (1980) *The Policing of Families*, London, Hutchinson.

Duman, D. (1979) 'The creation and diffusion of a professional ideology in nineteenth century England', *Sociological Review*, 27, 113-38.

Duman, D. (1981) 'The English bar in the Georgian era', in Prest, W., ed., *Lawyers in Early Modern Europe and America*, London, Croom Helm.

Duman, D. (1982) *The Gentlemen of the Long Robe*, London, Croom Helm.

Durkheim, E. (1964) *The Division of Labor in Society*, New York, Free Press (first published 1893).

Duster, T. (1970) *The Legislation of Morality*, New York, Free Press.

Eekelaar, J. M. (1973) 'What are parental rights?', *Law Quarterly Review*, 89, 210-34.

Eekelaar, J. M. and Clive, E. (1977) *Custody After Divorce: The Disposition of Custody in Divorce Cases in Great Britain*, Oxford, SSRC Centre for Socio-Legal Studies.

Eekelaar, J. M., Dingwall, R. and Murray, T. (1982) 'Victims or threats? Children in care proceedings', *Journal of Social Welfare Law*, 68-82.

Emerson, R. M. (1969) *Judging Delinquents*, Chicago, Aldine.

Emerson, R. M. (1981) 'Observational field work', *Annual Review of Sociology*, 7, 351-78.

Evans-Pritchard, E. E. (1937) *Witchcraft, Oracles and Magic among the Azande*, Oxford, Clarendon Press.

Fairburn, A. C. and Tredinnick, A. W. (1980) 'Babies removed from their parents at birth: 160 statutory care actions', *British Medical Journal*, 5 April.

Farquhar, I. and Bacon, R. (n.d.) 'Child abuse procedures: The gap between intention and practice', Cambridge, Child Care and Development Group, mimeo.

Fauconnet, J. (1928) *La Responsibilité*, Paris, Alcan, 2nd edn.

Feeley, M. (1979) *The Process is the Punishment*, New York, Russell Sage Foundation.

Fido, J. (1977) 'The Charity Organisation Society and social casework in London 1869-1900', in Donajgrodski, A. P., ed., *Social Control in Nineteenth Century Britain*, London, Croom Helm and Totowa, NJ, Rowman and Littlefield.

Filstead, W. J. (1970) *Qualitative Methodology*, Chicago, Markham.

Finnis, J. (1980) *Natural Law and Natural Rights*, Oxford, Clarendon Press.

Flood, J. (1978) 'Barristers' clerks: middlemen of law'. Unpublished Ll.M. thesis, University of Warwick.

Fontana, V. J. (1976) *Somewhere a Child is Crying: Maltreatment – Causes and Prevention*, New York, Mentor.

Frank, A. W. (1981) 'Therapeutic and legal formulations of child abuse', in Irving, H. H., ed., *Family Law: An Interdisciplinary Perspective*, Toronto, Carswell.

Franklin, A. W. (1982), 'Child abuse in the 80s', *Maternal and Child Health*, 7, 12-16.

Freeman, M. D. A. (1981) 'The rights of children when they do "wrong"', *British Journal of Criminology*, 21, 210-29.

Freidson, E. (1976) *Doctoring Together: A Study of Professional Social Control*, New York, Elsevier.

Friedman, S. B. (1972) 'The need for intensive follow-up of abused children', in Kempe, C. H. and Heifer, R. E., eds., *Helping the Battered Child and his Family*, Philadelphia, J. B. Lippincott.

Galanter, M. (1974) 'Why the "haves" come out ahead', *Law and Society Review*, 9, 95-160.

Garfinkel, H. (1967) *Studies in Ethnomethodology*, Englewood Cliffs, NJ, Prentice-Hall.

Geach, P. T. (1960) 'Ascriptivism', *Philosophical Review*, 69, 221-5.

Gelles, R. J. (1973) 'Child abuse as psychopathology: A sociological critique and reformulation', *American Journal of Orthopsychiatry,* 43, 611-21. (Reprinted in Gelles, 1979).

Gelles, R. J. (1974) *The Violent Home,* Beverly Hills, Sage.

Gelles, R. J. (1975) 'The social construction of child abuse', *American Journal of Orthopsychiatry,* 45, 363-71. (Reprinted in Gelles, 1979).

Gelles, R. J. (1978) 'Violence towards children in the United States', *American Journal of Orthopsychiatry,* 48, 580-92. (Reprinted in Gelles, 1979).

Gelles, R. J. (1979) *Family Violence,* Beverly Hills, Sage.

Gelles, R. J. (1980) 'Violence in the family: A review of research in the seventies', *Journal of Marriage and the Family,* 42, 873-85.

Gibson, H. M. (1977) 'Rules, routines and records: The work of an A & E department', unpublished Ph.D. thesis, University of Aberdeen.

Gil, D. G. (1975) 'Unravelling child abuse', *American Journal of Orthopsychiatry,* 45, 345-56.

Gil, D. G. (1978) 'Societal violence in families', in Eekelaar, J. M. and Katz, S. N., eds., *Family Violence,* Toronto, Butterworth.

Giovannoni, J. M. and Becerra, R. M. (1979) *Defining Child Abuse,* New York, Free Press.

Glaser, B. G. and Strauss, A. L. (1965) *Awareness of Dying,* Chicago, Aldine.

Glaser, B. G. and Strauss, A. L. (1967) *The Discovery of Grounded Theory: Strategies for Qualitative Research,* Chicago, Aldine and (1968) London, Weidenfeld and Nicholson.

Glastonbury, B., Cooper, D. M. and Hawkins, P. (1980) *Social Work in Conflict,* London, Croom Helm.

GMC (1977) *Basic Medical Education in the British Isles: Vol. II The Disciplines and Specialties,* GMC/Nuffield Provincial Hospital Trust, Oxford, Oxford University Press.

Goffman, E. (1975) *Frame Analysis,* Harmondsworth, Penguin.

Goldberg, M. and Neill, J. E. (1972) *Social Work in General Practice,* London, Allen and Unwin.

Goldie, N. (1977) 'The division of labour among the mental health professions – a negotiated or an imposed order?', in Stacey, M., Reid, M., Heath, C. C. and Dingwall, R., eds., *Health and the Division of Labour,* London, Croom Helm and New York, Prodist.

Goldstein, J., Freud, A. and Solnit, A. (1980) *Before the Best Interests of the Child,* London, Burnett Books.

Goodenough, W. H. (1957) 'Cultural anthropology and linguistics', in Garvin, P. L., ed., *Report of the Seventh Annual Roundtable Meeting on Linguistics and Language Study,* Washington DC, Georgetown University.

Graham Hall, J. and Mitchell, B. H. (1978) *Child Abuse – Procedure and Evidence in Juvenile Courts,* Chichester, Barry Rose.

Greenwood, R., Walsh, K., Hinings, C. R. and Ranson, S. (1980) *Patterns of Management in Local Government,* Oxford, Martin Robertson.

Hage, J. and Aitken, M. (1967) 'Relationship of centralization to other structural properties', *Administrative Science Quarterly,* 12, 72-92.

Hage, J. and Aitken, M. (1969) 'Routine technology, social structure and organizational goals', *Administrative Science Quarterly,* 14, 366-77.

Hague, D. C., Mackenzie, W. J. M. and Barker, A., eds. (1975) *Public Policy and Private Interests: The Institutions of Compromise,* Macmillan, London.

Hall, R. H. (1962) 'Interorganizational structural variation: application of the bureaucratic model', *Administrative Science Quarterly,* 7, 295-308.

Hall, R. H. (1963) 'The concept of bureaucracy: An empirical assessment', *American Journal of Sociology,* 69, 32-40.

Hall, S., Critcher, C., Jefferson, T, Clark, J. and Roberts, B. (1978) *Policing the Crisis: Mugging, the State and Law and Order,* London, Macmillan.

Hallett, C. and Stevenson, O. (1980) *Child Abuse: Aspects of Interprofessional Communication,* London, Allen and Unwin.

Handler, J. F. (1973) *The Coercive Social Worker: British Lessons for American Social Services,* Chicago, Markham.

Harris, N. and Palmer, E. (1976) 'How do social workers spend their time?', *Community Care,* 19 May.

Hart, H. L. A. (1951) 'The ascription of responsibility and rights', in Flew, A., ed., *Essays on Logic and Language,* Oxford, Basil Blackwell.

Hart, H. L. A. (1954) 'Definition and theory in jurisprudence', *Law Quarterly Review,* 70, 37-60.

Hart, H. L. A. (1968) *Punishment and Responsibility,* Oxford, Clarendon Press.

Hart, H. L. A. (1973) 'Bentham on legal rights', in Simpson, A. W. B., ed., *Oxford Essays in Jurisprudence, 2nd Series,* Oxford, Oxford University Press.

Hassall, C. and Stilwell, J. (1976) 'A study of the work of social workers', Worcester, Worcester Development Project.

Hawkins, K. (1983) *Environment and Enforcement: Regulation and the Social Definition of Pollution,* Oxford, Oxford University Press.

Hayek, F. A. (1960) *The Constitution of Liberty,* London, Routledge and Kegan Paul.

Heider, F. (1944) 'Social perception and phenomenal causality', *Psychological Review,* 51, 358-74.

Heifer, R. E. and Kempe, C. H. (1976) *Child Abuse and Neglect: The Family and the Community,* Cambridge, Mass., Ballinger.

Heraud, B. (1981) *Training for Uncertainty: A Sociological Approach to Social Work Education,* London, Routledge and Kegan Paul.

Hilgendorf, L. (1981) *Social Workers and Solicitors in Child Care Cases,* London, HMSO.

Hodges, J. and Hussain, A. (1979) 'La police des familles', *Ideology and Consciousness,* No. 5, 87-123.

Hoffman, C. W. (1927) 'Organization of family courts, with special reference to the juvenile courts', in Addams, J., ed., *The Child, the Clinic and the Court,* New York, New Republic.

Hoggett, B. (1981) *Parents and Children,* London, Sweet and Maxwell, 2nd edn.

Hohfeld, W. N. (1919) *Fundamental Legal Conceptions as Applied in Judicial Reasoning,* New Haven, Yale University Press.

Holter, J. C. and Friedman, S. B. (1968) 'Child abuse: early case finding in the emergency department', *Pediatrics,* 42, 128-38.

Home Office (1970) *Guide to Part I of the Children and Young Persons Act 1969,* London, HMSO.

Hoyles, M., ed. (1979) *Changing Childhood,* London, Writers and Readers.

Hughes, D. (1980a) 'Lay assessment of clinical seriousness: practical decision-making by non-medical staff in a hospital casualty department'. Unpublished Ph.D. thesis, University of Wales, Swansea.

Hughes, D. (1980b) 'The ambulance journey as an information-generating process', *Sociology of Health and Illness,* 2, 115-32.

Hughes, E. C. (1971) *The Sociological Eye,* Chicago, Aldine-Atherton.

Hull, D. (1974) 'Medical diagnosis', in Carter, J., ed., *The Maltreated Child,* London, Priory Press.

Huntington, J. (1981) *Social Work and General Medical Practice: Collaboration or Conflict?,* London, Allen and Unwin.

Ingleby Report (1960) *Report of the Committee on Children and Young Persons,* Cmnd. 1191, London, HMSO.

Jackson, J., Booth, M., and Harris, B. (1981) *Clarke Hall and Morrison on Children,* Second Cumulative Supplement to Ninth Edition, London, Butterworth.

Jeffery, R. (1979) 'Normal rubbish: deviant patients in casualty departments', *Sociology of Health and Illness,* 1, 90-107.

Johnson, J. M. (1981) 'Program enterprise and official co-optation in the battered women's shelter movement', *American Behavioral Scientist,* 24, 827-42.

Katz, S. N., McGrath, M., and Howe, R-A. (1976) *Child Neglect Laws in America,* Washington, American Bar Association.

Kempe, C. H. (1975) 'Family intervention: The right of all children', *Pediatrics,* 56, 693-4.

Kempe, C. H. (1976) 'Approaches to preventing child abuse: The health visitors concept', *American Journal of Disease in Childhood,* 130, 941-7.

Kempe, C. H. (1978) 'New vistas in the prevention of child abuse', in *Child Advocacy and Pediatrics,* Report of the Eighth Ross Roundtable on Critical Approaches to Common Pediatric Problems, Columbus, Ohio, Ross Laboratories.

Kempe, C. H., Silverman, F. N., Steele, B. F., Droegemueller, W. and Silver, H. K. (1962) 'The battered-child syndrome', *Journal of the American Medical Association,* 181(1), 17-24.

Kitsuse, J. L. (1962) 'Societal reaction to deviant behaviour: problems of theory and method', *Social Problems,* 9, 247-56.

Lasch, C. (1977) *Haven in a Heartless World: The Family Besieged,* New York, Basic Books.

Lawson, A. (1980) 'Taking the decision to remove the child from the family', *Journal of Social Welfare Law,* 141-63.

Levitt, R. (1980) *The Reorganized National Health Service,* London, Croom Helm, 2nd edn.

Light, D. (1980) *Becoming Psychiatrists,* New York, John Wiley and Sons.

Loventhal, D. (1972) *West Indian Societies,* London, Open University Press.

Lowe, N. V. and White, R. A. H. (1979) *Wards of Court,* London, Butterworth.

MacAndrew, C. and Edgerton, R. B. (1970) *Drunken Comportment: A Social Explanation,* London, Nelson and (1969) Chicago, Aldine.

MacCormick, D. N. (1976) 'Children's rights: A test case for theories of right', *Archiv für Rechts und Sozialphilosophie,* 62, 305-17.

McGlew, T. and Robertson, A. (1981) 'Social change and the shifting boundaries of discretion in medicine', in Adler, M. and Asquith, S., eds., *Discretion and Welfare,* London, Heinemann.

McHugh, P. (1968) *Defining the Situation: The Organization of Meaning in Social Interaction,* Indianapolis, Bobbs-Merrill.

McHugh, P. (1970) 'A common-sense conception of deviance', in Douglas, J. D., ed., *Deviance and Respectability: The Social Construction of Moral Meanings,* New York, Basic Books.

McIntosh, J. (1977) *Communication and Awareness in a Cancer Ward,* London, Croom Helm and New York, Prodist.

Macintyre, S. (1977) *Single and Pregnant,* London, Croom Helm and New York, Prodist.

Martin, F. M., Fox, S. J. and Murray, K. (1981) *Children Out of Court,* Edinburgh, Scottish Academic Press.

Martin, F. M. and Murray, K. (1976) *Children's Hearings,* Edinburgh, Scottish Academic Press.

Mauksch, H. O. (1966) 'The organizational context of nursing practices', in Davis, F., ed., *The Nursing Profession: Five Sociological Essays,* New York, Wiley.

Mayston Report (1969) *Report of Working Party on Management Structure in the Local Authority Nursing Services,* London, HMSO.

Mead, A. (1974) *The Actual and Potential Role of the Social Worker in the Primary Health Care Team*, London, DHSS.

Meyer, M. W. (1972) *Bureaucratic Structure and Authority: Co-ordination and Control in 254 Government Agencies*, London, Harper and Row.

Miller, J. K. (1976) 'Perspectives on child maltreatment in the military', in Heifer, R. E. and Kempe, C. H., eds., *Child Abuse and Neglect: The Family and the Community*, Cambridge, Mass., Ballinger.

Morris, A. and Giller, H. (1979) 'Juvenile justice and social work in Britain', in Parker, H., ed., *Social Work and the Courts*, London, Edward Arnold.

Morris, A., Giller, H., Szwed, E. and Geach, H. (1980) *Justice for Children*, London, Macmillan.

Mount, F. (1982) *The Subversive Family*, London, Jonathan Cape.

Mungham, G. and Thomas, P. A. (1979) 'Advocacy and the solicitor-advocate in magistrates' courts in England and Wales', *International Journal of the Sociology of Law*, 7, 169-96.

Murray, T., Dingwall, R. and Eekelaar, J. M. (1983) 'Professionals in bureaucracies: solicitors in private practice and local government', in Dingwall, R. and Lewis, P. S. C., eds., *The Sociology of the Professions: Lawyers, Doctors and Others*, London, Macmillan.

Newberger, E. H. and Bourne, R. (1978) 'The medicalization and legalization of child abuse', in Eekelaar, J. M. and Katz, S., eds., *Family Violence*, Toronto, Butterworths.

Newberger, E. H. and McAnulty, E. H. (1976) 'Family intervention in the pediatric clinic: A necessary approach to the vulnerable child', *Clinical Pediatrics*, 15, 1155-61.

Niederland, W. G. (1974) *The Schreber Case: Psychoanalytic Profile of a Paranoid Personality*, New York, Quadrangle/New York Times Book Co.

Packman, J. (1975) *The Child's Generation: Child Care Policy from Curtis to Houghton*, Oxford, Basil Blackwell.

Parker, H., Casburn, M. and Turnbull, D. (1981) *Receiving Juvenile Justice*, Oxford, Basil Blackwell.

Parry, N. and Parry, J. (1979) 'Social work, professionalism and the state', in Parry, N., Rustin, M. and Satyamurti, C., eds., *Social Work, Welfare and the State*, London, Edward Arnold.

Parton, N. (1979) 'The natural history of child abuse: a study in social problem definition', *British Journal of Social Work*, 9, 431-51.

Parton, N. (1981) 'Child abuse, social anxiety and welfare', *British Journal of Social Work*, 11, 391-414.

Pearson, G. (1975a) *The Deviant Imagination*, London, Macmillan.

Pearson, G. (1975b) 'Making social workers', in Bailey, R. and Brake, M., eds., *Radical Social Work*, London, Edward Arnold.

Pelton, L. H. (1978) 'Child abuse and neglect: the myth of classlessness', *American Journal of Orthopsychiatry*, 48, 608-17.

Pfohl, S. J. (1977) 'The "discovery" of child abuse', *Social Problems,* 24, 310-23.

Phillips, A. (1979) 'Social work and the delivery of legal services', *Modern Law Review,* 42, 29-41.

Phipson on Evidence (1976) edited by Buzzard, J. H., May, R. and Howard, M. N., London, Sweet and Maxwell, 12th edn.

Piliavin, I. and Briar, S. (1964) 'Police encounters with juveniles', *American Journal of Sociology,* 69, 206-14.

Pitcher, G. (1960) 'Hart on action and responsibility', *Philosophical Review,* 69, 226-35.

Pollner, M. (1975) '"The very coinage of your brain": The anatomy of reality disjunctures', *Philosophy of the Social Sciences,* 5, 411-30.

Prest, W., ed. (1981) *Lawyers in Early Modern Europe and America,* London, Croom Helm.

Punch, M. and Naylor, T. (1973) 'The police: A social service', *New Society,* 17 May, 35.

Rees, S. and Wallace, A. (1982) *Verdicts on Social Work,* London, Edward Arnold.

Richmond, M. (1917) *Social Diagnosis,* New York, Russell Sage.

Roberts, D. F., West, R. J., Ogilvie, D. and Dillon, M. J. (1979) 'Malnutrition in infants receiving cult diets: a form of child abuse', *British Medical Journal,* 1, 296-8.

Rosenfeld, A. A. and Newberger, E. H. (1977) 'Compassion vs control: conceptual and practical pitfalls in the broadened definition of child abuse', *Journal of the American Medical Association,* 237, 2086-8.

Rothman, S. M. (1981) 'Women's clinics or doctors' offices: the Sheppard-Towner Act and the promotion of preventive health care', in Rothman, D. J. and Wheeler, S., eds., *Social History and Social Policy,* New York, Academic Press.

Sacks, M. (1972) 'Notes on police assessment of moral character', in Sudnow, D., ed., *Studies in Social Interaction,* New York, Free Press.

Salmon Report (1966) *Report of the Committee on Senior Nursing Staff Structure,* London, HMSO.

Satyamurti, C. (1981) *Occupational Survival,* Oxford, Basil Blackwell.

Schutz, A. (1962) *Collected Papers I: The Problem of Social Reality,* The Hague, Martinus Nijhoff.

Schutz, A. (1964) *Collected Papers II: Studies in Social Theory,* The Hague, Martinus Nijhoff.

Schutz, A. and Luckmann, T. (1974) *The Structure of the Life-World,* London, Heinemann and (1973) Chicago, Northwestern University Press.

Scott, M. B. and Lyman, S. M. (1968) 'Accounts', *American Sociological Review,* 33, 46-62.

Scott, M. B. and Lyman, S. M. (1970) 'Accounts, deviance and social order', in Douglas, J. D., ed., *Deviance and Respectability: The Social Construction of Moral Meanings,* New York, Basic Books.

Sheridan, M. D. (1968) *The Development Progress of Infants and Young Children,* London, HMSO.

Silbey, S. (1981) 'Making sense of the lower courts', *The Justice System Journal,* 6, 13-27.

Skinner, A. E. and Castle, R. L. (1969) *78 Battered Children: A Retrospective Study,* London, NSPCC.

Smart, C. (1982) 'Regulating families or legitimating patriarchy? Family law in Britain', *International Journal of the Sociology of Law,* 10, 129-48.

Smith, D. (1974) 'Woman, the family and corporate capitalism' in Stephensen, M., ed., *Women in Canada,* Toronto, New Press.

Smith, G. (1980) *Social Need,* London, Routledge and Kegan Paul.

Stein, L. I. (1967) 'The doctor-nurse game', *Archives of General Psychiatry,* 16, 699-703.

Stimson, G. V. (1978) 'Treatment or control? Dilemmas for staff in drug dependency clinics', in West, D. J., ed., *Problems of Drug Abuse in Britain,* Cambridge, Cambridge University Press.

Stimson, G. V. and Webb, B. (1975) *Going to See the Doctor: The Consultation Process in General Practice,* London, Routledge and Kegan Paul.

Straus, M. A., Gelles, R. J. and Steinmetz, S. K. (1980) *Behind Closed Doors: Violence in the American Family,* Garden City, New York, Anchor/Doubleday.

Strong, P. M. (1979a) *The Ceremonial Order of the Clinic,* London, Routledge and Kegan Paul.

Strong, P. M. (1979b) 'Sociological imperialism and the profession of medicine: a critical examination of the thesis of medical imperialism', *Social Science and Medicine,* 13, 199-215.

Strong, P. M. (1980) 'Doctors and dirty work – The case of alcoholism', *Sociology of Health and Illness,* 2, 24-47.

Strong, P. M. and Horobin, G. W. (1978) 'Politeness is all – The forms, causes and consequences of medical gentility', Aberdeen, Institute of Medical Sociology, mimeo.

Sudnow, D. (1965) 'Normal crimes: sociological features of the penal code in a public defender office', *Social Problems,* 12, 255-76.

Sudnow, D. (1967) *Passing On: The Social Organization of Dying,* Englewood Cliffs, NJ, Prentice-Hall.

Sutton, A. (1981) 'Science in court', in King, M., ed., *Childhood, Welfare and Justice: A Critical Examination of Children in the Legal and Childcare Systems,* London, Batsford.

Taylor, L. (1972) 'The significance and interpretation of replies to motivational questions: the case of sex offenders', *Sociology,* 6, 23-40.

Taylor, L., Lacey, R. and Bracken, D. (1980) *In Whose Best Interests?* London, Cobden Trust/Mind.

Thane, P. (1981) 'Childhood in history', in King, M, ed., *Childhood, Welfare and Justice: A Critical Examination of Children in the Legal and Childcare systems*, London, Batsford.

Theophilus, A. (1973) *General Practitioners and Social Workers: Collaboration or Conflict*, Wiltshire Social Services Department, mimeo.

Thomas, P. A. and Mungham, G. (1983) 'Solicitors and clients: altruism or self-interest?', in Dingwall, R. and Lewis, P. S. C., *The Sociology of the Professions: Lawyers, Doctors and Others*, London, Macmillan.

Townsend, P. (1979) *Poverty in the United Kingdom*, Harmondsworth, Penguin.

Tredinnick, A. W. and Fairburn, A. C. (1980a) 'Left holding the baby', *Community Care*, 10 April, 22-5.

Tredinnick, A. W. and Fairburn, A. C. (1980b) 'The baby removed from its parents at birth: prophylaxis with justice', *New Law Journal*, 19 June, 498-500.

Tripp, J. H., Francis, D. E. M., Knight, J. A. and Harries, J. T. (1979) 'Infant feeding practices: a cause for concern', *British Medical Journal*, 2, 707-9.

Tutt, N. (1981) 'A decade of policy', *British Journal of Criminology*, 21, 246-56.

Voysey, M. (1975) *A Constant Burden*, London, Routledge and Kegan Paul.

Wald, M. (1975) 'State intervention on behalf of "neglected" children: a search for realistic standards', *Stanford Law Review*, 21, 985-1040.

Waller, W. (1936) 'Social problems and the mores', *American Sociological Review*, 1, 922-33.

Weber, M. (1947) *The Theory of Social and Economic Organization*, New York, Free Press.

Weber, M. (1954) *Law in Economy and Society*, Cambridge, Mass., Harvard University Press.

Whittington, C. and Bellaby, P. (1979) 'The reasons for hierarchy in social services departments: a critique of Elliott Jaques and his associates', *Sociological Review*, 27, 513-40.

Wigmore (1940) *Treatise on Evidence*, Boston, Little, Brown and Co., 3rd edn.

Wilson, J. Q. (1968) *Varieties of Police Behavior*, Cambridge, Mass., Harvard University Press.

Wolff, K., ed. (1950) *The Sociology of Georg Simmel*, New York, Free Press.

Zimmerman, D. H. (1969) 'Record-keeping and the intake process in a public welfare agency', in Wheeler, S., ed., *On Record: Files and Dossiers in American Life*, New York, Russell Sage Foundation.

Inquiries, Statutes, and Cases

INQUIRIES

Auckland (1975) *Report of the Committee of Inquiry into the Provision and Co-ordination of Services to the Family of John George Auckland*, London, HMSO.

Brewer (1977) *Wayne Brewer: Report of the Review Panel*, Taunton, Somerset Area Review Committee.

Brown (1980) *Report of the Committee of Inquiry into the Case of Paul Steven Brown*, Cmnd 8107, London, HMSO.

Chapman (1979) *Lester Chapman: Inquiry Report*, Reading, The County Councils and Area Health Authorities of Berkshire and Hampshire.

Colwell (1974) *Report of the Committee of Inquiry into the Care and Supervision Provided in Relation to Maria Colwell*, London, HMSO.

Fraser (1982) *Richard Fraser, 1972-1977: The Report of an Independent Inquiry*, London, London Borough of Lambeth/Inner London Education Authority/Lambeth, Southwark and Lewisham AHA (T).

Godfrey (1975) *Report of the Joint Committee of Inquiry into Non-Accidental Injury to Children with Particular Reference to the Case of Lisa Godfrey*, London, London Borough of Lambeth/Lambeth, Southwark and Lewisham AHA (T)/Inner London Probation and After-Care Committee.

Mehmedagi (1981) *Maria Mehmedagi: Report of an Independent Inquiry*, London, London Borough of Southwark/Lambeth, Southwark and Lewisham AHA (T)/Inner London Probation and After-Care Service.

Menheniott (1979) *Report of the Social Work Service of DHSS into Certain Aspects of the Management of the Case of Stephen Menheniott*, London, HMSO.

Page (1981) *Malcolm Page*, Chelmsford, Essex County Council/Essex Area Health Authority.

Peacock (1978) *Report of Committee of Enquiry Concerning Simon Peacock*, Cambridge, Cambridgeshire and Suffolk County Councils/Cambridgeshire AHA (T)/Suffolk AHA.

Pinder/Frankland (1981) *Report Concerning Christopher Pinder/Daniel Frankland*, Bradford, Bradford Area Review Committee.

Spencer (1978) *Karen Spencer: Report by Professor J. D. McClean*, Derby, Derbyshire County Council/Derbyshire AHA.

Taylor (1980) *Carly Taylor: Report of an Independent Inquiry*, Leicester, Leicestershire County Council/Leicestershire AHA (T).

STATUTES AND STATUTORY INSTRUMENTS

Adoption Act 1958 [7 Eliz. 2, c. 5]

Child Care Act 1980 [1980, c. 5]

Children Act 1948 [11 & 12 Geo. 6, c. 43]

Children and Young Persons Act 1933 [23 & 24 Geo. 5, c. 12]

Children and Young Persons Act 1963 [1963, c. 37]

Children and Young Persons Act 1969 [1969, c. 54]

Children and Young Persons Act (Northern Ireland) 1968 [1968, c. 34]

Civil Evidence Act 1968 [1968, c. 64]

Criminal Evidence Act 1965 [1965, c. 20]

Domestic Violence and Matrimonial Proceedings Act 1976 [1976, c. 50]

Family Law Reform Act 1969 [1969, c. 46]

Foster Children Act 1980 [1980, c. 6]

Guardianship of Minors Act 1971 [1971, c. 3]

Magistrates Court (Children and Young Persons) Rules 1970. [S.I. 1970 No. 1792 as amended by S.I. 1976 No. 1769]

Social Work (Scotland) Act 1968 [1968, c. 49]

CASES

A v. *Liverpool City Council* [1981] 2 All ER 385.

B v. *Gloucestershire County Council* [1980] 2 All ER 746.

C (R, S and K) (Minors) v. *M and others* [1982] 1 WLR 826.

Davis v. *Johnson* [1979] AC 264.

Essex County Council v. *TLR and KBR* [1979] 9 *Family Law* 15.

F v. *Suffolk County Council*, 79 LGR 554.

Humberside County Council v. *DPR* [1977] 1 All ER 964.

Lewisham London Borough v. *Lewisham Juvenile Court* [1980] AC 273.

Myers v. *DPP* [1965] AC 1001.

Re CB (a minor) [1981] 1 All ER 16.

Re D (a minor) [1980] AC 273.

Re K (Infants) [1965] AC 201.

R v. *Greenwich Juvenile Court ex p. Greenwich London Borough Council* [1977] *The Times* 10 May.

R v. *Milton Keynes Justices ex p.R.* (1979) 123 Sol Jo 321.

R v. *Welwyn Justices ex p.S.* [1978], *The Times*, 30 November.

R v. *Worthing Justice ex p. Stevenson* [1976] 2 All ER 194 (DC).

Shropshire County Council v. *PJS (A child)* [1975] 141 JPN 394. Discussed in (1979) 9 *Family Law* 60.

Southwark London Borough Council v. *C (A minor)* [1982] 2 All ER 636.

W v. *Nottinghamshire County Council* [1982] Fam 53, 3 WLR 959.

Index

[Page numbers below reference the original pagination of the printed 1983 and 1995 editions; this pagination is retained in this republication for continuity in citation and syllabus, consistency with the new ebook edition, and the convenience of the reader. The original pagination is found embedded into the present text by the use of brackets.]

285

Lay social theories 55-7

Lawyers, as a profession 104-5 (*see also* Solicitors; Barristers)

Legal aid 167, 173, 177-8, 227, 241, 261

'Liberal compromise' 91, 94, 218-19

Liberal values 77-8, 86, 90-1, 166, 204, 212-17, 263-4

and accountability 120-2

Licences 55, 103, 106, 108, 204, 207, 250

London, special problems in 240

Love, parental 72-6, 86-9, 164, 205, 218, 252-3

Lyman, S. M. 81-2, 198, 200, 202-3

Magistrates' courts 18-19, 228, 236-43

Material environment 57-65

Medical social work 255

Methodology 20-30

Mill, J. S. 216-17, 220, 263

Moral socialization 214-21, 264

Morris, A. 121, 208, 210, 245

National Health Service (NHS) 13-16, 38, 101

National Society for the Prevention of Cruelty to Children (NSPCC) 8, 16-17, 125, 208, 230-1, 247

Newberger, E. H. 33, 90, 92, 245, 249, 254, 263

'Normal family life', *see* Families

Nurses, in accident departments 37-8, 52-3

Official Solicitor 227

Optimism, rule of 69, 73, 76, 78-102, 218

Paediatricians 15-16

Parents

demeanour, importance of 44-6

excuses for deviance of 86-9, 202-3, 205

incorrigibility of 92-6, 191-6, 204-5

justifications of 198-202, 204

lack of representation 177-8, 241-2, 262

love, see Love, parental

moral character 77-8, 80-96, 150-2, 155-64, 182-3, 185-96

responsibility, perception of 58-62, 64-76, 79-82, 86, 185-96, 252

rights of 223-4

single 71-2, 251

Parton, N. 35, 208-10

Place of safety order 9-10

Playgroup 18

Police 16-17, 148, 230, 259

Poverty 2, 76-7, 247

Probation service 17

Professions 103-6, 120-1

Records

medical and nursing 256

production in court 242-3

social services 115-17, 256

Relativism, *see* Cultural relativism

Reporting laws 11

Resources, agency 117-18, 220, 256-7

Satyamurti, C. 61, 83, 118, 220, 251, 253, 255

Scott, M. B. 81-2, 198, 200, 202-3

Service families 253

Sex differences 101

Silbey, S. 179, 237-8, 261, 263

Smith, G. 61, 112, 220

Social inquiry reports 196-7

Social problem, concept of 2-3

Social regulation 213-21

Social services departments

Dingwall, Eekelaar & Murray

accountability of 108-11, 120-1, 143, 149, 234

allegations of expansionism 209

and lawyers 168-72

referrals to 111-20

Social workers

accountability of 108-11

as identifiers 12, 113, 256

as witnesses in court 182, 185, 187, 242

compared with health visitors 62, 65, 116-19, 257

conceptions of clients 111-13, 251

conceptions of normal family life 57-76

turnover 76, 180-1

Solicitors

private practice 105, 112, 172-8, 240, 261

local authority 105, 152-3, 166, 168-72, 181-2, 196-7, 227, 240, 260

representing parents 173, 177-8

representing the child 172-7

(*see also* Lawyers)

Standing Panels 143-7, 235-6

Statutes relating to child protection 7-9, 224-31, 245-6

Stevenson, O. 116, 118-19, 153, 209

Strong, P. M. 38, 40-1, 45, 87, 104, 209, 248, 250, 257-8, 263

Supervision orders 10, 196-7, 243

Tutelage 72, 217, 264

Violence, domestic 68, 71

Waller, W. 2, 55, 208

Wardship proceedings 10-11, 226-8, 242, 265

Weight charts 49, 154-5, 158, 160-1, 184, 260

Visit us at *www.quidprobooks.com.*

CPSIA information can be obtained at www.ICGtesting.com
Printed in the USA
OW04s1221200115

3587LV00001B/234/P

9 781610 272360